The United States and Cuba

The

United States

and

CUBA

Business and Diplomacy, 1917-1960

ROBERT F. SMITH

 COLLEGE AND UNIVERSITY PRESS
New Haven, Connecticut

© *Copyright, 1960, by Robert F. Smith*

Library of Congress Catalog Card Number: 60-53477

The material in Chapter II, section II, has previously appeared in
Discourse magazine, and is reprinted with their permission.

REPRINTED WITH PERMISSION OF BOOKMAN ASSOCIATES, INC.
BY COLLEGE AND UNIVERSITY PRESS, PAPERBACK DIVISION

MANUFACTURED IN THE UNITED STATES OF AMERICA BY
UNITED PRINTING SERVICES, INC.
NEW HAVEN, CONN.

To

My Wife

Alberta

Preface

This book might well be subtitled *The Prelude to Tragedy* because it provides a case study in a field of United States diplomacy which has been characterized by errors and short-sighted policies. The problems of Cuban-American relations have been directly related to the over-all approach of the United States to the so-called underdeveloped nations of Asia, Africa, and Latin America. In the twentieth century these areas have been shaken by nationalistic movements, cultural change, strivings for higher living standards, and programs aimed at curbing both political and economic subordination to industrialized nations. Change has been the essence of this century.

The foreign policy of the United States has been ambivalent toward these changes. While professing commitment to the ideal of national self-determination, the United States has often tended to support the status quo in these areas. The relatively stable era prior to World War I has become something of a "heavenly city" for American officials, and this has limited their ability to cope with change in the world. In the eyes of many people in the world the United States has, to a certain extent, abdicated its ideological leadership as champion of the idea that systems are made to serve men, and not men to serve systems. The tragedy of this situation has become especially apparent in the post World War II era. The United States has all too often enshrined stability in a period of rapid change, and as a result nations in Asia, Africa, and Latin America have begun to look elsewhere for ideological leadership and support. The problem of Fidel Castro's Cuban revolution is another chapter in the annals of political and economic change in this century.

There is an urgent need for Americans to understand the foreign policy of the nation, and the reasons for its development. One of the major factors behind this status quo policy in regard to underdeveloped areas is the world-wide business interests of the United States. Political revolutions against dictatorial governments are generally supported by the United States. In the twentieth century these revolutions have increasingly embodied social and economic changes, and when these threaten substantial economic interests the ardent support of the United States often begins to fade. In order to achieve some measure of economic independence, and to reform economic structures which had defied change for centuries, some nations have expropriated large holdings. Since the protection and advancement of American overseas economic interests is one of the major concerns of the United States Government, such developments have usually affected the government's policies in regard to such revolutions. This connection between business and diplomacy was concisely stated by a State Department official in 1930:

> The participation of American corporations in the development of Latin America involves an incalculable corrective to existing trade figures and implies a distinct and direct American influence in Latin American policies. Irrespective of the policy at Washington and the personality of statesmen, the operations of such enterprises as the United Fruit Company or the several American oil companies create independent political interests in the territories subject to their economic operations which supplement and often determine official policy both at Washington and in the various Latin American capitals.[1]

In one respect this business influence is natural in a country like the United States. Private business enterprise is the major concern of the nation, and most citizens are connected, either directly or indirectly, with some aspect of the economic system. In a representative system foreign policy is as subject as any other policy to the various interests of groups in the country. This is not due simply to business pressure. These do exist, and they often conflict with each other. Often, however, governmental officials share the economic views of certain groups and shape policy without undue pressure. Some of these officials have been in business prior to entering government service, and others have educational and social ties with business leaders.[2]

The interaction between the interests of various groups and party politics, especially in Congress, is another aspect of the rather complicated role which many parts of the governmental structure must play in serving as "broker" for the various interest groups in the country.

There is nothing wrong in America having overseas business interests. A large, industrial nation has no other alternative, and these interests often play a valuable role in the economy of other areas. The point must be stressed, however, that in a world of change, conflicts sometimes develop between economic interests and the national ideal of self-determination. It is not an easy matter to reconcile this conflict, but all too often the United States tends to support the status quo without trying to formulate alternative policies. Sometimes such policies have been belatedly developed, but in the interim American prestige has declined and American ideological leadership has been frittered away. Mexico and Egypt provide two such examples, and Cuba is now providing another.

Prior to World War II the United States had time to vacillate and wait for moderating developments—thirty years in the case of Mexico—but today the demand for change is too widespread, and another world power is seeking to gain ideological leadership and control. The imperial designs of the Soviet Union, and the power conflict this engenders, further complicates the formulation of American policy. The need for allies, strategic raw materials, and for measures to block the spread of Communist power must not blind Americans to the need for other policies to meet the needs of underdeveloped areas.

Positive policies of economic aid and active support for social and economic reform provide an alternative to complete loss of economic holdings and Communist domination. Of course, there is no guarantee that this would always work, but it is more realistic than a policy which ignores the aspirations and problems of the common people in a country, and which bases American friendship on the retention of existing economic arrangements. Expropriation of foreign holdings may not be the wisest course for Cuba and other countries to follow, but American failure to understand the economic realities in countries where the resources are controlled by a small minority will contribute to the demand for just such measures. The United States may well have to make short-term economic sacrifices for long-range friendships.

Strategic, moral, ideological, and economic factors have interacted to form the substance of Cuban-American relations. The tendency in many works dealing with diplomacy has been to stress the political side of foreign policy, and to rigidly segregate this from the economic side. This study is designed to develop the economic aspects of Cuban-American relations, and to show their relationship to diplomacy. If these at times seem to emerge as dominant elements, it is only because the State Department documents lead the way. Economic motives and pressures are not the only elements in the story, and there is nothing deterministic about the role of business in diplomacy. Diplomatic historians, however, have overdone the "ivory tower," "chessboard" approach to foreign policy. I have chosen to approach the subject from the standpoint of the market place and the political arena.

The situation in Cuba today has its roots deep in the past. Compound a mixture of sugar, tariffs, foreign loans, export markets, politics, and political stability and the result is an important insight into the nature of Cuban-American relations. These hit a depressing low in 1960, and the Cuban Government has drawn close to the Communist bloc. The United States must share the blame for the situation which erupted into the Cuban trek toward Moscow. The fact that the Communist bloc has taken advantage of the Cuban revolution does not explain away the past errors of the United States. It does mean, however, that these errors must be analyzed so that positive measures can be developed to prevent the spread of Communist influence in the hemisphere.

The present situation is even more tragic, since the United States is basically not an imperialistic nation. State Department officials do not want to run Cuba, nor do they have aggressive designs. If this were not the case, the United States would have absorbed the island years ago and thereby saved much money and diplomatic effort. The mote in the eye of United States policy toward Cuba and other underdeveloped countries has not been evil intent or goals of subjugation, but rather a profound lack of understanding coupled with the smug certainty of the overly virtuous. We have often mistaken surface prosperity and calm for the general well-being and contentment of the common people in a country. When this illusion has been destroyed we have been unwilling to face the possible need to sacrifice some immediate economic interests in order to retain the friendship of people seeking to improve their standard of living.

Herbert Hoover once argued that the American citizens who purchased foreign bonds during the 1920's, and who subsequently lost their investments through default, could console themselves with the thought that they had helped subsidize the American economy.[3] Perhaps today some Americans with foreign business interests could be expected to help subsidize the ideological leadership of the United States in a world of social change.

Another possibility is that of large-scale economic aid from the United States which would be specifically designed to speed peaceful reform. The State Department, in July 1960, announced the start of a new loan program for social reform projects in Latin America. This is a move in the right direction, but such a program is several years overdue, especially in the case of Cuba.

Any alternative to Communist influence will involve sacrifices on the part of all Americans: businessmen with overseas interests and average citizens. Admiral Hyman Rickover has written:

> No democratic nation can successfully pursue its international objectives unless its people are willing to subordinate private interest to national interest in all areas where the country's world position is at stake.[4]

The future of freedom is at stake in the underdeveloped nations today, and the national interest will require such subordination of private interests. If this study seems critical of the policy of the United States, it is only because the exaltation of private interests in the past has in some measure contributed to the crisis of freedom in the underdeveloped areas of the world.

Acknowledgments

The writing of this book has been greatly facilitated in various ways by others. I am deeply appreciative of the aid and advice given by friends and associates, but I take full responsibility for all interpretations and for any errors of fact or judgment. I would especially like to thank Dr. Fred Harvey Harrington, of the University of Wisconsin, for his criticism, advice, and support. To Dr. Thomas Le Duc, of Oberlin College, and to Dr. Richard Thompson, of Ohio University, I owe a debt of gratitude for advice during the early stages of research. My thanks also go to the Historical Division of the Department of State for permission to use State Department documents, and to the University of Wisconsin for financial aid. I am greatly indebted to Texas Lutheran College for the encouragement and assistance given during the writing of this book; especially to Dr. A. G. Wiederaenders and Dean E. B. Everitt for their close cooperation. Last, but certainly not least, I must express the feeling of deep gratitude for the help and support of my wife Alberta Smith. Her long hours of typing, translating (my handwriting), proofreading, and literary criticism have made this book possible.

ROBERT FREEMAN SMITH

August 1, 1960

Contents

CHAPTER ONE

Prologue: Cuban-American Relations, 1898-1919

I

Between 1898 and 1919 a pattern of Cuban-American relations developed which involved a rather close connection between investments, trade, and Cuban stability. An official of the State Department's Latin American Division—Boaz Long—noted this development in a memorandum to Secretary of State Robert Lansing in February 1918. In a summary statement of the period since 1898, Long enthusiastically reported:

> The total trade of Cuba with the United States just prior to the end of the Spanish rule over that island (1897) amounted to about twenty-seven million dollars per annum. During the decade following the termination of our war with Spain the island of Cuba, guided by American influence, increased her trade with us by leaps and bounds and brought it to the startling total in 1917 of something over four hundred and thirty million dollars. This unprecedented development of Cuba may serve as an illustration of what probably would take place in the Central American countries provided this Government extended to them aid of a practical character as it did to Cuba.

The "aid" that Long discussed in more detail consisted of the maintenance of stability, investments, loans, and trade.[1]

The protection of investments, the expansion of trade, and the stability of Cuba were mutually dependent parts of the pattern of relationships, and all in turn were linked to the influence of the United States Government. Intervention by various means in the affairs of Cuba, and the reciprocity treaty—which increasingly tied the Cuban sugar economy to the United States—were basic elements in this relationship. The nature of this pattern of Cuban-American relations was clearly illustrated by several events in 1917 and 1918.

Early in 1917 disturbances broke out in Cuba. The United States issued instructions that it would not tolerate armed revolt, and small detachments of marines were repeatedly landed from February to August in response to numerous requests from American business interests.[2] Destruction of property increased during April, however, and by May there was talk of sending a large body of American soldiers. President Mario Menocal disapproved of such a step,[3] but by the latter part of May the State Department had definitely decided to go ahead with this plan and had requested the War Department to begin preparations.[4] In order to salve Cuban feelings, and possibly the feelings of Americans who might disagree with a policy of occupying a friendly country, an artful plan was worked out. It was arranged for President Menocal to "offer" to the United States "sites for training camps . . . if it should be considered desirable to send troops to train in mild winter climate."[5] This would make it possible to "impress eastern Cuba with [the] fact of [the] presence of United States troops" through the guise of "extensive practice marches."[6] The American people were informed that the "friendly offer" had been accepted, and that it was proof of Cuba's desire to assist in the war with Germany.[7] An Associated Press article had hinted at the real reason for intervention and this disturbed the State Department. For, as Minister William Gonzales put it, "such publications . . . are embarrassing to diplomatic work."[8]

Camp sites were rented in Oriente Province,[9] and on August 16, 1917 it was decided to send a regiment of marines rather than a cavalry regiment.[10] The marines arrived in force later that month, and the State Department received periodic "training" reports from the marine commander.[11] Some historians have contended that this intervention was due to fear of German attempts to create trouble. There was one report of possible German activity, but it was received almost two months after the decision to send troops had been made.[12] Frank Polk, the acting Secretary of State in July 1917, stated that troops were being sent, "to aid in the protection of sugar properties and mining properties and in restoring complete order in the Oriente Province."[13] The Military Attaché, in a report written in 1921, said that at the time he was not advised of the reason for intervention but that it was generally understood that it was to protect American property.[14] In addition the marines acted as strikebreakers and strike preventers for the Cuba Railroad.[15]

During the summer of 1917 Cuba began negotiations with the United States for a fifteen million dollar loan. Secretary of State Robert Lansing informed Secretary of the Treasury William Gibbs McAdoo that Cuba's application for a loan offered a good opportunity to bring pressure on that government for a favorable settlement of the claims of the Ports Company of Cuba and the Cuba Railroad. Lansing noted that the loan should not be made until these issues were settled.[16] The Ports Company claim stemmed from the revocation of the "Dragado Concession" in 1913. The company had obtained a concession to dredge the ports of Cuba in 1911, and had planned to make over 200 percent profit on the operation. The Trust Company of Cuba—headed by Norman H. Davis—was deeply involved with the Ports Company.[17] The Cuba Railroad claimed that the Cuban Government owed it $250,000,000 for damages suffered during the 1917 revolt. The Cuban Government stated that it was willing to loan money to the company, but that it did not owe damages.[18]

Pressure was put on the Cuban Government to settle these claims. In October 1917 the Cuban Congress finally agreed to settle with the Ports Company, but the railroad claim was debated until the spring of 1918. The Cuban Government then agreed to pay the damage claims of the railroad out of the proceeds of the loan.[19] On April 3, 1918 the Cuban President signed a decree which, in effect, returned to the Ports Company all of its assets while the Cuban Government assumed its debts.[20] The first five million dollar advance to the Cuban Government was approved on March 27, 1918, and the two subsequent advances of like amounts were approved later that year.

During the summer of 1917 the price of Cuban raw sugar on the New York Market increased to 6.75 cents a pound—the highest price since the Civil War.[21] The United States Government then moved to assert control over the sugar market. The Lever Act of August 10, 1917 granted the executive the power to control the marketing and production of foodstuffs, and created the Food Administration. Herbert Hoover was picked to head the administration, and one of his first moves was to organize the machinery to control Cuban sugar marketing.

For all practical purposes Cuban sugar set the price for sugars sold at New York, and any attempt to control raw sugar prices had to eliminate much of Cuba's bargaining power. On August 31, 1917 Herbert Hoover wrote to the British Food Controller and outlined a program to accomplish this purpose. Hoover's plan consisted of several parts: (1) the British were to force the Canadians to withdraw from the Cuban sugar market; (2) the British and American purchasers were to agree to place their purchases with the New York Committee of five men—to be appointed by the United States and Britain; (3) this committee would have the power to set the price for raw sugar purchases and to apportion the Cuban crop among the purchasing nations.[22] Thus, the Cuban producers were to be told that they could sell their crop only to the committee, and for the price set by the committee.

The British agreed to Hoover's plan, and the International Sugar Committee was organized. The British Government appointed two members, and the United States Government appointed three. There was some surprise—and alarm—expressed by Cubans when Hoover picked Earl Babst, the president of the American Sugar Refining Company, to head the committee.

William A. Jamison of the Arbuckle Brothers Refinery and George N. Rolph of the Food Administration were the other two members. American refiners wanted a cheap raw material, and the Cubans believed that the American appointments to the committee were indicative of the influence of the refiner's point of view.[23]

The International Sugar Committee set the price of Cuban sugar at 4.6 cents a pound, plus freight to New York. The producers in Cuba vigorously objected to this price, and on November 20, 1917 the Cuban Minister stated this objection to Secretary Lansing.[24] Four days later Herbert Hoover requested State Department support in forcing the Cubans into line.[25] The American Minister to Cuba informed the department that the price of sugar, as fixed by the committee, would seriously affect the people of Cuba since the price of food—which Cuba imported from the United States—was inflated beyond the purchasing capacity of most Cubans. Minister Gonzales felt that it was only fair to compensate the Cubans with higher sugar prices.[26]

The Cuban producers held out until January 17, 1918, when they finally consented to the price set by the committee. There was some indication that this consent was the result of economic coercion. A report from Cuba in early January 1918, stated that there was no flour in Cuba, and that no bread was available. In addition, the supply of coal was almost exhausted. For some reason the Cubans had been unable to obtain import licenses for wheat and coal from the American Food Administration.[27] As soon as the contract for sugar purchases was approved the Cuban Minister contacted the State Department and urged that imports to Cuba be expedited.[28] The import licenses were soon forthcoming.[29]

During the 1918 sugar shortage hearings, several individuals were quizzed about the tactics used to fix the price of Cuban sugar. Earl Babst—and others as well—refused to answer the question in public since he said that it would betray the "diplomatic instructions and relationships" of which he was a part. The committee went into executive session to receive the answer, and the veil of secrecy descended.[30]

Thus, the events of 1917–18 illustrate the "practical" aid policy described by Boaz Long. American businessmen helped to interpret this policy, and derived profit from its application. The years 1917–18 represented the zenith in the use of armed force in Cuban-American relations. The pattern of relations, which was so vividly illustrated during this two-year span, had its roots in the Spanish-American War.

II

The United States' declaration of war on Spain in April 1898 marked the beginning of a new period in Cuban-American relations. Some Americans had been concerned over the turbulence in Cuba which resulted from the revolutionary outburst in 1895, since this threatened to damage investments and disrupt trade.[31] Although this concern may not have been the primary reason for the decision to fight Spain,[32] the Spanish-American War nonetheless marked the beginning of active American intervention in the affairs of Cuba. As President William McKinley expressed it in his war message: "We have . . . become . . . the guarantors of a stable and orderly government protecting life and property in that island."[33]

With the end of the war in 1899 the United States was faced with the problem of the status of Cuba. The Teller Amendment to the declaration of war had disclaimed any intent to annex the island, but the United States had no intention of handing Cuba over to the insurgents.[34] A military government was set up in Cuba, and governed the island until the Cubans formed a native government in 1903. Before the occupation ended, however, a thorough protectorate was established by the Platt Amendment. This amendment to the Military Appropriations bill for 1901–02 was passed with little debate, then added to the Cuban Constitution, and finally embodied in a permanent treaty between the two countries in 1903.[35] Thus, the United States became the "legal" guardian of the new republic.

With the end of the war the United States was also in a good position to work out the problems of Cuban-American trade relations. As one author wrote in 1899: "To the United States, among the chief advantages of the liberation of Cuba will be a commercial one." These advantages were spelled out in terms of rich fields for investment and greatly expanded markets.[36] American business interests began to discuss a reciprocity agreement as the best means of attaining both of these goals.[37]

As early as June 1899, General James H. Wilson reported to Washington that establishment of proper trade relations between Cuba and the United States was of greater importance than the establishment of proper political institutions.[38] This emphasis was repeated in General Leonard Wood's first annual report in 1900 in which he stressed the need for reciprocity in order to increase American exports.[39] The issue was first brought up in Congress in February 1900 when a joint resolution was introduced in the House to admit sugar and molasses duty free from Cuba and Puerto Rico. The Ways and Means Committee submitted an adverse report and the resolution was tabled.[40]

In his annual report for 1901, Secretary of War Elihu Root placed special importance on the commercial relationships between the two countries. He strongly urged a reduction in duties upon Cuban sugar and tobacco, and pictured a vast market potential for American goods which "would contribute far more to our prosperity than the portion of our present duties which we would be required to concede."[41] The movement for Cuban reciprocity gained momentum during the summer and fall of 1901. A delegation of prominent Cubans visited Washington and gave President Theodore Roosevelt the petition of the "united business interests of Cuba" calling for concessions in the tariff.[42] The President came out in favor of Cuban reciprocity in his first annual message of December 3, 1901. He repeated this in his annual message of December 2, 1902 and stated:

> I urge the adoption of reciprocity with Cuba, not only because it is eminently for our own interests to control the Cuban market and by every means to foster our supremacy in the tropical lands and waters south of us, but also because we . . . should make all our sister nations of the American Continent feel that . . . we desire to show ourselves disinterestedly and effectively their friend.[43]

The President's recommendations were referred to the House Commitee on Ways and Means and hearings began on January 15, 1902. In all, fifty-four people testified; sixteen in favor of reciprocity and thirty-eight opposed. Testimony for Cuba was received from eleven Americans, including the chairman of the Associated American Interests of Cuba, the president of the United States Export Association, a representative of the Merchant's Association of New York, a committee from the New

York Produce Exchange, the president of the National Sugar Refining Company, two sugar planters, and two officials of the military government—General Wood and Colonel Tasker Bliss.[44] This group represented a good cross section of American business groups interested in Cuba, and their arguments would be repeated many times in the coming years.

The heated Congressional battle over Cuban reciprocity was prolonged for several months as the domestic sugar interests used various stratagems to defeat it. The reciprocity bill died in committee when Congress adjourned on July 1, 1902, but Roosevelt then proceeded to negotiate a treaty with Cuba, which he submitted to the Senate in December 1902. The treaty was approved several months later and became effective in December 1903. As a result, Cuban sugar received a 20 percent preferential reduction in the American tariff, and various American products received from 20 to 40 percent reductions in the Cuban tariff.[45]

American trade with Cuba and the value of American investments in Cuba greatly increased after 1899. The United States became Cuba's best sugar market as Cuban production increased —especially after 1903—and the Cuban share of the American market increased from 17.6 percent in 1900 to 50.4 percent in 1913.[46] The value of American exports to Cuba increased from approximately $27,000,000 in 1897 to $200,188,222 in 1914. By 1914 Cuba was in sixth place among the customers of the United States.[47] In 1896 American investments in Cuba were estimated at $50,000,000—chiefly concentrated in mining and sugar properties.[48] This had increased to $265,000,000 by 1915, but European capital was still predominant in 1914. During World War I, however, the situation was reversed as American capital investments displaced European.[49]

Enterprising adventurers swarmed to the island and formed the spearhead of American economic penetration. Some of these men set up their own companies, some became agents for American companies, and others went into the sugar business. This group formed an economic interest which was greatly in favor of "gunboat" diplomacy and its efforts helped to set the tone for American-Cuban relations for several years.

One of the best examples of this group was Frank Steinhart. A regular army sergeant who became the "pet" of General Sheridan due to a fortuitous occurrence, Steinhart took his discharge in Havana in 1903 after closing up the accounts of the provisional government. He was immediately appointed United States Consul General in Cuba and held the post until July 1907. He became engaged in various enterprises including the Havana Electric railway—which later absorbed the Havana electric light system—and the Spanish Bank which was dominated by the Cuban "financier" Jose Lopez Rodriguez—"Pote" for short. Steinhart believed that the only hope for Cuba lay in American control and the use of American troops if necessary.[50] He acquired a great deal of influence among the Cubans as well as among American officials. Enoch Crowder, who had been a personal friend of Steinhart's since 1906, wrote concerning him:

> Undoubtedly he was a man of great influence with the Wood administration. In the second intervention, he actually controlled Magoon and was the invisible Government. He bid for the same kind of control with every American Minister appointed here, and he generally acquired it.[51]

The importance of Frank Steinhart, and the group of American enterprisers in Cuba of which he was representative, became clear in 1906. As Consul General he bombarded the State Department with requests for intervention during that year. Theodore Roosevelt was reluctant to send armed forces, but finally he sent a commission headed by William Howard Taft.[52] The commission, under the guidance of Steinhart, met Cuban political chiefs and tried to work out a settlement of the political controversy which threatened American property.[53] Estrada Palma, the Cuban President, and his cabinet resigned, however, and Taft proclaimed himself provisional governor. Charles E. Magoon succeeded Taft as provisional governor, and administered Cuba until January 1909 when the second intervention ended.[54]

Cuba remained relatively quiet until 1912, when the "race war" broke out. The State Department requested the Navy Department to send ships and marines to Cuba because "important

American interests" had asked for protection of their endangered property. The request was complied with and marines were landed on numerous occasions during 1912.[55] The Cuban Government defeated the Negro rebels, but the United States Government continued to keep a close watch over affairs in Cuba.

III

From 1900 to 1913 American exports to Latin America expanded slowly but steadily. As American businessmen and government officials became more conscious of the growing value of this trade, efforts to facilitate its development were increased. In September 1914, the Secretaries of State and Commerce called together representatives of the United States Chamber of Commerce, the Southern Commercial Congress, and the National Foreign Trade Council to discuss ways to increase trade with Latin America. The Secretary of Commerce appointed a committee on Latin American Trade to further this goal.[56] In 1915 the first Pan-American Financial Congress was held under the direction of Secretary of the Treasury McAdoo, and as a result the International High Commission on Uniform Laws was formed.[57] These and other activities were reflections of the growing interest of American businessmen in trade and investment opportunities to the south. The Latin American Trade Committee, which had been appointed by the Secretary of Commerce, reported in 1915 that:

> Your committee . . . believe that the *cessation or curtailment of our trade with Latin America will in itself be highly injurious to American industry,* just as we believe that *the extension of this trade would make for the prosperity of the country at large,* as well as for those directly interested.[58]

Great stress was placed on the need to invest capital in Latin America in order to increase trade. "Practical Pan-Americanism" and "profiting by the Monroe Doctrine" were terms applied to these aims.[59] As John Hays Hammond explained it to the National Association of Manufacturers in 1916, "It is obvious . . . that we must either curtail the capacity of our factories . . . or we must depend upon the exploitation of foreign countries for the relief of our congested home markets."[60] This required governmental action, and American businessmen worked for, and received, this cooperation.[61]

Despite the fact that American exports to Latin America were greatly increasing, so that by 1918 the United States was the leading exporter to that region, some businessmen were worried about the future of this trade. Ill will was also growing in Latin America as a result of the policies of the United States. The implications of this feeling were spelled out to the International Trade Conference by Francisco Escobar of the Bogota, Colombia, Chamber of Commerce: "Somebody has said here that trade follows the flag; but let that flag be clean and spotless, without any blots on it. It is up to you to wipe out that blot that somebody put on your flag through that unfortunate canal incident."[62] There was also widespread concern over the prospects of a postwar trade war with England and Germany, particularly for the markets of Latin America which had gone to the United States by default after 1914.[63] It was clearly recognized that European countries would put forth great efforts to regain these markets, and it was asserted that any loss of trade by the United States would raise serious domestic questions such as unemployment and socialist agitation.[64] It was also recognized that European countries would play on the anti-Yankee theme in this drive for markets.[65]

These were all factors behind the Long memorandum of 1918. Long stressed the necessity for modifying the "big stick" policy in the postwar years since European powers would be making great efforts to discredit the United States. As he suggested:

The business of these countries and the friendship of their people will almost certainly be obtained and conserved through the adoption of practical and humanitarian measures of notable advantage, and American prestige be injured by advancing thoughts of ultimate intervention or domination. Intervene when necessary, but do not threaten or talk of it in advance.[66]

The ideas expressed in this memorandum were part of the pattern of Cuban-American relations which developed after 1919.

In the period 1898–1919 American business groups helped to set the general pattern for Cuban-American relations. The export groups interested in Cuba were, generally, satisfied after 1903. Refining interests were also taken care of by the treaty since the duty on raw sugar declined from 1903 to 1920. American investors were the one group with definite demands after 1903 and the trend of American policy reflects these. This was the "frontier" stage of economic enterprise, so to speak, and most American investors were in the early stages of developing their interests. As one historian expressed it, "The small enterpriser running great risks in hope of enormous profits upon his slender capital, and anxious for special political favors at Havana or Washington,"[67] was the chief figure during this era. Frank Steinhart, Horatio Rubens, and Herbert C. Lakin were examples of this group.

The complexion of American investments began to change prior to World War I. This struggle helped increase the American stake in Cuba and hastened the change in the type of capital enterprise predominating in the island. Forces in the domestic economy also created new problems for American business groups with Cuban interests. The response to these changes and forces constitutes another chapter in Cuban-American relations— the period from 1919 through 1933.

CHAPTER TWO

The Economic Setting

I

The economy of Cuba was primarily dominated by sugar with tobacco, the second ranking Cuban export, playing a less important role. The story of Cuban economic development during these years was characterized by increased American penetration and control. As a result, the Cuban economy reflected some of the trends developing in the United States. The Cuban economy, however, was affected by the change in status of the United States and the legislative reaction to it. Here was the dilemma of American business interests during the period from 1919 through 1933. As American business became dominant in Cuba the value of Cuba's exports to the American market began to decrease, and the prosperity of Cuba depended on this market.[1]

American investments in Cuba increased 536 percent between 1913 and 1928.[2] In 1913 the American stake was estimated at $220,000,000, which was 17.7 percent of all American investments in Latin America.[3] By 1929 this had grown to an estimated $1,525,900,000, or 27.31 percent of the total Latin American in-investment.[4] American-owned sugar mills produced approximately 15 percent of the Cuban crop in 1906 and 48.4 percent in 1920.[5] By 1928 various estimates placed American control of the sugar crop between 70 and 75 percent.[6]

At the close of World War I the sugar industry was booming. As a result, a marked tendency toward integration was accelerated and many sugar companies borrowed heavily to expand production. Some of the larger producing companies bought up both small producers in Cuba and refineries in the United States.[7] The American, National, Warner, and Revere—owned by

the United Fruit Company—sugar refining companies expanded
their holdings in Cuban sugar centrals.[8] The American Refining
Company attempted to buy up the National Company and to
merge all important refining interests in the New York City
area, but the Justice Department blocked the sale.[9] In 1927 the
National Company purchased the refinery of the Warner Sugar
Company.[10] In addition, several manufacturing concerns in the
United States began to buy sugar-producing properties in Cuba.
The Hershey Chocolate Company had pioneered in this respect
prior to the war and were followed by the Hires Root Beer
Company and the Loft Candy Company.[11]

The sugar market started its spectacular downward spiral in
the summer of 1920. The price fell from twenty-two and a half
cents a pound to four cents a pound in less than six months. As
a result many sugar centrals went into bankruptcy and were
taken over by American banks. Others had to turn to these
banks for funds. An executive committee of bankers even took
charge of the powerful Cuba Cane Sugar Corporation.[12]

The National City Bank of New York went deeply into the
sugar business after 1920. The bank loaned money to sugar
planters even before it established a branch in Cuba in 1915.
During the 1920–1921 crop year the bank had between thirty
and thirty-five million dollars out in loans which could not be
paid. The bank asked Gordon S. Rentschler, an Ohio manufacturer of sugar mill machinery, to go to Cuba and look over
the mortgaged sugar properties. In February 1922 the bank
approved Rentschler's plan, and he organized the "really sound
properties" into the General Sugars Company.[13] In some cases
adjoining estates were purchased to round out the properties,
and by 1923 the new company produced 5.1 percent of the
sugar crop in eleven active mills.[14] Gordon Rentschler became
a director of the bank—in charge of sugar interests—in 1923, a
vice-president in 1925, and president of the bank in 1929.[15]
Besides going directly into the sugar business, the National City
Bank floated fifteen bond issues for American companies in
Cuba between 1921 and 1931. Of these, six were for sugar companies—including Cuban American and Cuban Dominican—and
six for railroads.[16]

This era of "bank-controlled corporations and bank-admonished syndicates" in the Cuban sugar industry was also one of increased production. The sugar companies hoped to overcome the low price by more efficient production and greatly increased volume. American capital poured into Cuba to help effect this program of expansion, modernization, and reorganization which began in the early 1920's.[17] This served to reduce further the number of independent sugar producers. Edwin F. Atkins wrote in 1926 that, "While many individual or family interests still remain, they are generally being absorbed by corporate ownership."[18] These were prophetic words, for by 1928 the old Atkins interests had passed to the syndicate of Lowry, Thayer, and Havemeyer.[19]

Many other types of enterprises attracted American capital after 1919. The Electric Bond and Share Company began in 1921 to buy up properties throughout the island, and the International Telephone and Telegraph Company through its subsidiary, the Cuban Telephone Company, controlled the communications of the island.[20] The principal railroads, except the British-controlled system, were merged in 1923 into a holding company known as the Consolidated Railroads of Cuba. This represented the integration of the Cuba Railroad and its subsidiaries with the interests of Colonel J. M. Tarafa—the Cuba Northern Railways Company. The new group was controlled by the Cuba Company, which was the parent company of the Cuba Railroad.[21] This monopolistic control of rail transportation was authorized by a special act of the Cuban Congress known as the "Tarafa Bill." This act authorized trade to be carried on only through ports served by the Consolidated Railroad. The large sugar companies protested and as a result the law firm of Sullivan and Cromwell, with the support of the State Department, worked out a compromise agreement with the railroad interests.[22]

American banks also floated securities for the government of Cuba. J. P. Morgan and Company and the Chase National Bank—with its associates—handled the loans. Morgan and Company handled the fifty million dollar issue of 1923 and the nine million dollar issue of 1927.[23] The Chase Securities Corporation in conjunction with Blair and Company, Equitable Trust Company, and the Continental Bank and Trust Company handled the public works securities which were marketed between 1927 and 1932.[24]

The value of American exports to Cuba declined from the 1920 zenith—when the United States supplied 73 percent of all Cuban imports—until 1922. There was a brief upturn which lasted until 1925 when American exports again declined.[25] This downward trend continued into the 1930's and was not typical of the American trade pattern prior to 1929. Cuba was America's fourth best customer in 1924—taking 66.1 percent of her imports from the United States—but declined steadily to sixteenth place in 1933.[26] By 1929 the United States was only supplying 59 percent of all Cuban imports.[27] The value of American exports to Cuba declined not only absolutely but also relatively to the exports of other countries.[28]

The major reason for this decline was the depressed state of the Cuban sugar economy. The price of sugar fell to 1.6 cents a pound in 1921. In 1923 the price went up to 6 cents a pound, and there was a brief boom. This ended, however, in 1925 and the price of Cuban sugar began a steady decline which continued until 1934. Rising Cuban production competed with increased crops from other areas, and this competition helped to depress the price.[29] The American tariff act of 1922 acted initially to depress the Cuban price rather than raise the New York price of sugar,[30] and Cuban sugar came into the United States in greater quantities during 1922. The quantity of Cuban sugar imported into the United States dropped in 1923; then began a gradual rise in 1924, 1925, and 1926; declined in 1927 and 1928; increased in 1929; and then dropped off sharply from 1930 to 1934. The peak of the 1926 and 1929 increases, however, were not as high as the 1922 amount.[31] After 1926 the insular possessions of the United States began to supply an increasingly greater share of American sugar imports, and this trend continued until 1934.[32] The tariff on Cuban sugar imports into the United States was an important factor in this trend.[33] In 1924 the United States took 83.3 percent of all Cuban exports, but this declined to 68 percent in 1933. The over-all value of Cuban exports to the United States followed the same downward trend from 1924 to

1934.[34] After 1929 Cuban sugar exports to the United States dropped sharply, both in terms of value and quantity.[35]

American loans and investments probably prevented a greater decline in American exports to Cuba.[36] There was a limit, however, to this process since the value of these investments was based on Cuba's ability to sell sugar at a profitable price. The attempt by the sugar producers to offset the depressed price by increased and more efficient production likewise had a practical limit. In the end, the sugar industry became a heavily overcapitalized structure which was extremely vulnerable to depression.

The value of American investments in Cuba declined sharply after 1929. By 1936 these investments were estimated to be $666,000,000.[37] This substantial decline resulted primarily from the revaluation of assets, and the reorganization of overexpanded corporate activities, especially in the sugar industry.[38] Bank ownership and operation of the Cuban sugar industry greatly increased as numerous sugar mills went into bankruptcy.[39] The value of Cuban Government bonds, however, generally retained a good market value until 1933, but this was an artificial process involving financial manipulations by American bankers and the Cuban Government.

II

The facts concerning trade and investments are necessary to any study of this type, but it is also necessary to consider how businessmen and government officials looked at the economic setting. The facts and figures take on meaning as they are interpreted and applied by the dominant groups in the country.

The problem of surplus production in the American economy had been developing for several years prior to World War I. As American industries speeded up to fill the increasing markets created by the war, more businessmen began to accept the idea that a growing export trade was vital to American prosperity. The National Foreign Trade Council had been saying this since 1912, but their national secretary stated, "One week of the European war did more than ten years of campaign discussion to convince the American people that foreign trade is a vital element in domestic prosperity."[40] Businessmen expressed a growing concern over the war-stimulated increase in American productivity and one commercial journal wrote:

> For the first time in our history as a nation the assurance of our continued prosperity rests with the future of our foreign trade. . . . Our industries were expanded and speeded up during four years of war to supply not only our own markets but also to meet a share of the world's demands. A decline from that level is desirable, but a return to the pre-war basis would result in serious industrial disturbance. We have surpluses to sell.[41]

The attitude was expressed many times during the 1920's. Mayor James M. Curley, of Boston, warned that American factories could serve the domestic market by producing only seven months out of the year, but that foreign markets must be found to consume the production of the other five months or else social unrest would flare.[42]

American businessmen stressed several ways of increasing trade. Some discussed the need to increase imports and the reciprocal nature of trade,[43] but in the face of domestic clamor for protection greater stress was placed on foreign lending. "Trade follows investment" was an oft-repeated theme.[44] Some attacks were made on this policy by businessmen who had no export interests, but such attacks were not numerous. The tariff increases after 1920 provided protection from import competition which these men desired.[45]

The markets and investment opportunities in Latin America became increasingly important to American business during this period. An official of the National City Bank wrote in 1920:

> If these new forces [the increase of industry to meet war demands], in addition to those in operation before the war, are now to be kept in productive activity, it becomes incumbent upon the United States to develop foreign outlets to take over the surplus to be expected from this production.
> It is the realization of this future probability . . . which has radically changed our attitude toward foreign business and particularly towards the trade of South America.[46]

The markets to the south were pictured as vital outlets for the surplus production of the United States, and the role of investments in expanding those markets was emphasized. One manufacturer stated that the statistics for American trade with Latin America emphasized the argument for building trade through loans,[47] and another called foreign loans the "key to foreign trade expansion" in Latin America.[48]

A cloud hung over this otherwise bright picture of profits and prosperity. European competition to regain these markets cast a continual shadow and helped to spur American businessmen into formulating various means of wooing Latin America. The British frankly announced that they were out to take back their prewar markets,[49] and the Germans soon added to American fears. A trade journal editorialized in 1921:

> Confronted as American steel exporters now are with unfavorable financial and trade conditions and with the possibility of competition from Germany, which before the war did a large business with South America, the need of the right attitude at Washington toward our customer nations on the south is evident.[50]

Better political relations, better business methods, lower tariffs, and more American investments were discussed as ways to hold and expand the Latin American market. The Pan Americanism that developed in the business community of the United States was dedicated to the expansion of American economic interests in the face of increased competition from Europe.[51]

Cuba was an example of how these various ideas were applied. The Cuban market was extolled by exporters, and the National Foreign Trade Council pointed out to manufacturers "the potentialities of the Cuban market, which is easily accessible but yet characteristic of the vast markets in the republics further south."[52] A writer in 1923 pointed out that American trade with Cuba had greatly increased in the past twenty years, and that this was only an example of the total market provided by Central America.[53] The National City Bank in 1919 published a pamphlet which described the profitable investment opportunities in Cuba and stated that "trade follows invested capital."

This publication ascribed the large growth of American exports to the fact that about one-half of Cuba's greatest industry was controlled by American capital, and the remaining interest was held by Cubans who were friendly toward the United States—"an avowed protector of safe and sane governmental authority."[54]

The spectre of European competition appeared in 1919, and American manufacturers were warned by commercial organs not to take the Cuban market for granted.[55] The American Minister to Cuba wrote to the State Department that British industries, backed by the British government, were taking definite steps to secure the trade of Cuba. Gonzales further reported that other countries were trying to secure Cuban trade. Thus, he wrote:

> In order to strengthen the position of our interests in Cuba, at my call a large and representative body of American citizens met at this legation on the afternoon of July 15, 1919, for the purpose of organizing here an *American Chamber of Commerce.* . . . . It is in capable hands, and later it may be found to be of valuable assistance in the advancement . . . of trade relations between the United States and Cuba.[56]

The Chamber of Commerce prospered, but the threat of competition continued. In 1925 Julius Klein, Chief of the Bureau of Foreign and Domestic Commerce, noted that Europeans were making "forceful" efforts to get the trade of Cuba. He warned that the share of the four leading European countries in Cuba's import trade was greater in 1923 than for the five-year average 1919–1923.[57] In 1929 the editor of the *Havana Post* and the *Times of Cuba* warned the State Department that the British were getting ready to "make a determined effort to gain the Cuban market." British purchases of Cuban sugar had doubled since 1928, he reported, and British interests had offered to buy his newspapers for twice their value.[58]

Many of these ideas and arguments received even greater stress after the onset of the depression in 1930. In addition, the place of Latin America in the export trade future of the United States received increased emphasis. The formation of the Committee on Inter-American Relations in March 1930 was symbolic of this trend.[59] This committee operated in conjunction with the National Foreign Trade Council, and Chairman Palmer Pierce stated that the committee was motivated by the belief that "our future important trade lanes will run north and south rather than east and west."[60] Thus, the argument that exports to Latin America—as well as the export trade in general—were vital to American prosperity appeared especially valid to many business-men after 1929.[61]

American economic interests in Cuba—as well as in the rest of Latin America—were of real concern to American business-men. Whether the interests involved concrete gains or potential worth, businessmen believed they were valuable and that they played a definite role in American prosperity. These concepts influenced business thinking about all phases of American re-lations with Latin America and contributed to the formulation of American policy.

III

American businessmen with overseas interests not only acted in accordance with the views described, but they made these views known to the United States Government, and requested specific action. J. Walter Drake, the president of Hupp Motor Company, spelled this out very clearly:

> Foreign trade, essentially a national business, is the ag-gregate of private effort carried on through organizations in which the government furnishes certain elements and performs certain definite functions. . . . The influence of diplomacy must be exerted from the very beginning and continued to the end. The men both at home and abroad engaged in this enterprise demand not only that the govern-ment actually foster and encourage their efforts, but they rely upon the support of the nation through diplomatic relations to continually assist and protect them. Diplomacy is inseparably linked with foreign trade.[62]

In this case these views were definitely made known to the government since Drake became Assistant Secretary of Com-merce in 1923.

In the spring of 1921 businessmen expressed much concern

over the matter of governmental action to push American economic interests overseas. An official of the Guaranty Trust Company wrote to Herbert Hoover expressing the opinion of a group of businessmen who had been meeting at the Union League Club. This group had been discussing how to provide foreign markets for American surplus production, and they believed that a lower tariff—especially for South America—was one answer.[63] Hoover wrote that this letter was typical of "many such" that he received.[64]

Secretary of State Hughes had a conference with Percival Farquar, an associate of Minor C. Keith, in which the economic pattern of the next eight years was very concisely outlined. The heart of Farquar's argument was that the American investing public must supply the funds for overseas investments, but that a pronouncement should be made by the government to the effect, "That it is opportune and in the interest of the country to make American industrial investment abroad, and that such investment will have the moral support of the government."[65] Farquar stressed the necessity for investments in order to push exports, but his primary interest was a mining project in South America. The bankers backing the project wanted to float a bond issue in the American market, and they wanted the government to help with the public relations. Bankers found that the export angle made a better talking point, in terms of "the national interest," than profit alone. The Foreign Trade Advisor of the State Department noted that such a pronouncement should be made since it would help American businessmen.[66]

On May 21, 1921 the Harding Administration, in an announcement, linked foreign loans and investments to the stimulation of American exports and industries.[67] This was followed by a semisecret dinner attended by eight leading bankers and Secretaries Hoover and Mellon. This was the first of a series of conferences which the administration held with financial interests to obtain their cooperation in using foreign loans to stimulate the export trade. The promotion and protection of American investments overseas were discussed, and the bankers pledged their support to the administration's economic policy.[68] Some of the bankers even suggested a plan which later came to be called "collective security," but administration officials were not prepared to guarantee the political security of every nation receiving American capital.[69]

The opinions of governmental officials concerning these issues appeared in numerous statements and publications. These opinions reveal the great affinity of views held by businessmen and officials of the government, and provide an important clue to the nature of American foreign policy.

Woodrow Wilson stated that he had been interested in carrying the enterprise of American businessmen to every quarter of the globe long before he was "suspected of being a politician."[70] Warren Harding said that the basis of foreign relations was the "struggle for commercial and industrial supremacy," and Calvin Coolidge's terse dictum on the business of America concerned the same idea.[71]

Charles Evans Hughes told the United States Chamber of Commerce in 1922 that:

> The Department of State is carrying the flag of the twentieth century. It aims to be responsive in its own essential sphere to what it recognizes as the imperative demands of American business. It aims at the coordination of the work of all departments bearing upon the same great object of American prosperity.[72]

In 1930 the American Ambassador to Germany, Frederic M. Sackett, stated that the prosperity of the United States depended on exports and that the growth of the export trade, "gives a clue to the economic reasons which influence America's foreign policy."[73] Career men in the State Department voiced the same opinions. Joseph Grew noted in his diary that Americans were not concerned with happenings on the Lithuanian border, but only in the ability of the service "to insure business, better business, bigger business."[74] The Assistant Secretary of State, J. Butler Wright, told the National Foreign Trade Convention in 1925 that all major differences between countries were economic in basis, and that the official policy of the government was to promote, support, and protect American enterprise abroad.[75]

Similar statements poured forth from other governmental

agencies. The Secretary of Commerce added up the American stake in the export trade and predicted a severe depression if foreign commerce diminished.[76] The Navy Department even joined in the clamor, and in a series of publications modestly pointed out the Navy's role in pushing exports. Even "errands of mercy" helped to open up "new fields for our commerce."[77]

The halls of Congress also resounded to export arguments. A representative from De Queen, Arkansas, proclaimed, "The future contains the real conflict, the real battle that is to be fought; and that is the battle of economic competition in the markets of the world."[78] During debate on the bill to reorganize the foreign service, speaker after speaker hammered on the need to sell American surplus production. Finally, Senator Tom Connally arose and commented: "All of our foreign policy seems to be motivated . . . by the dollar mark."[79]

Government officials consistently stressed American economic interests in Latin America and their importance to American prosperity. Joseph Grew told the Consular Association in 1924 that:

> Since beginning my duties here there has come forcibly and strikingly to my notice, the volume and importance of our work in Latin America. Our material interests in that section of the world are immense and are constantly increasing. . . . We must now . . . consider that Latin America must have the best of our thoughts, the best of our energies, and the best of our men.[80]

Grosvenor Jones, of the Commerce Department, told the National Association of Manufacturers that "if we do not enter the Latin American field we shall fail to maintain our position in international trade."[81] In 1924 Julius Klein, of the Bureau of Foreign and Domestic Commerce, called for additional offices in foreign countries, particularly in the Caribbean region and South America. These areas were singled out for special attention, Klein said, because of the great American commercial interest and the growing European competition there.[82]

Such opinions were voiced by many individuals. Presidents, cabinet members, departmental officials, and Congressmen voiced the belief that Latin America was vital to the economic well-being of the United States.[83] The words of Herbert Hoover, however, provided a concise summary of these views of the period:

> Great masses of people, both in our country and Latin America, would be irretrievably impoverished if our foreign trade were suspended for more than a few months. I would go further and say that we could not keep the whole of these huge hordes of humanity alive nor this civilization from anarchy if it were to cease.[84]

IV

This was the economic setting of the period 1919 to 1930. Economic statistics revealed a growing American stake in Central and South America, the Caribbean area, and Cuba. Statistics in themselves do not reveal the entire picture, however. They must be interpreted and understood, at least in part, by men before actions and policies can be formulated. The views of businessmen and government officials which were presented, reveal several concepts: (1) that the American economy was characterized by a surplus production which could best be sold abroad; (2) that foreign investments and loans were vital to continued prosperity; (3) that Latin American markets and investments, both actual and potential, were vital to the economy of the United States.

CHAPTER THREE

Sugar Tariff Battle:
First Phase, 1920-1928

I

The postwar slump in the economy of the United States produced an increased demand for an upward revision of the tariff. Many industries clamored for protection of their domestic market from foreign competition. Tariff revision was also seen as a possible means of alleviating the depressed condition of farmers, and the large farm organizations were as vigorous in their demands for protection as the chemical and textile industries.[1] The beet sugar growers and refiners were typical of this group. They had increased production to meet the war-stimulated demand, and the drastic collapse of the sugar market in 1920 hurt them as much as it did the Cuban producers. The beet sugar producers knew that Cuban sugar could undersell their product in a glutted market because of lower production costs. Transportation costs made little difference in the competitive position of Cuban raw sugar, so the domestic producers demanded an increase in the tariff in order to garner as much of the American market as possible.

At the beginning of the tariff debate in 1921 the effective rate on Cuban sugar was 1.0048 cents a pound; or 20 percent less than the full duty. The Underwood-Simmons Tariff Act, which had set this rate, had also provided that sugar should be placed on the free list on May 1, 1916. The domestic producers had managed to have this provision repealed on April 27, 1916, but the remaining duty was not an important issue as long as the market expanded. When competitive market conditions returned in 1920 the domestic producers once more discovered that they were to a considerable extent dependent on the tariff.[2]

The laboring oar in the tariff battle was pulled by the beet sugar producers. The states of California, Colorado, Michigan, Nebraska, and Utah were the principal producing areas, while the states of Idaho, Ohio, and Wyoming held secondary positions.[3] The Congressmen from these states were responsive to the demands of the beet sugar interests. Senator Reed Smoot, of Utah, was chairman of the Senate Finance Committee, and Representative Joseph Fordney, from the beet sugar section of Michigan, was chairman of the House Ways and Means Committee. Both were able champions of higher sugar duties. Cane sugar was produced in Louisiana, but this interest played a minor role in the campaign.

The House Ways and Means Committee began to hold hearings on tariff revision in January 1921, and the curtain rose on a struggle which lasted over a year and a half. This opening skirmish was brief. The beet sugar producers presented their demands, and these were countered by the Warner Sugar Refining Company of New York City and Edwin F. Atkins.[4] Both of these briefs attacking an increased sugar duty stressed the probable effect of such an increase on American exports to Cuba. Both pointed out that an increase in the tariff would raise the cost of raw sugar and thus hamper the competitive position of their refineries. In addition, Atkins told the committee that the Cuban Insurrection of 1895 had been caused by an increase in the American sugar tariff, and he plainly implied that a similar outbreak—resulting in great damage to American property—might be provoked if the duty were again raised.[5] The committee, however, recommended an increase in the sugar duty to 1.6 cents a pound on Cuban raw sugar.

The Harding administration soon after coming into office, called for the enactment of stopgap tariff legislation to halt the recession. This "Emergency" Tariff Act was rushed through a special session of Congress with the understanding that it would be kept on the statute books until a more detailed act could be framed. The Emergency Tariff raised the duty on Cuban sugar to 1.6 cents a pound, but the domestic producers wanted it set still higher.

By August 1921 both sides were warming up for the second-round battle. American businessmen interested in Cuban sugar accused Congress of hindering the efforts of bankers and the State Department to relieve conditions in Cuba.[6] The *Wall Street Journal* in a similar vein urged that the duty on Cuban sugar be lowered, and said that the beet sugar people were trying to "destroy Cuba."[7] The Cuban Government tried a different approach by sending a Commercial Commission to Washington to try to negotiate a change in the reciprocity treaty. The commission did not attack the American tariff directly, but suggested that increased preferential reductions be granted on a reciprocal basis.[8]

Business support for the Cuban proposal quickly became evident. Most of the letters received by the State Department, either directly or from Congressmen, stressed the factor of increased German competition. One manufacturer wrote:

> We have been doing considerable business with the Sugar Factories Construction Company, Havana, Cuba, and were recently advised through their New York Office that unless some modification of the existing treaty as to tariff is arranged there will be very little opportunity of securing any more business, for competitive prices offered by German manufacturers are such that they are at least 33% below American prices.[9]

The vice-president of the International General Electric Company stated his support of the proposed 50 percent differential reduction, and was informed by the State Department that copies of the Cuban commission's memorandum had been sent to members of the Congressional Committees concerned.[10]

Other American business groups sent communications to the government attacking the sugar tariff. The American Manufacturer's Export Association passed a resolution noting the effect of German competition on American trade with Cuba, and calling for favorable consideration of the memorandum of the Cuban Commercial Mission.[11] A similar resolution was sent by the Tampa, Florida, Board of Trade,[12] and letters of protest were sent by officials of Rotary International, a brick company, and an iron foundry.[13]

In October 1921 the American Committee on Cuban Emergency was organized in New York City. This group, composed "of American business interests whose trade with Cuba is seriously affected by the present industrial depression in the island," proposed to work for a reduction in the tariff.[14] Among the industrial and commercial groups represented were the Berwind-White Coal Mining Company, the Coca-Cola Company, the American Trading Company, the Westinghouse Electric Company, the American Car and Foundry Company, the Baldwin Locomotive Works, and numerous sugar companies.[15] The American Chamber of Commerce of Cuba worked with the committee. The Chamber urged its members to write to their "connections" in the United States—businessmen and Congressmen—and request them to cooperate with the Cuban Emergency Committee. The Chamber also supplied a sample letter for its members to use, and informed the State Department of its campaign.[16]

As the year 1921 drew to a close, the Cuban proposal for a revision of the reciprocity treaty was set aside. Businessmen with Cuban interests focused their attention on the tariff fight in Congress which was coming to a climax. This was probably the most expedient course, since throwing open the whole question of Cuban reciprocity could have resulted in the loss of even the 20 percent preferential at the hands of the protectionist-minded Congress.[17]

The Senate Committee on Finance began its hearings early in 1922. The major beet sugar companies and the American Farm Bureau Federation supplied the case for higher duties on sugar.[18] The argument for a lower tariff came from Edwin F. Atkins, representing E. Atkins and Company; Edwin P. Shattuck, representing several sugar companies which had organized as the American Producers of Cuban Sugar;[19] Horatio Rubens, representing the American Committee on Cuban Emergency; Frederic Craycraft, of the American Steel Company of Cuba; and representatives from the Cuban-American Sugar Company and Arbuckle Brothers' Refinery.[20] Their arguments chiefly consisted of the following points: (1) an increase in the tariff would seriously harm the American export trade with Cuba; (2) such an increase might provoke political disturbances and attacks on American property; (3) American investments of all kinds would be jeopardized.[21]

For all practical purposes, however, these elaborate arguments were a waste of time, since the beet sugar Congressmen were determined to increase the tariff.[22] The hearings did reveal which American business interests were concerned over the tariff. One significant group was missing: the bankers. The National City Bank finally made one public attack on the tariff in June 1922[23]— the General Sugars Company had been organized by that time. Otherwise, this group took little action in the antitariff campaign. It was working to protect its interests, however, in a series of behind-the-scenes maneuvers.

The beet sugar interests wanted to limit Cuban sugar production. Herbert Hoover sided with them on this issue, and tried to encourage the Cuban sugar interests to reach an agreement with the domestic producers. In the fall of 1921 the Cuban Government received several notes from the Commerce Department which strongly recommended the restriction of Cuban sugar production. Various plans for such restriction were proposed in these notes, but the Cuban Government rejected all of them.[24] By November 1921 the National City Bank, the Royal Bank of Canada, and J. P. Morgan and Company were ready to dissolve the Sugar Finance Commission—an experiment in controlled marketing which had been organized in February. The Commission had proved to be too restrictive for the bankers, however, and had helped to block a plan—formulated by the bankers and the sugar refiners—to dispose of the raw sugar held in storage.[25] The Cuban Government dissolved the Commission on December 21, 1921. By this time most of the Cuban sugar on hand had passed into the hands of the American bankers, and restriction was the last thing they wanted.

Dwight Morrow had several conferences with Herbert Hoover in November and December 1921. On December 11, 1921 Morrow sent Hoover a memorandum entitled "Sugar Restriction in Cuba." In this document Morrow stated the bankers' opposition to either production or marketing restrictions, and suggested that a conference of "leading banks" be called by Hoover to work out some method of stabilizing the sugar market. Morrow wrote that it was undesirable to work for a lower tariff because of the "various conflicting interests." In this respect Morrow agreed with Hoover, and suggested that the government work out a policy to protect investors in Cuban sugar and in domestic beet sugar.[26] The House of Morgan had loaned money to beet producers also.[27]

Later that month the bankers began to work out a plan, and Herbert Hoover went to New York City to confer with them.[28] The plan that emerged involved the organization of a corporation under the Webb-Pomerene Act. With the backing of the New York bankers several large companies formed the Export Sugar Company in December 1921.[29] The American Sugar Refining Company, B. H. Howell and Son, the Cuban-American Sugar Company, and the United Fruit Company formed the pool.[30] They agreed to take 500,000 tons of unsold Cuban sugar, refine it, and ship it to Europe. The refineries would then collect a toll of 90 cents a hundred pounds for the sugar which they sold.[31]

While the banks and some of the large sugar companies were protecting their interests by unloading the Cuban surplus, Horace Havemeyer carried on negotiations with the beet sugar executives. Havemeyer's American Sugar Refining Company worked for a compromise solution rather than attacking the tariff directly, since the company held 7.3 percent of the beet sugar industry —in addition to its Cuban holdings.[32] Other sugar companies worked with Havemeyer for a compromise, but still continued to fight the tariff through their lobby groups. The domestic producers, however, demanded that Cuban crop restriction be a part of any agreement, and the American producers and refiners of Cuban sugar did not want that. Senator Smoot and Herbert Hoover wrote to General Crowder asking him to impress on the Cuban Government the need for such restriction. Smoot even stated that if the Cuban Congress would restrict the 1922–23 crop to 2,500,000 tons he would try to have the tariff on Cuban sugar lowered to 1.4 cents a pound.[33] The Senate Finance Committee recommended a tariff of 1.6 cents, but when it became evident that the Cuban Government was not going to restrict production Senator Smoot introduced an amendment—which was passed—raising the rate on Cuban sugar to 1.84 cents a pound.[34] The final rate in the Fordney-McCumber Tariff Act of September 1922 was 1.7648 cents, a compromise between the Senate rate and the House rate of 1.6 cents.

Senator Smoot had originally favored the plan devised by the bankers and sugar companies to sell the surplus Cuban crop in Europe, but he believed that restriction of the Cuban crop would also be supported by the bankers.[35] When instead the bankers opposed restriction and dumped the Cuban surplus on the market,[36] Smoot cried "Wall Street Plot." On August 7, 1922 Senator Smoot ripped into the Wall Street bankers and the eastern refiners, and publicly accused them of trying to destroy the beet sugar industry.[37] Thus, a residue of mutual suspicion was all that remained of Herbert Hoover's hope of balancing interests.

II

Soon after the enactment of the Fordney-McCumber Tariff the National Defense Committee was formed in Cuba to fight the higher duty. This group hoped to work in cooperation with American refiners and manufacturers, and was primarily concerned with propaganda activities. Horatio Rubens advised the committee to concentrate on modification of the reciprocity treaty rather than on lowering the tariff.[38] Although the committee did little to push this plan, Rubens continued to advocate it as the best way of decreasing the duty on Cuban sugar. Rubens hoped that export interests in the United States would take the lead, and put pressure on the State Department. Obviously, this method of lowering the duty on sugar would have the advantage of bringing the State Department directly into the picture.[39]

The Cuban sugar interests had some hope at first that the flexible provisions of the tariff law might be utilized to lower the duty. The United States Tariff Commission, at the request of President Harding, began an investigation of the sugar tariff in March 1923.[40] After sixteen months of investigation, intergroup controversy, and pressure from various business interests the

Commission submitted two reports. The majority report recommended a lower duty on sugar.[41] President Coolidge shelved the report for ten months. Finally, in June 1925, he issued a long statement in which he refused to lower the duty. The President stated that American farmers should adjust their production to the domestic market rather than the foreign markets, and the domestic market should therefore be protected. He especially hoped that the excessive wheat acreage would be displaced by sugar beet production.[42] The Coolidge decision, according to a prominent firm of sugar merchants, "finally settles the matter until further Tariff legislation is introduced into Congress, which is not likely for the next few years, that is to say, with any hope of passing Congress."[43]

The average New York price for Cuban sugar had increased in 1923 and 1924, but had dropped in 1925. Thus, agitation for changing the reciprocity treaty began to increase in 1926. On May 5, the Cuban Government addressed a note to General Crowder proposing the negotiation of a new treaty.[44] On May 13, the business support for this proposal was noted by Dr. Manning of the State Department's Latin American Division. In a memorandum on the subject, Manning quoted extensively from an article in the May 12, New York *Journal of Commerce*, and cited a speech given before the Foreign Commerce Group meeting of the United States Chamber of Commerce by the president of the American Chamber of Commerce of Cuba.[45] A few days later this latter group formally addressed its views to the State Department in a resolution supporting the proposal of the Cuban Government.[46]

The State Department did not make a formal reply to the Cuban Government, and the matter drifted until February 1927. The Cuban Ambassador to the United States, Orestes Ferrara, broached the subject to Stokeley W. Morgan, and stated that Cuba wanted a stable, nonfluctuating price for sugar. He stated that a customs union or an increase in the preferential to 40 percent would be best for Cuban interests, but that the sliding scale preferential—the preferential to be high when the price was high, low when the price was low—would be more expedient.[47] The State Department considered this proposal for several months, and the memorandums concerning it generally expressed the desire to modify the treaty in some way.[48] Most of these also expressed a great reluctance to tangle with a hostile Congress and Executive over the sugar issue.[49]

The Department continued to check on business opinion to see what support was developing for the Cuban proposal. *Nation's Business* featured two articles on the Cuban problem,[50] and in September 1927 the Department learned that the American Chamber of Commerce of Cuba intended to submit a brief on the subject to the convention of the United States Chamber of Commerce.[51] In December the Cuban Government sent two proposals for revision of the reciprocity treaty to the Department. Both of these embodied increased preferentials on American and Cuban goods, and restriction of American sugar imports from the Philippines.[52] The Department Economic Advisor, Arthur N. Young, said that neither of these offered a practicable basis for revision due to the strength of American domestic producers.[53]

The Cuban Government tried to put pressure on the United States by manipulating its import duties. Generally this involved upward revisions, but in one case they drastically cut the tariff. The duty on gasoline was reduced from 16.39 cents a gallon to 0.1 cent, and the Standard Oil Company of New Jersey complained that this nullified their 20 percent preferential.[54] Dr. Manning called this an "insidious plan" to destroy the preferential treatment enjoyed by American exports,[55] but the Department realized that the Cubans were really trying to force the revision of the treaty.[56] A formal protest was not made, only "discreet" inquiries. In 1927 the Machado Government proclaimed a program of national self-sufficiency, and Orestes Ferrara told the 1928 National Foreign Trade Convention that this program was forced on Cuba by the American sugar tariff. Ferrara also warned this group that Cuba would try to industrialize if the United States continued its sugar policy.[57]

III

Although numerous groups took part in the tariff fight of 1921–22, excitement rapidly dwindled after the act was passed.

Some of the sugar producers and refiners continued to make sporadic protests to the Tariff Commission, but this interest group generally followed the lead of the bankers. From 1919 on the bankers and the producers put their reliance on expanded and more efficient production. They believed that Cuba would continue to supply at least 25 percent, or more, of the world's sugar production. In 1919 the National City Bank stated that European beet sugar production was completely disorganized, and that world consumption could be expected to double in the coming decade. Thus, it optimistically concluded that "the enlarged demands upon Cuba will continue indefinitely."[58] The bankers generally stayed out of the Fordney-McCumber Tariff battle while warding off demands that Cuban production be restricted. From 1926 on, however, they were faced with restriction attempts by the Cuban Government. While not averse to raising the price of sugar, American interests did not want decreased production.[59] The most serious threat was the Tarafa law passed in October 1927. This law was intended to control marketing and production, but protests from American producers and bankers forced President Machado to suspend all restrictions in August 1928.[60] Thus, until 1929 the bankers concentrated on large crops rather than the tariff.[61] Many of the refiners and producers followed this pattern also. The increase in duty had been passed on to the American consumer, and the market appeared to have adjusted to the Fordney Tariff without any ill effects.[62]

American manufacturers interested in the Cuban market generally lost interest in the sugar tariff after 1922—with the exception of some who were connected with the American Chamber of Commerce in Cuba. The increase in Cuban trade during 1923 convinced many that the Fordney Tariff was not harmful, and the decline after 1925 was generally masked by domestic prosperity. Some interests were no doubt reluctant to raise the tariff issue in times of general prosperity for fear of rocking the economic boat. The National Automobile Chamber of Commerce in 1927 was most eager to assure Senator Smoot that they were not working for a lower sugar tariff. They protested, however, that Smoot's accusation had forced them into the "embarrassing" position of having to make such a denial, since it would now appear as if they were taking sides in the controversy.[63] Some exporters did see the effect of the Tariff on Cuban purchasing power,[64] but many others either did not make this connection or believed that investments were the real answer to the problem.[65] Even Cuban attempts to create pressure by manipulating the import duties had little effect until 1929.

The State Department was to a considerable extent on the sidelines during the tariff battle of 1921–22.[66] Subsequently the Department generally shared the views of the exporters. While some officials were sympathetic to the idea of lowering the rates on sugar, most expressed reluctance to tangle with the protectionist-minded "farm bloc" in Congress. There were also some, such as Arthur N. Young, who saw no relationship between the tariff and Cuban purchasing power.[67]

The one group which consistently campaigned for lower duties was the American Chamber of Commerce of Cuba. This group was largely composed of Americans with direct investments in Cuba, though some bankers and exporters held membership also. Edwin F. Atkins expressed the general views of this group when he said that the reciprocity treaty was as vital to the protection of investments as the Platt Amendment.[68] These people were, as a rule, closer to the situation in Cuba than other groups, and thus could more readily see the relationship between Cuban prosperity and their own profit. By 1928 some members of this group were convinced that the Democratic party was more sympathetic to their interests than the Republican. As one individual declared: "The election of Mr. Hoover as the next President of the United States banishes hope, entertained by many of our people, that his opponent, Mr. Smith, would or could, lower the tariff against Cuban sugar."[69] The American Chamber of Commerce of Cuba helped to keep interest in the tariff alive, however, and were in a position to lead the campaign which began in 1929.

CHAPTER FOUR

Sugar Tariff Battle:
Second Phase, 1929-1933

I

By the fall of 1928 various industrial and agricultural groups were again agitating for an increase in the tariff. The domestic beet sugar producers were among the most outspoken advocates of higher duties. In the case of sugar three things had happened in order after 1922: (1) the domestic price increased while the foreign price was depressed; (2) domestic production increased; (3) both the domestic and the foreign price declined to a point where the domestic producers were again unable to make a profit.[1] While the beet sugar producers were increasing their output, they were supplying a decreasing proportion of the American market. During the period 1927–30 the domestic producers supplied 18.4 percent of the sugar consumed in the United States, while Cuba supplied 49.4 percent and the insular areas supplied 31.8 percent.[2] This represented a gain for the latter group, and a decline for Cuba and the beet sugar interests. Thus, the demand for more protection and the vigorous opposition to this demand were both stimulated by the same factors.

Five distinct lobby groups were engaged in the sugar tariff battle of 1929–30. Two of these, the domestic producers and the insular producers, generally worked together against the Cuban interests. Both were interested in cutting down the Cuban share of the American market, and therefore cooperated on some issues. On the other hand, both were competitors and consequently opposed each other on other issues.

The Cuban interests were represented by two groups. The first group to begin operations was composed of the American Chamber of Commerce of Cuba and the United States Sugar Association. The Chamber of Commerce represented Americans with direct investments in Cuba—excluding the sugar companies— such as railroads, branch factories, and business establishments.[3] The Sugar Association represented the W. J. McCahan Refining Company, the National Sugar Refining Company, the Hershey Corporation, the Fulton Iron Works of St. Louis, and many of the leading sugar companies.[4] In addition, the Association of Mill Owners of Cuba cooperated with this group.[5] All of these business groups were directly interested in the Cuban economy, and almost all of them had property in Cuba.

The second lobby was composed of the American Bottlers of Carbonated Beverages, the Hershey Corporation, and the H. H. Pike sugar brokerage firm.[6] This group was primarily interested in the price of sugar on the American market. The Hershey Corporation had a hand in both lobbies due to the diverse nature of its interests. It owned a candy factory in Pennsylvania and a sugar company in Cuba. There was another factor, however, which placed Hershey in a class by itself. Hershey was the major American company which refined sugar in Cuba for shipment to the United States, and this placed the company directly in competition with the American refiners. The H. H. Pike Company marketed the refined sugar which Hershey did not use in its candy factory.

The fifth lobby was composed of some of the seaboard refining companies, and usually entered the battle during the hearings to ask for higher duties on refined sugar. Most of the refining companies in this group had no direct interest in Cuba.[7]

II

The organization of the Chamber of Commerce–Sugar Association group was effected in December 1928. Word reached Cuba that the domestic sugar producers had held a meeting in Kansas City, Missouri, and had decided to fight for an increase in the sugar tariff to 3 cents a pound—which would be 2.4 cents on

Cuban raw sugar.[8] As a result, the American Chamber of Commerce and the Cuban Government held a conference, and the Chamber was authorized to act in behalf of Cuba during the forthcoming tariff controversy. Herbert C. Lakin, the president of the Cuba Company, was put in charge of the operation. Later in December Lakin went to New York and effected a working alliance with the United States Sugar Association. A publicity bureau was set up in Washington, D. C., and began to issue material under the name of either the Chamber of Commerce, the Sugar Association, or the Cuba Company.[9] In addition Lakin raised a "tariff defense fund" of over $95,000 and hired Edwin P. Shattuck to assist in the lobbying effort.[10]

The House Ways and Means Committee began hearings on the tariff bill in January 1929. An imposing array of domestic and insular sugar producers called for a higher duty on raw sugar, and several seaboard refining companies called for a higher duty on refined sugar. The Farm Bureau Federation also asked for the limitation of sugar imports from the Philippine Islands.[11] The attack on an increased sugar duty was largely conducted by Herbert C. Lakin and Edwin P. Shattuck. Representatives of two American firms testified that their export business to Cuba would be ruined by a tariff increase, and the testimony of Lakin and Shattuck stressed the trade argument also.[12] Most of the other arguments which had been used in the 1921–22 campaign were presented, but in addition a new point was presented. As the Lakin-Shattuck brief expressed it:

> The increase in American exports to the Latin American countries during the past few years is the result of a program of development of Latin American markets, and the chief necessity for the preservation of this market is Latin American good will.
>
> Events of the past few months show that distinct efforts are being made by our representatives to cultivate this good will, and to bring about a better understanding with Latin America.
>
> What therefore shall be said of a policy which is aimed directly at crippling one of the chief Latin American countries?[13]

This argument was particularly aimed at the incoming Hoover administration with its fervent professions of friendliness toward Latin America.

The principal efforts of the Lakin-Shattuck group were carried on behind the scenes. By personal contact and adroit maneuvering they tried to play both ends against the middle. On the one hand they worked to prevent an increase in the tariff, and on the other they worked for a compromise arrangement with the domestic producers to raise the price of sugar.

In January 1929 Lakin visited Dwight Morrow in Mexico—at Morrow's invitation—to apprise him of the situation. Lakin thought that Morrow would be the next Secretary of State, but this hope soon vanished.[14] Another contact, however, proved to be more valuable. On January 29, Lakin wrote to General Crowder, who was helping the Cuban lobby:

> By great and good fortune I find that Shattuck . . . is perhaps Hoover's closest legal friend. He is the personal attorney for Hoover and all his family. I think I have persuaded him to undertake a confidential mission first to convince Hoover, and secondly to work on the committees and members of Congress, on behalf of Cuba.[15]

Edwin Shattuck had worked with Herbert Hoover on the Sugar Equalization Board, the American Relief Administration, the European Children's Fund, and other charitable organizations.[16] Lakin hoped to utilize this friendship, and offered Shattuck a responsible retainer's fee for his services. Shattuck tentatively accepted the offer, and went to Miami, Florida, to see Herbert Hoover upon his return from the South American tour. Hoover assured Shattuck that the proposed arrangement would not "embarrass" him, and the two men had several conferences during the month of February.[17]

Lakin and Shattuck hoped to make good use of the Latin American good will argument which they had presented to the House Committee. Lakin wrote on February 1, 1929: "I really have some hope that it may be possible to persuade President Hoover to insist that the duty on sugar be not raised. My hope is based on making use of his desire to foster good will with

Latin America."[18] This group, however, did not intend to stop with mere argument. They encouraged various groups in Cuba to send briefs attacking the United States and its tariff policy to newspapers and leading citizens throughout Latin America. Thus, Lakin hoped to stir up the evidence which he could point to as proof that an increase in the sugar duty would antagonize the rest of Latin America and threaten the American export trade.[19]

The Cuban interests also hoped to work out an undercover deal with the domestic producers to raise sugar prices, and if possible to drive a wedge between the insular and domestic interests. Early in January 1929 Lakin proposed his first idea.

> My notion is that we could secretly put some such plan [rebate to domestic producers] up to Smoot, Petriken, and Carlton, and get them to thinking in terms of protection against not only the Philippines, but also Hawaii and Porto Rico. Meantime, of course, our technical defense before the Ways and Means Committee would proceed, as if no such plan were in contemplation. It seems to me that secrecy is important.[20]

Lakin made these proposals to Senator Smoot and the beet sugar interests, and they were introduced into the House Committee's discussion.[21]

The Lakin-Shattuck group continued to work on more definite plans. W. A. Chadbourne suggested an extensive plan, but on February 9, 1929 Edwin Shattuck submitted several modifications which Lakin and President Machado believed to be more practicable.[22] This revised plan consisted of three parts: (1) consent to an increase in the full sugar duty to 3 cents; (2) amend the reciprocity treaty to give Cuba a 50 percent preferential reduction on 2,400,000 tons; (3) limit the free importation of Philippine sugar to 500,000 tons each year, the remainder to pay the full duty.[23] This was an ambitious plan indeed, as Lakin realized when he wrote to Shattuck that "nobody but you with your special connections could hope of success."[24] This plan represented one of the first attempts to stabilize sugar marketing by a proportionate division of the American sugar market.

Another plan was under discussion, however, which had some

support from Herbert Hoover. This was the sliding scale of duties: the tariff would fluctuate with the price of sugar. In a series of conferences held in Miami, Florida, just prior to his inauguration, Hoover had told both Shattuck and Senator Smoot that he wanted to work out a plan to protect both the Cuban and the domestic sugar interests.[25] Hoover suggested the sliding scale as offering a possible solution, and asked Shattuck to confer with Smoot and try to work out the details.[26] Lakin and Shattuck were not sure of Smoot's reaction to the idea until General Crowder reported on March 22 that he had conferred with Smoot and the Senator was working on a sliding scale proposal. Crowder further stated that the time was ripe for making suggestions to Senator Smoot.[27] Both sides continued to work on such proposals, but no specific plans were developed for several months.

The beet sugar producers had hoped to obtain some agreement as to Cuban crop restriction in 1921, and they soon indicated that restriction of some kind would have to be part of any compromise. There was one significant difference between conditions in 1921 and 1929. Some of the important Cuban interests were convinced that control of some variety was a necessity. In February 1929 Colonel Deeds, the president of General Sugar Company, and S. R. Noble of the Royal Bank of Canada contacted the Cuban Government and stated the need for controlled marketing through a "single sales agency."[28] The control scheme was held in reserve, however, while Lakin and Shattuck pushed the plan to limit the importation of sugar from the Philippines. The domestic producers appeared to be going along with this idea until it ran into serious opposition from Secretary of State Henry L. Stimson, who had been governor-general of the Philippines from 1927 to 1929. Stimson testified before the House Ways and Means Committee in April and accused the Cuban interests of trying to undermine the Philippines.[29]

By April the domestic producers were bringing Cuban restriction into the discussion. W. L. Petriken, president of the Great Western Sugar Company, told General Crowder that there was no longer any hope for a flat Philippine restriction to 500,000 tons. Instead, Petriken said that his group was pushing a sliding restriction plan for both the Philippines and Cuba. This proposal would set importation quotas of 500,000 tons for the Philippines and 3,000,000 tons for Cuba. If Cuba sent more than her allotted tonnage to the United States the Philippines might increase their importations by one-sixth of the Cuban increase. Thus, Cuba would be penalized for exceeding the stated limit, and Petriken said that the beet producers preferred this arrangement to a single sales agency controlled by Cuba.[30]

This plan died also, but the Cuban interests continued to work on the single seller plan. Colonel Tarafa informed Herbert Lakin that President Machado was ready to impose 100 percent control as soon as Lakin informed him that the time for compromise had arrived.[31] Consultation with Senator Smoot convinced Lakin and Tarafa that the single sales agency was an acceptable part of the compromise. It was agreed not to have any aspects of the plan discussed in the House, and to spring it in the Senate at the last minute.[32] This plan also involved the sliding scale duty on sugar, and both sides began work on the technical composition of the schedule.[33]

Thus, by the middle of May the backstage compromise maneuvers between the Lakin-Shattuck group and the domestic producers appeared to be fairly successful. There was still some hope that the imports of Philippine sugar could be limited, but the basic plans involved the single sales agency to restrict Cuban exports, and the sliding scale tariff.

III

The Lakin-Shattuck lobby carried on a separate campaign to prevent the tariff from being raised. This was primarily directed toward the House of Representatives, and to a lesser extent toward various groups throughout the country which in turn might pressure Congressmen. Of course, there were some hazards involved in working on two separate—and incompatible—campaigns at the same time. As Herbert Lakin observed in a letter to Shattuck:

It might be dangerous to approach them [the Consumer's League] if we have any hope of working out an arrangement which will enable everybody to get a little better price for sugar; but if we have no such hope and decide merely to attempt to prevent the duty from being raised the league might be interested in our argument that the beet people are attempting to make the American consumer pay $84,000,000 in order to benefit the beet people by less than $9,000,000.[34]

Thus, the Lakin-Shattuck group concentrated on the Congressional part, and left most of the propaganda and group contact effort up to the Pike-Baldwin lobby.[35]

The Cuban interests had two important contacts on the House Ways and Means Committee: Cordell Hull of Tennessee, and James Frear of Wisconsin. Lakin had even decided to try to employ Hull as a lobbyist if Hull retired in March 1929.[36] Hull decided against retiring, and continued to leak information concerning committee discussions to Lakin.[37] James Frear had several conferences with Herbert Lakin and General Crowder, and told them in advance of his plan to introduce a bounty proposal.[38] On April 17, 1929 Frear presented his bill calling for bounty payments to beet growers and for a lower duty on sugar.[39]

About the middle of April Hull informed Lakin that the Ways and Means Committee was split over the sugar duty, and that more pressure should be applied, especially on Congressmen Isaac Bacharach, Harry Estep, and Henry W. Watson.[40] Lakin contacted Junior Owens of the Bottler's Association, and asked him to utilize his lobby also. In addition, several other men were contacted and requested to put pressure on the Congressmen involved. Owens later stated that he sent out a night letter to his members in the congressional districts concerned, and asked them to urge their representatives to vote against an increase in the tariff.[41]

On May 7 the House Committee presented the tariff bill. The pressure had not been effective enough, however, and an increase in the duty on Cuban sugar to 2.4 cents a pound had been recommended. The United States Sugar Beet Association declared its support of the bill—even though it had hoped for

higher rates and Philippine restriction.[42] Cordell Hull called the
sugar duty increase "an economic outrage,"[43] and James A. Frear
sent a letter to all of the House members urging them to force
the issue on the floor so that a separate vote could be taken on
the sugar duty.[44] The two Cuban sugar lobbies had been discussing floor tactics for several weeks. Junior Owens and Herbert Lakin decided that it would be a good idea to get Con-
gresswoman Ruth Pratt of New York to lead the fight. Owens
said that Mrs. Pratt could rally the women of America to defend their sugar bowls, and that this appeal would make every
paper in the land. He concluded with a sage comment regarding
the ways of lobbyists and lawmakers:

> In my opinion such a move would be of untold value to
> Mrs. Pratt, provided she is ambitious to be one of the out-
> standing women of America. It is one of those cases where
> it is six for her and six for us. . . . We would furnish her all
> the material she needs to make this fight and, of course,
> we would be mighty glad to do it.[45]

Mrs. Pratt made her maiden appearance before the House by
reading a letter attacking the sugar tariff from William Green,
of the AFL, to Representative Frear.[46] On May 20, Mrs. Pratt
delivered a stinging attack on the beet sugar producers. Mrs.
Gladys Jones, who was in charge of the Lakin-Shattuck lobby's
publicity bureau, helped her to write it.[47]

The sugar tariff was stirring up so much dissension that the
Republican party decided to submit the bill to a party caucus
before reporting it to the House for action.[48] Two days prior
to the caucus Stephen Love and Harry Austin, of the beet
sugar interests, were called to Speaker Nicholas Longworth's
room where they were informed it would be impossible to get
the 2.4 rate through the caucus, and that they would have to
accept the sliding scale or get nothing at all.[49] Austin replied:

> Coming at the eleventh hour, you can imagine that this
> threw a bombshell into our camp. Our answer to this was
> a farm block caucus, the day preceeding the regular Republi-
> can caucus. Seventeen beet-sugar States were represented by
> about 50 Congressmen, who voted unanimously to stand by

the 2.40 rate and oppose the opening of the sugar schedule on the floor of the House for amendment. This made the administration leaders sit up and take notice, and you have been advised of the result.[50]

The farm bloc strategy worked, and on May 28 the House passed the bill setting the duty on Cuban sugar at 2.4 cents a pound.

IV

William H. Baldwin was the chief lobbyist for the Bottler's Association-Hershey-Pike group. In conjunction with Junior Owens of the Association and H. H. Pike, Jr., he engaged in a wide range of contact activities. Propaganda, group contact, and public relations in general were conducted by Baldwin. Lakin and Shattuck had some contact with the editor of the *Washington Post,* through General Crowder,[51] but to a great extent they let Baldwin handle this side of the campaign. Baldwin was in touch with such organizations as the Federal Council of Churches, the Leonard Wood Memorial for the Eradication of Leprosy, the Foreign Policy Association, and the Daughters of the American Revolution. Some of these contacts proved fruitful. Baldwin submitted resolutions attacking the sugar tariff to his contacts in the New York State Chamber of Commerce and the American Association of Exporters and Importers. Both groups approved the resolutions.[52] Baldwin also supplied material to Raymond L. Buell for the Foreign Policy Association's study on Cuba and the tariff, and took credit for instigating William Green's letter to James A. Frear—which had been read to the House by Mrs. Pratt.[53] The National Catholic Welfare Council was encouraged to attack the beet producers on the grounds of exploitation of Mexican labor; the American Federation of Labor and the National Child Labor Committee were brought into the attack on child labor in the beet fields; and numerous consumer and women's clubs were contacted.[54]

The path of the lobbyist, however, was obstructed by numerous pitfalls. Baldwin had hoped to get one of the candidates for the national presidency of the D.A.R. to link the limitation of sugar imports from the Philippines with continental defense, but:

> We did not get word to go ahead with Mrs. Talmadge
> . . . until it was too late for the D.A.R. presidency. . . .
> Anyway, Mrs. Talmadge lost the election and thereby any
> news value.[55]

Some concern was expressed by P. A. Staples over stirring up
the AFL, because any close investigation would reveal that
workers in Cuba were paid low wages and worked twelve hours
a day.[56] On another occasion the Cuban interests paid all the
expenses of a Cuban vacation for a *Time* magazine editor and
his wife. The editor returned to New York to write a very non-
committal article about Cuba, while his wife continued to "live
it up" in Havana at Lakin's expense. Mr. Lakin commented, "I
fear that our investment in her was not especially profitable."[57]

These lobby groups had very little contact with the State
Department. On one occasion the editor of the Havana *Post*
visited the department and informed Walter C. Thurston, of the
Latin American Division, that any increase in the sugar tariff
would result in the loss of American trade.[58] On June 8, 1929
the Secretary of State sent a memorandum to President Hoover.
This memorandum discussed the probable influence of tariff
increases on relations with other countries, and the only part
of the document which attacked the tariff was that prepared by
the Latin American Division. This section, which was also the
longest, stated that the "commercial competitors" of the United
States were fomenting anti-American feeling, and that tariff increases would only give this element fresh ammunition. Cuba and
the sugar tariff were used as an example.[59] Thus, the State Department echoed the arguments of the Cuban interests, and supported their position.

The scene of action shifted to the Senate in June 1929. Preparations for the Senate hearings were started in May. H. H. Pike, Jr.
drew up plans concerning which individuals were to testify,
what points each should make, the order of their appearance,
and the attitudes of the members of the committee.[60] As Pike explained, "the main thing is to stage a good program."[61] During
the course of these preparations, however, the Pike-Baldwin group
began to discover the dual activities of the Lakin-Shattuck
group. Pike complained that the latter group was not cooperating

with him, and that apparently they were not going to make much of a fight before the Senate Finance Committee. He further stated that this group was "flirting" with the sliding scale idea, and that he believed that Shattuck was in "very close touch" with the other interests. He concluded that, "This rather tends to hurt our confidence in these people when we are supposed to be working with them and they fail to tell us the truth about people with whom they are working."[62] By the time the Senate hearings on sugar began, the alliance between the two groups had been broken.

The Senate Finance Committee conducted hearings from June 13 to July 18. The Farm Bureau called for abrogation of the Cuban reciprocity treaty while the beet producers repeated the arguments which they had presented at the House hearings.[63] Edwin Shattuck, John Snyder of the Hershey Corporation, and G. R. Parker of the American Exporters and Importers Association testified in favor of lower sugar duties.[64] The hearings were rather beside the point since the desires of the groups concerned were already well known, and the committee did not critically examine any of the testimony.[65]

The real issue in the sugar controversy was the much discussed sliding scale. It was generally known that Senator Smoot was working on such a plan, but the details were not revealed until the latter part of July. Smoot would not consult with Lakin and Shattuck either, and all of the sugar interests awaited Smoot's announcement with some apprehension.[66] Herbert Hoover was reported as favoring the sliding scale, and the National City Bank indicated that it favored the compromise also.[67]

When Smoot finally announced his plan a storm of protest broke out, and the Senate Finance Committee announced that it would reopen the hearings to consider the plan. Senator Smoot's sliding scale provided for a full duty of 1 to 3 cents, the duty to go up as the price went down. Willett and Gray, sugar statisticians, even declared that most of the sugar trade considered it unworkable.[68] The hearings reopened on August 7, 1929. The Farm Bureau Federation and the beet producers attacked the plan, and declared that the rates were too low.[69] H. H. Pike, Jr. called it a "dangerous step toward communism," because the rates were too high. Herbert Lakin, who attended the hearings but did not testify, also believed that the scale was too high.[70] On August 11 the Republican members of the committee presuaded Smoot to drop the sliding scale idea and to work for a flat rate. Compromise between the Cuban and domestic sugar interests had once more proved to be difficult.

The Republican committee members went into secret session, and after an extensive debate they compromised on a rate of 2.2 cents for Cuban sugar. This rate was written into the tariff bill and the completed bill was introduced into the Senate on September 4, 1929.

Herbert Lakin renewed his lobbying efforts in an attempt to get the sugar duty lowered by the Senate. He wrote to President Machado that the hopes of the Cuban interests lay with the Democrats and the insurgent Republicans, but that great efforts had to be made to counteract the logrolling tactics of the regular Republicans. Thus, Lakin had conferences with Senators William Borah of Idaho and Pat Harrison of Mississippi to discuss strategy. Borah was considering a bounty amendment, while Harrison was preparing an amendment to lower the proposed duty.[71] Lakin also wanted Shattuck to continue to talk to Herbert Hoover. As Lakin saw it, there were four courses of action open to Hoover. He could openly attack an increased sugar duty; he could secretly notify the Republicans in Congress that the duty must not be increased; he could veto the tariff bill; or he could utilize the proposed flexible provision to lower the sugar duty after it was passed.[72] Lakin recognized that as a matter of practical policy Hoover would probably not follow the first and third courses. The fourth course was eliminated when the Senate rejected the flexible provision.[73] Thus, the Cuban interests were faced with the task of persuading Hoover to put pressure on his party leaders in Congress.

In January 1930 the fight was resumed in the Senate. Senator Borah's bounty amendment was defeated,[74] but Senator Harrison's amendment to retain the 1.76 cents duty on Cuban sugar was passed.[75] The Packard, Essex, Hudson, and White automobile dealers of Cuba, and Metro-Goldwyn-Mayer de Cuba immediately sent congratulatory cables;[76] but the battle was far from finished. The lobby investigation, which had been conducted late in 1929, provided ammunition for Senator Smoot. The report of the committee was read to the Senate,[77] and Smoot delivered a bitter attack on all the groups working for a lower sugar tariff—especially the National City Bank. Of course the Senator ignored the domestic sugar lobby, but he solemnly declared:

> Oh Mr. President, if I could only tell the whole story of the intrigues and the rotten deals connected with this matter it would surprise the Senate. I would refer to the fact that a decision was reached at one time to destroy the sugar industry in the United States. I know the story.[78]

Senator Smoot did not stop with oratory, but went on to introduce an amendment to raise the duty on Cuban sugar to 2.0 cents a pound. This amendment was passed when nine Senators who had voted for the Harrison amendment switched to the Smoot camp.[79] Representative Willis C. Hawley was not satisfied with the Senate rate, but the House agreed to cut their proposed rate to 2.2 cents. On May 2, however, the low tariff group in the House pushed through an amendment cutting the House proposal to 2.0 cents. An attempt was made by the domestic refiners to reopen the sugar schedule in order to raise the duty on refined sugar, but this attempt failed.[80] Thus, the Hawley-Smoot Tariff Act carried a duty of 2.0 cents a pound for Cuban sugar.

V

The sugar tariff battle of 1929–30 left a residue of unsatisfied wants and burning animosity. Almost every group involved felt that it had been betrayed or wrongly used. The residue of battle settled on groups not directly connected with sugar. Senator John J. Blaine of Wisconsin even asked for an investigation into the influence of the Mormon hierarchy on the sugar tariff vote in the Senate.[81]

Although the calculated attempts to compromise broke down, the end result was actually a compromise. Herbert Hoover took the credit for the final settlement. He had told Harry Guggenheim in November 1929 that he strongly opposed the proposed increase, and he later stated that he believed the ¼ cent compromise was just to both sides. Hoover himself, however, pronounced the verdict when he said: "However, there will be little consolation in that, because no one is ever grateful for negative blessings."[82]

The sugar schedule, which the editor of the *New York Times* called the most controversial in the entire bill,[83] was received as Hoover predicted. Some of the Cuban interests did express relief that the rate only went up ¼ cent, but this attitude changed within a few months. Actually, the Cuban sugar interests had won something of a victory with, or in spite of, their concentrated activity. The Farm Bureau Federation had asked for a duty of 3.0 cents on Cuban sugar,[84] and even the protectionist members of the House were not able to keep the 2.4 rate. The "sons of the wild jackass" had frankly announced that if industrial groups attacked agricultural tariffs they would fight to pull down the entire tariff structure.[85] Against such farm bloc strength, and with little to offer in the way of bargains, the Cuban interests needed all the influence and pressure they could muster to keep the increase as low as they did.

During the course of the debate the Cuban interests became increasingly allied with the Democratic party and the insurgent Republicans. James Frear and Cordell Hull in the House, and William Borah and Pat Harrison in the Senate worked closely with the Cuban interests. In addition some of the lobbyists worked with the publicity director of the Democratic National Committee, and some of the material originated by the lobby was issued by the committee.[86] This alliance would prove to be most significant after March 1933.

Two arguments put forward by the Cuban interests assumed increasing importance in the debate of 1929–30 and in the years following. The first of these was the argument that an increased sugar duty would seriously injure the American export trade with Cuba. More export groups came out publicly in support of a low sugar tariff in 1929 than had done so in 1921. By 1929 many exporters could clearly see that trade with Cuba was declining, and they could document their case with facts and figures.[87] The second argument was that American relations with Cuba affected the attitude of the other Latin American countries toward the United States. This in turn, it was argued, would affect the American export trade with all of this area. The National City Bank, Senator La Follette, Herbert Lakin, and many others stressed this point.[88] Lakin even encouraged the other Latin American countries to attack the tariff policies of the United States, and thus furnish the Cuban interests with proof of the argument. Many of these countries did not need much encouragement.[89]

Most of the American refining companies were displeased with the tariff because it did not increase the differential on refined sugar imports—the differential being the percentage of additional duty based on the raw sugar duty. When the duty was set at 2.0 cents on Cuban raw sugar the duty on Cuban refined automatically became 2.12 cents, in accordance with the fixed differential. In the earlier tariff acts this had not been a problem, but after 1924 Cuba began to produce refined sugar for export. As a result most of the refiners in 1929 were more concerned over increasing the duty on refined Cuban sugar than over keeping the duty on raw sugar down. The McCahan and the National refining companies, however, went along with the Cuban lobby, and stayed out of the refined sugar controversy. Some interests were split. The United Fruit Company backed the Cuban lobby while its subsidiary, the Revere Refining Company, worked with the seaboard refiners. The same thing was true of the Lowry Company and the Pennsylvania Sugar Refining Company. The Hershey Corporation worked for lower duties on both raw and refined sugar. This internecine strife probably weakened the influence of the lobbies concerned.

By 1929 the groups with significant economic stakes in Cuba had decided that price stability was of major importance. The American Chamber of Commerce of Cuba and the United States Sugar Association represented these groups. In addition some of the New York banks were allied with this faction.[90] The Chamber of Commerce–Sugar Association group supported plans involving some form of controlled marketing combined with lower duties and restriction of insular area imports into the

United States. In some cases these plans also contained bounty payment provisions for the beet producers. As a result of this shift in attitude toward control, the Cuban interests—with the exception of many refiners—were able to attempt a compromise with the domestic producers in 1929.[91] Compromise was a distinct possibility, since the beet sugar interests were also thinking in terms of stable prices and control. Definite terms were never worked out, however, and when Senator Smoot's sliding scale was rejected by all concerned the controversy once more centered on the sugar duty.

VI

After the enactment of the Hawley-Smoot Tariff Act the Cuban sugar interests again tried to work out a market stabilization plan. On August 30, 1930 a conference was held in New York City under the leadership of Thomas L. Chadbourne. Representatives of all parts of the sugar industry were present, including beet and domestic cane sugar men. Chadbourne stressed the need for cooperative action to save investors in every phase of the sugar business, and Dr. Viriato Gutierrez then proposed the plan which had been devised by the Cuban interests. Under the proposed "Gutierrez plan" Cuba would limit her sugar exports to the United States to a maximum of 2,800,000 long tons for 1931—with proportional increases in later years if consumption increased—if the growers in the United States, Puerto Rico, Hawaii, and the Philippine Islands agreed not to exceed the crops made in 1930. In addition, Cuba would try to further an international conference among the other producers of the world's sugar, with a view to a general stabilization of the industry.[92] The domestic and insular producers liked the idea of Cuban restriction but they could not agree on restricting their own production. Thus, the Gutierrez plan did not go into effect.[93]

The Cuban interests decided to go ahead with the international conference plan, however, and on November 21, 1930 a delegation headed by Thomas L. Chadbourne departed for Europe. Early in February 1931 agreements were made by the representatives of seven countries after a series of conferences in Amsterdam, Brussels, and Berlin. Cuba, Java, Germany, Czechoslovakia, Poland, Belgium, and Hungary agreed to restrict their sugar exports for a period of five years.[94] The Cuban interests soon discovered that restriction by producers of 45 percent of the world's sugar was not the final answer to their problems, especially in regard to the United States market. The domestic and insular producers took an increasing proportion of that market after 1930, at the expense of the Cuban producers. The Cuban share of the American market dropped from 49.4 percent in 1930 to 25.3 percent in 1933. For the same period the domestic share rose from 18.4 percent to 26.6 percent, and the insular share rose from 31.8 percent to 47.9 percent.[95] It was soon obvious to the Cuban producers that improvement of their marketing position in the United States depended, in part, on the restriction of their chief competitors.[96]

The American business groups interested in Cuba continued to stress tariff revision and the revision of the reciprocity treaty. In June 1931 Guerra Everett, of the Cuban Chamber of Commerce in the United States, delivered a resolution of the Chamber to President Hoover. The document pointed out the drop in American exports to Cuba, and stated that increased preferentials would enable the United States to dominate the Cuban market.[97] Thomas L. Chadbourne addressed the Institute of Public Affairs of the University of Virginia on the same subject on July 7, 1931. Chadbourne had this speech printed in pamphlet form, and mailed to individuals and groups throughout the country. In this address Chadbourne called for cooperative action on the part of the sugar producers, as well as for reduction of the tariff.[98]

The Fourth Pan American Commercial Conference met in October 1931, and Thomas L. Chadbourne and Guerra Everett addressed the meeting. Chadbourne delivered a speech similar to the one given in July. Everett called for the sympathy of the Latin American delegates and the active support of the North American delegates in the campaign to revise the reciprocity treaty.[99]

A note of humor crept into the propaganda on occasion. A letter calling for the immediate end of the sugar tariff, closed on a poetical note:

Cuban freeman	No, I'm not,
Cuban freeman	No, I'm not,
What's the matter	Can't be free
What's the matter	As can be,
With you?	Till my sugar,
Aren't you free,	CUBAN SUGAR
Aren't you free,	IS FREE TOO.[100]
As can be?	

Another organization entered the picture in October 1932 when the World Trade League organized a committee on Cuba. Several men who had been active in the tariff campaign were members of the committee. H. H. Pike, Jr. was chairman, and some of the other members were A. D. Hutcheson, the President of the Cuban Chamber of Commerce in the United States, Guerra Everett, and William H. Baldwin. This committee attacked the tariff act of 1930, and called for downward revision.[101] H. H. Pike, Jr. presented these views to the 1933 National Foreign Trade Convention. In addition, Pike attacked the domestic refiners for their efforts to raise the tariff on refined sugar.[102]

The domestic refiners had been agitating for an increase since June 27, 1930. The Tariff Commission held several hearings on the issue, but the requests of the domestic refiners were not recommended. The refiners also sent memorials to President Hoover and to Congress.[103] In addition, the refiners attacked the Chadbourne plan and all attempts to stabilize the sugar market through the restriction of raw sugar sales or production.[104]

Thus, by 1933 American businessmen interested in Cuba were acutely aware of the related problems of the tariff and market stabilization. Furthermore, these groups had generally become convinced that the Republicans would not furnish solutions for these problems. The interests of these groups, combined with the export demands of many manufacturers, furnished the economic background for the New Deal approach to Cuban-American relations.

CHAPTER FIVE

The Mail Order Trade, Cigars, and the Struggle for the Parcel Post Convention

I

Tobacco was the second major export product of Cuba, and the relationship between tobacco exports to the United States and American exports to Cuba provided the stage for another important controversy over policy. This controversy, however, was not based on the tariff. Instead, it was based on the Parcel Post Convention and sections 2804 and 3402 of the Revised Statutes of the United States. Cuba was primarily interested in the export of tobacco products such as cigars and cigarettes. The United States market for these goods consisted, for the most part, of dealers who ordered, in relatively small quantities, directly from Cuba. In addition, there were numerous American firms which shipped goods by mail to Cuba. In the absence of a parcel post agreement all of these goods had to be sent by first class mail, which was more expensive and subject to weight limitation. Thus, both American exporters and Cuban tobacco manufacturers were interested in the negotiation of a parcel post convention.

As early as 1920 the National Foreign Trade Council cited the great need for the establishment of a parcel post service between the United States and Cuba in order to "cement" the business relationships developed during the war.[1] The agitation for such an agreement continued to grow,[2] but Cuba refused to negotiate a parcel post convention with the United States. The reason for the Cuban refusal was found in sections 2804 and 3402 of the Revised Statutes of the United States, which prohibited the importation of cigars and cigarettes by parcel post in quantities of less than 3,000.[3] This law nullified in advance any benefits which Cuba might hope to derive from a parcel post convention, since most American firms—and individual purchasers—did not buy in such quantity.

On December 8, 1924 the Post Office Department notified the State Department that plans were being made to hold a postal conference with Cuba.[4] This conference was held in January 1925, and a temporary parcel post convention was worked out. The Post Office Department could not promise the Cuban Government that the cigar limitation statute would be repealed, but several concessions were offered to Cuba in an attempt to overcome this objection. The United States agreed to pay Cuba twenty-five cents for each package sent to Cuba, and to handle many of the routine postal duties which normally would have been handled by the Cuban postal authorities. American exporters were to be benefited by a provision raising the parcel weight limit from four pounds six ounces to eleven pounds. The temporary convention was to become effective on July 1, 1925, if ratified by both countries, and was to last for fourteen months.[5]

American business interests supported the proposed agreement. The Rochester, New York, Chamber of Commerce urged that it be ratified "as soon as possible,"[6] and Julius Klein, of the Commerce Department, stated that the convention would help to divert Cuban trade from Europe.[7] The 1925 National Foreign Trade Convention went a step further and called for the negotiation of a permanent convention and the repeal of the cigar importation statute. The final declaration stated:

> Cuba has a parcels post trade with Europe of more than thirty million dollars a year. American manufacturers are effectively barred from that market through the operation of this statute.[8]

The effective date of the agreement had to be postponed by the Post Office Department, but on October 31, 1925 the convention was transmitted to the State Department for ratification by the President.[9] Thus, the temporary convention became effective on November 1, 1925.

Even before the ratification of the convention the State Department's Latin American Division had expressed the opinion that Cuba had only agreed to the temporary convention as a means of impressing American manufacturers with the advantages of such an agreement. Then, Dr. Manning stated, the Cubans hoped that a great deal of pressure would be exerted to secure the repeal of the cigar limitation statute—a *quid pro quo* for the continuation of the convention.[10] Manning, however, was pessimistic over the prospects for repeal due to the "remarkably widespread influence" of the domestic tobacco interests.[11] The events of the next five years proved the accuracy of this forecast.

II

In February 1926 a bill to repeal the cigar limitation statute was introduced into Congress at the request of the Treasury and Post Office departments.[12] Hearings were held by a special subcommittee of the House Ways and Means Committee early in March. Cigar manufacturers testified in opposition to the bill, while representatives of the Treasury and Post Office departments testified in favor of the bill. In addition, favorable statements were made by the Merchants' Association of New York, Montgomery Ward and Company, a clothing manufacturer, and other interests.[13] William R. Vallance, of the Office of the Solicitor, contacted the secretary of the subcommittee's chairman and told him that the Secretary of State favored the bill, and that reports of Department opposition were incorrect. Vallance further explained to the secretary that the State Department had not entered into the discussions because the Secretary of State believed that the issue primarily concerned the Treasury and Post Office departments.[14]

During the hearings several witnesses intimated that Cuban threats to abrogate the temporary convention were nothing but bluff, and that it was not necessary to repeal the cigar limitation statute in order for American exporters to enjoy the benefits of the agreement. Thus, the Cuban Director of Posts sent General Crowder a personal letter stating that Cuba did intend to abrogate the temporary convention at the end of the trial period if the cigar limitation statute was not repealed. The Ambassador told the State Department that this was not a bluff.[15] On May 15, 1926 the intentions of the Cuban Government were publicly outlined in the *Havana Post*.[16]

As soon as the hearings ended the American export interests began to organize a campaign to push the repeal bill through Congress.[17] The National Foreign Trade Council took the lead in the campaign. The final declaration of the April 1926 convention demanded the repeal of the cigar limitation statute.[18] The New York State Chamber of Commerce and the Chamber of Commerce of the United States passed similar declarations.[19] The Congressional session ended, however, before the committee reported on the repeal bill. The American interests welcomed the delay between sessions, and began to capitalize on the Cuban abrogation threat.[20] O. K. Davis, the secretary of the Foreign Trade Council, stepped up the campaign in October 1926. On October 5, Davis sent to the State Department a brief on the Cuban parcel post controversy, and informed the department of his plans for the coming Congressional session. In closing he declared, "Yours for the battle—if they want one."[21] By this time the Foreign Trade Council's fight for the repeal bill had attracted widespread comment. The *New York Times* wrote that the Council was striving to save the mail order trade with Cuba,[22] and the *National Business Review* stated that the outcome of the campaign "will demonstrate what a large and important part the National Foreign Trade Council plays in the affairs of the nation."[23]

The Chamber of Commerce of the United States continued to work for the repeal bill also. The board of directors of the Chamber met in Havana, Cuba in February 1927, and publicly stressed the connection between its fight for the repeal bill and its close connection with the American Chamber of Commerce of Cuba—the only foreign member of the board of directors was a member of this latter group. President John W. O'Leary of the Chamber also sent a brief to Congress outlining the great

increase in parcel post trade with Cuba.[24] The National City
Bank did not play an active role, but an official informed the
State Department of the bank's support of the repeal bill.[25]

The House Committee on Ways and Means reported the repeal
bill on January 19, 1927, and recommended that it be passed
without amendment. The committee's recommendation was
based on two points: (1) the need to expand the export trade;
(2) the need to protect American investments in Cuba.[26] This
represented the combined influence of the National Foreign
Trade Council, the Chamber of Commerce of the United States,
and the American Chamber of Commerce of Cuba. There was
no debate, and Congress adjourned on March 4, 1927, without
acting on the bill. The Cuban Government notified the United
States on April 7, that it would abrogate the convention on June
30, 1927. A modus vivendi was signed on April 13, however,
which extended the convention to March 1, 1928.[27] The 1927
National Foreign Trade Convention cited this development in
its final declaration, and once more urged the repeal of sections
2804 and 3402 of the Revised Statutes.[28]

During the 1926–27 fight over the repeal bill the State Department played the part of a cautious cheerleader. The department was in close contact with O. K. Davis of the National
Foreign Trade Council, and even offered to show him dis-
patches from Cuba so he could use the information in the
campaign.[29] The State Department wanted the repeal bill passed,
but it was very cautious in matters dealing with Congressional
prerogative. When the Chamber of Commerce of the United
States offered its services to the department in May 1926, Dr.
Manning, of the Latin American Division, wanted to reply
with a favorable comment. He noted, however, that if the letter
were made public it might be construed as an effort of the
department to influence legislation, and thus arouse hostile
criticism which in turn would adversely affect the pending
measure.[30] In April 1927 the Latin American Division discussed
the possibility of negotiating a protocol with Cuba exempting
cigars and cigarettes from the provision of the statutes, but this
idea was not pursued due to the fear of encroaching on the
prerogatives of Congress.[31]

III

Between Congressional sessions there was a lull in lobbying activity. In November 1927 the American Chamber of Commerce of Cuba sent out a circular letter to manufacturers and exporters in the United States. The letter warned that American business was going to lose some eight to ten million dollars worth of trade annually unless Congress repealed the cigar limitation statute. The Chamber of Commerce also stated that European nations would take over much of the trade with Cuba, and asked: "Are the tobacco interests of the United States any better organized than you are? Cannot your powerful influence be felt at Washington too?"[32] From December 1927 through March 1928 numerous letters were sent by American business groups to Congressmen, the State Department, and the President. The Senate Finance Committee received twenty-six letters and resolutions from businesses and chambers of commerce. Some of the groups represented were the Philadelphia Board of Trade, the Maritime Association of the Port of New York, the Cambridge Rubber Company, the Gillette Razor Company, several shoe manufacturers, and several cotton clothing manufacturers.[33] Many of these letters expressed the arguments of the circular letter, and applied these specifically to the interests concerned.[34]

President Calvin Coolidge, in his annual message of December 6, 1927, called for the repeal of the cigar limitation statute.[35] A month passed, however, and still no repeal bill had been introduced into Congress. Thus, the American interests tried a new approach. President Coolidge was planning to attend the Sixth Pan American Conference, which was to be held in Havana, Cuba. The United States planned to send an impressive delegation in an attempt to calm the anti-Yankee feeling in some sectors, and President Coolidge was scheduled to give the opening address on January 16, 1928.

On January 9, Hugo Hartenstein, of the American Chamber of Commerce of Cuba, sent a telegram to Coolidge stating that the introduction of a repeal bill into Congress prior to the President's arrival in Havana, would greatly "improve local sentiment."[36] The next day the manager of the Foreign Trade Department of the Chamber of Commerce of the United States visited the State Department. He repeated Hartenstein's warning to the President, and intimated that the Cuban public might express their feelings when the President arrived in Havana. The Chamber representative explained that his organization as well as the Foreign Trade Council and the Merchant's Association of New York were eager to support a repeal bill, but none of them wanted to urge Congressmen to introduce the bill. In addition, he stated that these groups felt that this was an administration matter, and that it should be sponsored as such. The purpose of the visit was to make sure that the State Department was fully aware of the situation, and to urge that administration influence be utilized to obtain the introduction of a repeal bill before the President's arrival in Havana.[37]

On January 12, Representative Henry W. Watson, an administration Republican from Pennsylvania, introduced a bill to repeal the cigar limitation statute. The National Foreign Trade Council immediately urged the passage of the bill.[38] The House Ways and Means Committee reported the bill early in February and recommended that it be passed without amendment. The committee report declared that the bill was supported by the Chamber of Commerce of the United States and "virtually every commercial organization in the United States." In addition the report cited the recent parcel post convention negotiated between Cuba and Great Britain, and pointed out the fact that Cuba was the only Latin American country which had no parcel post arrangement with the United States.[39] Later that month the Cuban Government served notice that the parcel post convention would definitely terminate on March 1. O. K. Davis tried to put on more pressure,[40] but the repeal bill was being kept off the Congressional calendar through the effective action of the tobacco interests and tobacco labor organizations working through Democratic Congressmen. Davis visited the State Department late in February and complained that the department had not been too active in supporting the repeal bill. The matter was discussed in the department, but Under-Secretary Robert Olds stated that no action could be taken at the time.[41]

The repeal bill did not reach the debate stage in Congress.

Democratic Representative Henry F. Rainey of Illinois was one of the leading opponents of the bill. He had a heated exchange of correspondence with Hugo Hartenstein between February 21 and March 6. Rainey declared that the Cubans were bluffing about their threat to continue the parcel post embargo, and he told Hartenstein that the United States would be "better off if the American Chamber of Commerce in Cuba could be persuaded to quit functioning."[42]

The temporary parcel post convention was terminated on March 1, 1928 by Cuba. Some protests were sent to Congressmen and to the State Department,[43] but in general the campaign for the repeal bill appeared to have hit a snag. The final declaration of the 1928 National Foreign Trade Convention—which met in April—urged that the bill be passed, not only because of the importance of the Cuban market but also because of the effect of the issue on relations with all of Latin America.[44] Congress, however, ended its session on May 29, with the repeal bill still on the shelf.

The Latin American Division of the State Department then began to consider ways to get around the statutes by diplomatic action. The division had been keeping in touch with public sentiment in Cuba, and was convinced that something should be done to alleviate the ill will created by both the parcel post controversy and the sugar tariff. Thus, Dr. Manning, with the concurrence of Division Chief Stokely W. Morgan, proposed that:

> If the Department would now take up at leisure during the Congressional recess the negotiation of a treaty excepting Cuba from the operation of the old law . . . and would invite the Cuban Ambassador to sign such a treaty it would be an irrefutable proof that the executive of this country is not in sympathy with the persistent failure of Congress to do anything to meet the Cuban demand.

Manning stated that even if the Senate failed to ratify such a treaty at least the Cubans would see the good intentions of the State Department. Any negotiations, however, were to remain confidential until after the fall election. The proposed treaty did not get beyond the planning stage, and the parcel post issue continued to plague Cuban-American relations.[45]

In the fall of 1928 Great Britain signed a parcel post convention with Cuba, which the United States Merchants' Association declared was prompted by the failure of Congress to repeal the cigar limitation statute. In addition, this development was cited as proof that European nations were taking over the Cuban market, and as an indication of the importance of a parcel post convention.[46]

The repeal bill was briefly debated in the House of Representatives in January 1929. Henry W. Watson, Republican from Pennsylvania, spoke in favor of the bill while Tom Connally, Democrat of Texas, attacked it.[47] No action was taken on the bill before Congress adjourned on March 4, but at the next session—which began on April 5—the proponents of the bill adopted a different approach. The provisions of the repeal bill were written into the proposed tariff readjustment act by the Republican members of the House Ways and Means Committee. Henry W. Watson was a member of the committee.[48] There was some indication that the proponents of the bill used the argument that something should be done to mollify Cuba, due to the proposed increase in the sugar tariff, as a lever to get the repeal bill included in the tariff act.[49]

During the hearings of the Senate Finance Committee on the tariff act, the repeal provision was attacked by Matthew Woll—a labor representative—and by Representative John J. Cochran—Democrat of Missouri. The Chamber of Commerce of the United States submitted a memorandum defending the provision.[50] The Senate committee included the repeal provision in its proposed act, and as a result the Hawley-Smoot Tariff Act of 1930 repealed sections 2804 and 3402 of the Revised Statutes. The National Foreign Trade Convention, which met in May 1930, then called for the prompt negotiation of a parcel post convention.[51]

The domestic tobacco interests, however, did not give up the fight. A resolution was introduced in Congress calling for the prohibition of cigar imports in packages of less than three hundred. The House Ways and Means Committee held hearings on the resolution on June 18, 1930. Michail J. Flynn of the Cigar

Makers' International Union and Senator Park Trammell, Democrat of Florida, testified in behalf of limitation.[52] The Chamber of Commerce of the United States and the Merchants' Association of New York sent briefs opposing the resolution, while Postmaster General Walter F. Brown testified against it.[53] The Republican members of the committee generally opposed the resolution. Representative Carl Chindblom interrupted Senator Trammell's defense of the resolution to declare:

> Every merchant in the United States, every manufacturer who tries to build up a market in Cuba has been injured in his prospects for business in Cuba by the sentiment and feeling that has been created in Cuba because of this discrimination against her. We are losing business in Cuba.[54]

The committee did not recommend passage of the resolution.

On July 24, 1930 a permanent parcel post convention between Cuba and the United States was signed. The convention went into effect on September 1, and was more favorable for American exporters than the temporary convention had been, since the parcel weight limit was raised to twenty-two pounds. Thus, the decade-long controversy over the parcel post convention had ended in victory for the American business groups interested in Cuba.[55]

The campaign to repeal the cigar limitation statute was primarily a product of American export interests. Some support was furnished by American investment interests, as represented by the American Chamber of Commerce of Cuba, but the sugar interests were not active. The opposition was a coalition of domestic tobacco interests and labor groups which found its chief political expression in the Democratic Party. Thus, the groups working for the repeal bill worked with elements of the Republican Party. The repeal bill was in effect a statutory lowering of the protective wall on a single item, and as such it was not enthusiastically received in Congress. When elements of the majority party writing the bill inserted it in a bulky bill dealing with numerous tariff items, then it passed with little difficulty. Business pressure coupled with political maneuvering and Congressional action, had opened the door for diplomatic negotiations.

CHAPTER SIX

Political Stability, Investments, and the First Loan Cycle

I

One of the primary goals of American policy toward Cuba was the maintenance of a stable Cuban Government. Such a government was expected to be friendly to the United States, and to preserve peace and order in the island. One of the principal motives behind this policy was the American investment stake. The Cuban Government was expected to protect this stake by the preservation of order and stability. With such protection, it was believed, American capital would continue to flow to Cuba, and this in turn would help provide an increasing market for American exports. The Commercial Attaché in Cuba, Chester Lloyd Jones, clearly pointed out this economic relationship in 1921 when he wrote:

> In the case of Cuba, encouragement of capital investment should be a national policy to the extent by which it tends to strengthen the economic and political basis of the government of the island.
>
> . . . .
>
> Capital investment should be encouraged when it will through the business connections established help to increase the market for American goods in Cuba.
>
> Capital investment should be encouraged in Cuba to a greater extent than in other foreign countries, because of the political arrangements existing between the two republics and through the proximity of the island to the United States, it is easier to guarantee the protection of the rights of the investors than is the case in other countries.[1]

Political stability, investments, loans, and trade were vitally connected in helping to shape the course of American-Cuban relations. Various techniques of policy were used by the United States to effect a salubrious blending of these elements, and the period from 1919 to 1933 was characterized by the use of techniques which did not involve the use of armed force.

II

A fairly chronic source of unrest in Cuba stemmed from the laboring class. The wave of strikes and disorders—accompanied by the threat of revolution—had been an important reason for the American intervention in 1917. Wartime prosperity helped to alleviate labor discontent, but early in 1919 another large strike began in Havana. During the course of the disturbance the United States Navy sent a cruiser, two gunboats, and some ten submarine chasers to the port city.[2] The Cuban Government was able to control the situation, so no marines were landed. The American Minister reported that the Cuban Congress had complied with the president's request for suspension of the constitutional guarantees and the establishment of the "law of public order." Now, the Minister wrote, the government could "legally proceed" against strikers and labor agitators. The Minister was also pleased to note that the Chamber of Commerce was supporting the actions of the government. This dispatch closed on a rather triumphant note which was symbolic of American policy toward Cuba—"No disorder anywhere."[3]

Elections in Cuba were also periods of unrest since the animosities and ambitions of the various factions came to a head during these "legal" struggles for power. The major complaint of the "out" groups was that the elections were controlled by the "in" group. Thus, the threat of revolution and the actual violence of campaign maneuvering characterized many Cuban elections. The United States tried to correct this situation by tinkering with the electoral machinery. In March 1919 General Enoch Crowder was sent to Cuba to revise the electoral code. The revised code was adopted by the Cuban Congress, but the State Department still believed that supervision of the 1920 elections was necessary due to the rumblings and threats of the opposition party.[4] The precipitous decline in the sugar market during the summer of 1920 provided more fuel for the growing agitation and gave more serious overtones to the revolutionary threats of the "out" groups.

On September 19, 1920 Boaz Long, the Minister to Cuba, requested that the marine force stationed at Camaguey be increased to five hundred men.[5] Upon receiving Secretary of State Bainbridge Colby's request for more details,[6] Long outlined the basis for his fears:

> Request for additional marines [at] Camaguey based on necessity for protection [of] sugar interests owned by Americans in four eastern provinces. It is estimated that a considerable percentage of total sugar production of 1920 crop controlled by American interests. . . . It is openly stated by partisans of both parties that in event of revolution or other disturbances American interests will be [the] first to be destroyed.[7]

President Menocal assured the United States that his government could protect these interests, and further explained that any act of intervention might provoke wholesale attacks on American property.[8] The opposition party continued to issue threats of rebellion,[9] but Woodrow Wilson decided that Menocal's appraisal of the situation was correct. Wilson advised Norman H. Davis, the Under-Secretary of State, that the United States would intervene in case of a revolution, but that a premature move would, "bring about the very thing we want to prevent."[10]

The elections were held on November 1, 1920 and Alfredo Zayas was listed as the winner by a narrow margin in five of the six provinces. The opposition party, however, brought fraud charges in numerous districts, and appealed to the United States to supervise the post-election review. Political turmoil appeared to be very close. The economic situation further complicated the Cuban problem. The banking system of the island was in desperate straits; the moratorium of October 10, and the subsequent embargo on the shipment of currency out of Cuba antagonized many creditors in Cuba and in the United States, and virtually halted business activity on the island; the congestion of merchandise in the ports of Cuba was increased by the moratorium; and finally the Cuban Government was in poor financial condition. This complex situation threatened all aspects of American business interests in Cuba. The Cuban economy was prostrate, and the government was slipping fast.

The State Department was well aware of the feelings of American business interests, and expressed its support of them. An official of the Chamber of Commerce of the United States informed the Standard Scale and Supply Company that the State Department was cooperating with American banking interests to better conditions in Cuba—in regard to debts owed to American companies.[11] The Chamber was in contact with the State Department, and the department assured them that the problems were being "attacked."[12] Early in January 1921 the vice-president of the National City Bank and the manager of the Royal Bank of Canada complained to the department that attacks on their Cuban branches by the Cuban press had started runs, and forced some of the branches to close. Norman H. Davis, the acting Secretary, told the American Minister to direct the Cuban Government to "take immediate and forceful steps" to end these attacks.[13] Long spoke to President Menocal, and efforts were made to end the propaganda.[14] The press attacks on the foreign banks continued, however, and Menocal called in representatives of the Havana press and told them not to attack the banks. Drastic measures were promised for those who continued "to annoy" the banks. Long requested the State Department to inform the bankers of this action, and to assure them that the matter was settled.[15]

Other problems, however, proved to be more difficult to settle. The Cuban Government contacted J. P. Morgan and Company early in November 1920 and requested a loan. The bank gave the Cuban Minister a memorandum concerning such a proposed loan and advised the State Department of the meeting. The proposed loan was not to exceed fifty million dollars, and the Cuban Government was to provide certain safeguards—a banker-appointed committee to manage the proceeds of the loan being the only one definitely stated in the memo.[16]

The State Department decided to combine financial reform with the loan negotiations, and suggested to the Cuban Government that former Assistant Secretary of the Treasury Albert Rathbone be employed as "financial advisor."[17] As soon as the Cuban Government decided to accept this suggestion, the State Department wrote, then Rathbone and Colonel Jose Tarafa could proceed to discuss a loan with the bankers.[18] Rathbone went to Cuba on December 10, 1920, stayed two weeks, and left after recommending that Cuba should negotiate a large loan. With the failure of the Rathbone mission the loan proposal lapsed for several months.

Meanwhile, the banking situation in Cuba continued to degenerate in spite of the moratorium. Boaz Long was convinced that the native bankers—such as W. A. Merchant, "Pote" Rodriguez, and Jose Marimon—were too corrupt to back any serious attempts at banking reform. Long suggested that:

> If upstanding American Bankers come into this field now they can save much for American businessmen, make money out of the transaction and put future banking operations in this rich Island on a sound basis.[19]

Long was also in contact with Colonel Tarafa, and both men generally agreed on the need for financial reform. In December 1920 Tarafa introduced a project of law which would give the United States the opportunity to establish the Federal Reserve System in Cuba.[20] This was not passed at the time, but both of these ideas had important implications for the future.

By late December 1920 it was evident to Woodrow Wilson and Norman Davis that the political and financial crisis in Cuba was becoming more acute.[21] On December 31, 1920 Davis directed General Enoch Crowder to proceed to Cuba and try to settle the outstanding problems. Crowder was instructed to attack the election issue first, and to emphasize that the flotation of a loan depended on the peaceful settlement of the election. The instructions stated that the American bankers were concerned over the political unrest stemming from the unsettled election, since this could result in "serious disturbances." In addition, Crowder was to further emphasize that disturbed conditions were proving harmful to commercial intercourse between the countries.[22] Crowder informed the Cuban Government of the wishes of the United States, and bluntly stated that unless the election issue were settled, intervention under the Platt Amendment would be "difficult if not impossible to avoid."[23]

The election issue proved to be a difficult problem, but it was resolved without revolution or intervention. General Crowder, Sumner Welles, and Norman Davis hoped that the rival candidates—Gomez and Zayas—would withdraw from the race in favor of a compromise candidate. Welles and Crowder drew up a list of six desirable characteristics for a Cuban president to possess, and the Alpha and Omega were: "First, his thorough acquaintance with the desires of this Government. . . . Sixth, his amenability to suggestions or advice which might be made to him by the American Legation."[24] Crowder believed that Zayas would be a weak president, but when neither candidate offered to withdraw the by-elections were held on March 15, and Zayas was recognized as president-elect on April 17, 1921.

American businessmen had been clamoring for the payment of commercial debts since the moratorium of 1920. In order to meet these demands the Torriente bills were pushed through the Cuban Congress with very little debate. These bills provided for the gradual lifting of the moratorium, with merchants and banks paying their creditors in installments, and for the reorganization of the banks. General Crowder was consulted about proposed changes in the bills, and he was able to protect the interests of American creditors by successfully opposing an amendment which would have assured the Cuban Government a preferred position as to its deposits in the endangered banks.[25]

The economic situation continued to deteriorate, however. American business interests complained to the new Secretary of State, Charles Evans Hughes, of their inability to collect debts and of the general instability caused by the severe financial strain. Frank Steinhart, representing the American Chamber of Commerce of Cuba, declared that it was absolutely necessary for General Crowder to remain in Cuba and to oversee the enactment of legislation "for the financial betterment and stabilization of commercial conditions in Cuba."[26] Further reform was believed to be necessary by business groups, and they requested that General Crowder be retained in Cuba. The Torriente laws were not effective, and eleven banks failed during May and June 1921. Thus, with the leading banks gone, the National City Bank and the Royal Bank of Canada became the leading banking houses on the island by default.

III

Late in June 1921 the State Department and the bankers renewed their talks concerning a Cuban loan. J. P. Morgan and Company stated that certain controls were necessary before the loan would be considered. The first Morgan proposal was for the creation of a Cuban finance commission which would supervise the expenditure of the loan proceeds as well as the repayment of the principal and interest.[27] The bankers informed the State Department that they wanted to help with the Cuban problem, but that they were unwilling to go ahead without the formulation of "a constructive plan having the hearty support of the Department of State."[28] The department insisted that certain reforms be instituted in Cuba prior to the floating of a loan. Hughes believed that a loan was necessary, but he stipulated that the Cuban budget be reduced so that the loan could be serviced out of the regular revenue of the government.[29] The bankers were in agreement with the department on this point since it concerned the general financial stability of the Cuban Government.[30]

Sumner Welles conferred with Norman Davis and several representatives of Morgan and Company in late July 1921. Welles reported that the major portion of his conversation with the Morgan group was confined to a discussion of what control American bankers would have over the revenues of the Cuban Government. Welles was of the opinion that they wanted a customs receivership—as in Nicaragua—but that they had finally agreed that the financial commission plan would be better. Such a commission, Welles stated, would have complete control over the collection of a portion of the revenue, but it would allow the Cubans to do the "actual physical collecting," thus soothing Cuban feelings.[31]

In September 1921 the Cuban Government asked Morgan and Company for a short-term loan of five million dollars. Norman Davis and Dwight W. Morrow sent a memorandum to the State Department stating that the bank was willing to make such a loan if it were the "preliminary step in constructive reform in the administration of Cuba's finances." The bankers further declared that they would cooperate with the department in using the Cuban loan application as a tool to force the Cuban Government to institute such desired reforms as budget reduction and revision of the tax laws. In addition, the memorandum stated that the bank would be willing to send a partner to Cuba to work with Crowder on the matter. The department indicated its approval of this memo and informed Crowder of the contents.[32] Shortly thereafter Norman Davis and Dwight Morrow departed for Cuba after a visit to the State Department.

After several days of discussion, Morrow and Davis reached an understanding with President Zayas on October 7, 1921. Among other things this understanding included a limit on the Cuban budget, adjustment in the revenue laws to bring in more taxes, and the future negotiation of a fifty million dollar loan.[33] Zayas agreed with this statement except for some of the details regarding the budget. He stated that he would try to reduce the budget to the prescribed amount—$59,000,000—but that he could not promise such a reduction.[34] Morrow was satisfied with Zayas' reply, and wrote that the bank was willing to proceed with the loan as soon as the State Department gave its approval.[35] Crowder, however, believed that Zayas should give more definite commitments concerning the desired reforms.[36] The bankers requested formal approval for the loan, and on October 20, 1921 Hughes notified them that he was satisfied with the assurances given by Zayas. Hughes further stated that as soon as the Cuban Congress approved the loan contract the State Department would sanction the loan.[37]

The Morgan firm notified the department on October 25, that the Cuban Congress had approved the contract. The department replied that as soon as it received formal notification of the action it would sanction the loan.[38] General Crowder convinced the department, however, that President Zayas was not sincere in his reform assertions, and the formal approval was delayed while Crowder tried to pressure the Cuban President into "more definite commitments."[39]

American export interests had been expressing their interest in the proposed loan since August. Most of the letters and resolutions received by the department stressed the need for an American loan to rehabilitate the Cuban economy and thus provide a better market for American goods.[40] On the other hand, American investment interests wanted the State Department to insist on extensive controls and reforms in Cuba before giving approval to the loan.[41] One prominent merchant wrote:

> Either our government at Washington should initiate a more aggressive program, or let us know there is no such hope. American business with Cuba has counted on Washington. We ourselves can carry on with sales of several millions of dollars a year of American manufactured articles and can pay our creditors in reasonable time, or we can die game.
>
> . . . .
>
> May we not hope that you will influence for the life of Cuba and of us here who serve the business and investment of America in Cuba, a policy from Washington that may be definite and aggressive for good and efficient government in this Island.[42]

Secretary of Commerce Herbert Hoover wrote to President Warren Harding on December 13, 1921 and recommended the immediate settlement of the loan contract. Hoover warned that American businessmen were apprehensive of the possible bankruptcy of the Cuban Government, and suggested that the requirements prescribed by the United States be liberalized.[43] Hughes defended the actions of the State Department on the basis of effective long-range stability for Cuba through financial reforms. He was able to tell President Harding that Zayas was going to revise the current budget downward by presidential decree, thus paving the way for approval of the loan.[44]

Secretary Hughes was caught between conflicting business opinions. General Crowder was very close to the American investment group residing in Cuba, and this tended to influence him in favor of the tougher policy. On his advice the State Department had hedged on approval in November. Other business groups—even some which wanted reforms, such as the bankers—believed that Cuba was near bankruptcy, and needed the five million dollar loan as soon as possible. Long-range reforms could come after the government had been stabilized, and the payments made on the foreign debt. Morgan and Company wanted a "moralization program" but not absolute American control over the Cuban Government. This meant that the bankers partially disagreed with some of the American residents in Cuba who seemed to want American officials to take over part of the government, and see to it that debts were paid at full value.[45] Dwight Morrow wrote to Crowder that "We ought not to use the Platt Amendment to collect the debts, or to enforce the contracts of private individuals."[46] Charles Evans Hughes was more in favor of this moderate approach, rather than the tough policy advocated by the resident investors. The five million dollar loan was finally agreed to by Hughes in spite of Frank Robin's cry, "God help us merchants in Cuba."[47]

On January 11, 1922 the State Department notified Morgan and Company that the loan would be approved.[48] The loan was negotiated later that month and Cuba was probably saved from defaulting on her foreign debt. Shortly thereafter General Crowder handed President Zayas the first of his famous "Fifteen Memoranda" dealing with political and financial reforms.[49]

The reduction of the Cuban budget was a central part of the "moralization" program. Budget reform had been one of the main points in the Morrow-Zayas negotiations for the five million dollar loan, and one of the basic requirements for stability in the eyes of the State Department and the bankers.[50] In March 1922, Dwight Morrow and Edward L. Stettinius—of the Morgan Company—went to Cuba and discussed the budget with General

Crowder. Crowder then informed the department that he intended to make demands for specific reforms to be accomplished
within specified time limits. In addition, he recommended that
an ultimatum threatening intervention accompany the two memoranda on budget reform.[51] The matter was discussed in the
State Department, and Dana Munro—Chief of the Latin American Division—recommended that the memoranda be approved
without the ultimatum.[52] As a result, Secretary Hughes told
Crowder to deliver the memoranda, but to delete any threat
of intervention for failure to comply with the demands.[53] The
general subject of budget reform was discussed again in Memorandum no. 13 of July 21, 1922. This memorandum was entitled,
"Conditions Precedent to Approval of a Loan," and signified the
renewal of loan negotiations. Crowder informed the Cuban
Government that these reforms were regarded as important by
the bankers as well as by the State Department.[54]

Crowder also pressured Zayas into making a sweeping cabinet
reorganization in June 1922. The General did not suggest any
names for the new cabinet, but he set the qualifications and
passed on all of the president's recommendations.[55] As a result
the "Honest Cabinet" was composed of men who were in
sympathy with the American reform program.

Another prerequisite for the approval of a larger loan was
tax revision. An extensive tax proposal was submitted to the
Cuban Congress in June 1922, but the American Chamber of
Commerce of Cuba protested against almost every provision.
The one item recommended by the Chamber was the one percent
gross sales tax. The Chamber particularly objected to the four
percent net profits tax.[56] A new tax law was prepared with the
assistance of the American and Cuban Chambers of Commerce.
This "Cuban Loan and One Percent Tax Law" was designed to
raise sufficient funds to meet the interest requirements, and to
provide a sinking fund for the proposed bond issue.[57] The department informed the Cuban Government that a serious situation would result if the law were not passed as written.[58]

By the end of August 1922 the Cuban Congress had adopted
the $55,000,000 budget, and a few weeks later the gross sales
tax law was enacted. The State Department had continually

stressed these issues as two of the most important reform demands. Although other elements of the "Fifteen Memoranda" had not been acted on—some never were—the department nonetheless gave its approval to formal loan negotiations as soon as budget reduction and tax reform had been enacted.

During the course of the negotiations the bankers contacted the State Department about the proposed wording of the loan prospectus and contract. Julius Lay, of Speyer Brothers, wanted to use a statement which would be more reassuring to investors than the stock reply which had been employed since March 1922.[59] The Chief of the Latin American Division noted:

> Mr. Lay feels that the expression "has no objection to offer" is too colorless to be of any assistance in selling the bonds and he states that should the bankers know in advance that they could make a statement like the one he proposes they would perhaps feel justified in giving Cuba a slightly better rate than they could otherwise do.

Lay had suggested that the statement read: "Pursuant to the Permanent Treaty between the United States and the Republic of Cuba, the Department of State has been advised of the negotiations of this loan and has given its consent thereto." The department changed "consent" to "acquiesced," and informed the bankers that such a statement could be used.[60]

Dwight Morrow contacted Secretary Hughes on December 28, 1922 and stated that the assurance by the department that General Crowder would remain in Cuba for at least two more years would "materially improve the disposition and the prospect of the proposed bond issue."[61] Hughes informed Morrow that he had taken the matter up with the President, and that the President had asked Senator Henry Cabot Lodge to introduce the necessary legislation to "provide for Crowder in a diplomatic capacity."[62]

Sealed bids were submitted for the loan contract, and on January 12, 1923 the loan was awarded to a syndicate headed by J. P. Morgan and Company. This syndicate bid 96.77 which was 3.25 points higher than the Speyer bid.[63] On January 13, Dwight Morrow telephoned Secretary Hughes and inquired whether the secretary had any objection to inserting in the prospectus a paragraph, which was read to the secretary. This paragraph summarized the first three articles of the Platt Amendment, and ended with the statement, "Issued with the acquiescence of the United States Government under the provisions of the treaty dated May 22, 1903." The Secretary of State approved the use of this paragraph.[64] In its final form the loan prospectus had this statement at the top of the page.

This loan prospectus represented the capstone to the cooperative efforts of the State Department and the bankers which had begun in the fall of 1920. The extensive use of the Platt Amendment was, for all practical purposes, a written guarantee backed by the United States Government. The advertisement accompanying the prospectus spelled this out in more detail. It stated that the credit of Cuba was based on Cuba's ability to supply a basic product, the proximity of Cuba to its principal market, and the "special interest" taken by the United States in the maintenance of peace and prosperity on the island. Special mention was also made to the Crowder mission and the reforms which had been effected as a result.[65] This was a clear statement—with State Department approval—that the protection of American investments in Cuba was a part of the foreign policy of the United States Government.

IV

General Enoch Crowder went to Cuba as a Special Representative of President Wilson and was retained in this capacity by President Harding. Boaz Long, the Minister to Cuba, left his post in June 1921 and later resigned from the diplomatic service. Crowder, however, continued to fill the rather enigmatic role of Special Representative. American businessmen began contacting the State Department in 1921, urging that Crowder be retained in Cuba and that he be given diplomatic status. According to law this would have entailed a special act of Congress, since military personnel were prohibited from holding diplomatic posts.

In September 1921 a prominent New York lawyer, Severo

Mallet-Prevost, asked the State Department to recommend such a special act to Congress in order to give Crowder "real diplomatic standing."[66] Secretary Hughes replied that, "present conditions make it impossible to make any change in General Crowder's status."[67]

During 1922 the problem of Crowder's retention became more serious, since the General was due to retire in February 1923. Herbert C. Lakin wrote to Secretary Hughes about this problem in August 1922, and stated that it would be a "calamity" if Crowder left Cuba.[68] In December 1922 the agitation to retain General Crowder picked up momentum. Colonel John Carrol—a lobbyist for numerous railroads and the Cuba Company, and a friend of Crowder—visited the department and told Under Secretary William Phillips that Crowder was anxious for a decision as to his future status. Phillips thought that Crowder should be appointed Minister, but he stated that the elevation of the Cuban post to an Ambassadorship was "slightly absurd."[69] Dwight Morrow wrote to Secretary Hughes on December 28, 1922, and stated that the bankers wanted General Crowder to remain in Cuba as the diplomatic representative. Morrow also wrote that the "goodness" of the loan depended, "to a large extent upon the ability of the American representative, backed by the Department of State, to guide the Cuban administration."[70]

The American Chamber of Commerce of Cuba sent a statement to businessmen in the United States requesting them to back the diplomatic appointment of General Crowder. The Chamber outlined the various reforms which had been accomplished, and frankly stated that the continuance of the Crowder mission was essential to the protection of American investments in Cuba.[71] These arguments were repeated—often verbatim—in the letters received by Congressmen and the State Department during the month of January 1923.[72] Several Senators were influenced by these arguments, and repeated them also.[73]

Secretary Hughes took the matter up with President Harding, and the President asked Senator Lodge to introduce the necessary legislation.[74] Congress passed the bill which made it possible for Crowder to have diplomatic status without resigning from the Army—although he was prohibited from drawing his retirement pay while on diplomatic duty—and on February 14, 1923 Enoch Crowder became the first ambassador to Cuba. The pressure of American business interests was not the sole factor behind this action, but the letters and statements of these business groups helps to illustrate their close connection with the Crowder mission.

V

The last part of the reform program was completed in the summer of 1923. Proposals for the stabilizing of the Cuban banking system had been in the air since the Tarafa project of law of December 1920. Most of these involved the Federal Reserve System of the United States, but no agreement could be reached as to how this system would be instituted in Cuba. In September 1921 the Federal Reserve Bank of New York appointed the National City Bank its correspondent and agent in Cuba.[75] This was not a solution to the problem, however, and Crowder's Memorandum no. 12 was concerned with the subject. In it Crowder expressed the hope that any central bank established in Cuba would function "in harmony with the Federal Reserve System and share the credit of the system."[76]

By May 1923 General Crowder believed that some action should be taken to overcome the growing influence of the Royal Bank of Canada. Crowder related how this bank was absorbing many private Cuban banks, and as a result was threatening to completely overshadow the American banks. In addition, he stated:

> In my opinion the establishment here of [an] active agency of [the] Federal Reserve Bank would meet with favor among businessmen and would add to the potential influence of the United States here where at present our banking influence is apparently on the wane.

Thus, Crowder urged that the Federal Reserve System be used to back up American banks in Cuba, and to help "save American banking prestige."[77] The legality of such a move was debated by the Federal Reserve Board, but on June 29, the board approved a plan under which the Federal Reserve banks of Atlanta and Boston would open agencies in Havana.[78]

During 1923 President Zayas began to pursue a more independent course, and General Crowder's active interference in the affairs of the Cuban Government came to an end. Zayas dismissed several members of the "Honest Cabinet" in April, and by June the entire cabinet had been reorganized. Crowder was quite concerned over the return of Cuban politics to its normal channels, and stressed the need for a "much more aggressive attitude" by the United States.[79]

In October 1923 the issue of what to do in Cuba came up for discussion when John M. Draper of the Borden Milk Company visited the State Department. Draper told Francis White—Chief of the Latin American Division—that as a result of the Crowder mission his company had experienced a "greater facility in making collections." In conclusion, Draper stated that the "old tendency" was returning, and that Crowder should have more power. White then discussed the matter with Under Secretary Phillips. Both men agreed that only two courses of action were open: (1) take a strong stand; (2) adopt a "hands off" attitude, and watch the situation until the Cubans "force intervention upon us." It was agreed that the time had passed for the first, and that Crowder should observe conditions with a view to drawing up a comprehensive indictment in case conditions of disorder and instability returned.[80] On November 15, Secretary Hughes told the Cuban Ambassador that the United States had no intention of intervening as long as the Cuban Government proved to be stable and sound.[81]

The years 1923 and 1924 proved to be relatively quiet ones for Cuba. An organization known as the Veterans' and Patriots' Association began to agitate for reform in 1923. The Association threatened revolution, and did start a minor uprising near Cienfuegos on April 30, 1924. President Calvin Coolidge placed an embargo on shipments of arms and munitions to Cuba, and the War Department made three sales of such commodities to the Cuban Government.[82] The State Department did not become too disturbed, however, since the movement was poorly organized and easily broken up by the Cubans. No American property was destroyed, and Zayas proved his ability to maintain stability with routine American aid.[83] The Association had been demanding some of the same reforms that Crowder had been advocating, but when faced with a choice between reform and stability the United States chose the latter.

VI

The period from 1919 to 1925 appears on the surface to have been one of shifting policies. Several historians have stated that the United States "abandoned" the "right of preventive intervention" in 1923, thus giving rise to a new policy.[84] The active "moralization" program did grind to a halt in 1923. But, did this constitute a basic shift in policy? This question can best be answered through an examination of the reasons behind the modification of Crowder's mission.

The technique of using foreign loans as a tool to obtain desired results in other countries was inherited from the Wilson administration by Secretary Hughes. The State Department used the need for a loan as a tool to obtain the "favorable" settlement of the Ports Company claim and the Cuba Railroad claim in 1917–18.[85] This tool was utilized again when the Cuban Government asked J. P. Morgan and Company for a loan during the crisis of 1920.

Secretary Hughes continued this policy toward Cuba. The use of the foreign loan as a policy tool was an accepted part of the department's Latin American policy, and Cuba was a specific example of this general policy. In a memorandum discussing the use of loans to settle "pending questions" in Central America and the Caribbean area, Dana Munro stated:

> In general it may be said that the immediate objects which we desire to obtain in Central America are political and financial reforms which will make for greater stability of Government and which will provide a safer field for American commerce and investments.

Munro then proceeded to enumerate specific political reforms which he hoped would provide the stability needed by American commercial and investment interests. In addition, Munro included numerous economic matters—such as favorable customs regulations and concessions to American corporations—which could be settled through loan pressure.[86]

Another memorandum was drafted by Sumner Welles and other men in the Latin American Division, which applied the use of the foreign loan as a policy tool to all of Latin America. In the introduction Welles pointed out that many countries to the south needed to borrow money, and that the United States was the only market for their securities. "On the other hand," Welles declared:

> The United States Government, on behalf of its nationals, seeks in these South American countries reasonable opportunities and protection in commercial intercourse, in obtaining concessions, in profitable investment, and in all undertakings that will be mutually beneficial to American citizens and to the citizens of the South American countries concerned.
>
> In brief, the countries mentioned are looking to the United States for money, and the United States is looking to them for profitable commercial and investment opportunities.[87]

Thus, the Cuban Government's need for a loan was used by the State Department as a tool to secure reforms conducive to stability. This was a specific application of the department's larger policy. The State Department repeatedly told the Cuban Government that the floating of a loan depended on the reforms enacted. General Crowder at one time advised the department to base its reform demands more on the Platt Amendment and less on the sanction for a loan. Crowder was afraid at the time that Zayas would let the Cuban Government go into bankruptcy in order to avoid reforms.[88] Morgan and Company cooperated with the department since the bankers also wanted stable conditions.

After the consummation of the fifty million dollar loan in 1923 the State Department no longer had this important policy tool to use in Cuba. The Platt Amendment remained, but the State Department from 1920 had preferred the loan tool since

in the final analysis the Platt Amendment rested on the threat
of force, and the United States—especially after March 1921—
was extremely reluctant to use armed force in Cuba. Crowder
went to Cuba threatening intervention, and told Sumner Welles
on March 1, 1921 that further intervention was very probable.[89]
The State Department, however, on several occasions after this
stated its reluctance to use armed force or even to push the
Cuban Government too hard—for fear that the officials might
resign.[90] Crowder's proposed ultimatum of April 1922 was
eliminated out of fear that the Cuban Government would not
enact the suggested reforms, thus forcing the United States to
enforce its threat.[91]

This attitude was, in part, connected to the attitude of American businessmen interested in Cuba. Reforms were demanded,
but most of the men involved expressed the same reluctance
toward the use of force unless actual outbreaks occurred. Frank
Steinhart told Crowder that he was "opposed to a Government
of intervention," and Dwight Morrow wrote to Crowder that,
"good government is not a substitute for self government."[92]

The State Department was also influenced by the desire not
to antagonize the other Latin American countries. General Crowder wrote to Secretary Hughes in September 1921 explaining
that the taxation and budget problems could be easily solved by
actual intervention. Crowder went on to say that he realized
that the department wanted to avoid such a course, and would
prefer to work with the Zayas administration. This document
concluded:

> I realize that the policy to be pursued here will be pro-
> foundly influenced by our own general Latin American
> policy and that the Department, out of deference to that
> policy, may find it necessary to modify the more important
> recommendations that I have . . . made or which I may
> make in the future.[93]

Reluctant to use force and bereft of its most effective instru-
ment of policy, the State Department watched the unravelling
of parts of the "moralization" program with mixed emotions.
Economic conditions began to improve quite preceptibly in 1923,

however, and the Cuban Government remained stable. With the return of some degree of prosperity American business interests began to look with more favor on the Zayas administration. In August 1923 Charles E. Mitchell of the National City Bank hailed Cuba as "a solvent nation enjoying an excellent administration."[94] That same month Cuba paid to the United States the principal and accrued interest of the 1918 "war loan."

At the beginning of the 1923 reaction in Cuba some businessmen wondered if instability would soon follow. Elliot C. Bacon, of Morgan and Company, wrote to General Crowder on January 22, 1923 and voiced the concern of the bankers. The dominant note in this letter was fear of instability, and "anything that will weaken the guaranties of the issue." Repudiation was also feared if the rumored changes in the Cuban Government were to bring to power a group of ultra-nationalists.[95] Zayas hastened to reassure the bankers concerning the status of the bonds, and payments continued on schedule.[96] Other business groups discovered the compatability of the Cuban Government. Through the Tarafa Bill the Cuba Company was able to obtain the right to consolidate several of the important railroad lines of Cuba. In effect this meant that American and Cuban business interests were joining together in cooperation with the government. Zayas also used force to break strikes for American businesses, and even exiled certain union leaders.[97]

Zayas was able to keep order, with the help of more prosperous conditions. The Veterans' revolt was quickly crushed, and the election of 1924 was fairly peaceful. American business groups responded favorably, and began to support the growing nationalism which, in some respects, was quite friendly to business interests.[98] Business protests to the State Department about conditions in Cuba dropped to practically nothing in 1923.

Thus, the State Department actually did not make a policy change. Conditions in Cuba improved, American business interests were satisfied, so there was no occasion for further action. Crowder continued to talk about reform, but few people were interested. The Cubans were warned not to let "corruption and extravagance" bring on another crisis or else another dose of preventive intervention might be necessary.[99] Active reform campaigns, however, were reserved for periods of crisis when stability was jeopardized by governmental policy. As long as the Cuban Government could meet the payments on its foreign debt and maintain stability, the United States did not press the issue of honesty and democracy in government. This general policy was explained by Francis White in November 1924. White's memorandum on how the United States could bolster political stability and discourage revolutions in this general area stated the policy in these words:

> The United States will get better results if we do not make long pronouncements but let the natives work out their solution with help and assistance from our diplomatic representatives, but without tying our hands to any given course of action should the people of the country be able to come to some solution which gives promise of affording a period of stability even though it should not fall in with our ideas of a republican democratic constitutional government and even should it not be in accordance with their own written constitution.[100]

In Cuba, as in other parts of Central America and the Caribbean, stability covered a multitude of sins.

CHAPTER SEVEN

Concessions to Cuban Nationalism: The Price of Co-existence

I

The Crowder mission, the increase in the sugar tariff, and the increasing control of the sugar industry by American bankers all contributed to a development of anti-American feeling in Cuba. The first symptoms of this feeling appeared in 1921, and after the first few months of the 1922 "moralization" program the public protests against American policy increased.

After the cabinet reorganization in June 1922, one Havana newspaper came out with double-page headlines declaring, "HATRED OF NORTH AMERICANS WILL BE THE RELIGION OF CUBANS." This paper went on to warn that, "the day will have to arrive when we will consider it the most sacred duty of our life to walk along the street and eliminate the first American we encounter."[1] An American writer in Cuba reported that there was a growing fear of actual intervention and complete American domination. This writer further stated that this Cuban fear of losing their independence was stimulated by the Crowder mission and the absorption of the sugar industry by American banks. The resulting anti-American feeling was even displayed in the advertisements of Cuban firms selling American goods.[2]

On June 20, 1922 the Cuban Senate adopted a set of resolutions protesting against American interference in the affairs of the Cuban Government, and calling for adherence to the Root interpretation of the Platt Amendment. This action reflected the general feeling of the Zayas administration. President Zayas had

103

exhibited a veiled dislike for the Crowder program, but had reluctantly complied with some of the proposals. The State Department had been concerned for some time over the problem of how far the Cuban Government could be pushed, and was quite conscious of the Cuban reaction to American policy and activities.[4]

American business interests in Cuba also were aware of Cuban feelings. In May 1921 fifty resident managers of American concerns signed a protest against a Hearst newspaper attack on Cuba, and delivered it to the American legation.[5] After an inspection tour of the National City Bank's holdings in Cuba, President Charles E. Mitchell stopped in Havana, and made a speech praising Cuba. Mitchell received a standing ovation when he attacked the sugar tariff, and gave the Zayas administration the credit for the economic recovery of Cuba.[6] Dwight Morrow made similar gestures to President Zayas.[7] The threat of an anti-American, nationalistic movement which would repudiate debts and confiscate property was always present in the thinking of American interests.[8]

Faced with a nationalistic reaction on the part of Cubans, the State Department made certain concessions to Cuba. The Isle of Pines Treaty, the removal of the marines from Camaguey, and the immigration concession were, in part, designed to calm the spirit of resentment. None of these involved substantial American interests, but they were all extremely important to the Cuban nationalistic feeling which continued to develop after 1922. In effect, the United States gave to Cuba a *quid pro quo* for the continued protection of American interests.

II

In July and August 1917 a sizable marine force was sent to Camaguey Province. By April 1921 this force had been reduced to 350 men, but the presence of American troops on Cuban soil was a constant source of irritation to the Cubans. The 1917 pretense that the marines were "training" on the island as part of the "war effort" had worn rather thin by 1921. The marines remained, however, and continued to fulfill the mission for which they had been sent. Herbert C. Lakin, the President of the Cuba Company, explained the mission as follows:

> The Marines were sent to Camaguey in July 1917, immediately after our railroad and constituent companies had suffered a seven million dollar damage in the Cuban Revolution of Jose Miguel Gomez against President Menocal. Their camp is on our property, near our railroad shops. They have been of very material assistance to us at various times and their presence there has saved us from much more trouble than we have had, and from actual property damage. That section of Cuba is a hotbed of Bolshevism. The Bolshevists are inclined to destroy property. The presence of the Marines has prevented them.[9]

In April 1921 Herbert C. Lakin made a special trip to Washington, D. C., to counteract Cuban requests for the removal of the marines. Lakin visited Secretary of the Interior Albert B. Fall, and Secretary Fall wrote to Under Secretary of State Henry Fletcher requesting an interview for Lakin. Fall stated that Lakin's request for protection was "well founded," and asked Fletcher to help Lakin.[10] Lakin talked to Fletcher, and also with Assistant Secretary of War J. Mayhew Wainwright—whom he called "a personal friend of mine"—and Senator George Moses. Secretary Hughes later informed the Secretary of the Navy that he wanted the marine force retained at Camaguey.[11]

The marines, however, wanted to withdraw the force to Guantanamo Bay for reasons of economy.[12] Hughes was informed of this recommendation, and referred the question to Crowder. The General reported that the marine force was needed to protect American property, and Hughes informed the Navy Department that "General Crowder states that at the present time railroad labor troubles are again threatening, particularly on the Cuban–American Railroad [the Cuba Railroad]." Thus, Secretary Hughes again asked the Navy Department to continue the maintenance of the Camaguey garrison.[13]

An incident occurred in August 1921 which stimulated more Cuban dissatisfaction over the marine issue. Two former employees of the Cuba Railroad who had been dismissed for strike agitation attacked the assistant general superintendent of the railroad. The official was seriously injured, and several marines entered the house of the assailants in an attempt to arrest them.[14] The agitation resulting from the "Foster incident" prompted Herbert Lakin to contact the State Department, and Hughes reassured him that the department had no intention of withdrawing the garrison.[15]

On December 5, 1921 the Cuban House of Representatives passed a resolution calling on the United States to withdraw the marines. Crowder also reported that several newspapers had attacked the marine "intervention" as well as his mission, and that these attacks could not be "entirely disregarded." In a memorandum concerning the issue, General Crowder stated that he had advised against removal in June 1921 because he believed that the "dead season" between cane harvests would be a period of strikes and disorders. The season had passed, however, with no disturbances so Crowder wrote that it was no longer necessary to keep the marines at Camaguey. He did advise the department not to relieve the garrison immediately as this might be interpreted as a victory for anti-American propaganda. Crowder concluded that the department should wait until a "more opportune moment," and that it should advise the Cuban Government that public agitation of the question would only delay such action.[16]

Herbert Lakin told Henry P. Fletcher that he had no objection to the removal if the Cuban Government would protect the railroad.[17] On January 3, 1922 Lakin tried to head off the pending removal, however, by appealing to the department's desire to avoid full intervention. He wrote to Crowder, and stated that if the marines were withdrawn that "anarchists" would start trouble, and force the United States to take over Cuba.[18]

General Crowder returned to the United States in January 1922 to prepare for the forthcoming "moralization" demands. On January 23, Crowder informed Sumner Welles that he was anxious for the withdrawal instructions to go into effect before he returned to Cuba. The obvious implication of Crowder's recommendation was that the marine withdrawal would make the "moralization" program more palatable to the Cuban Government. The General stated that there were no disturbances in

Camaguey, and that if any developed the marines could be rushed back from Guantanamo within forty-eight hours. Thus, the Cuba Railroad would still have recourse to marine protection, if needed.[19]

The State Department requested the withdrawal of the marine garrison on January 24, and on January 26, 1922 the Navy Department replied that such orders would be issued immediately.[20] No additional protests were made by the Cuba Railroad, and in August 1922 Lakin informed the department that he was satisfied with conditions in Cuba.[21] The withdrawal of the marines from Camaguey did not sacrifice any American interests, yet it was as an important concession in the eyes of Cubans.[22]

III

Article six of the Platt Amendment, as embodied in the Permanent Treaty of May 22, 1903, specified that the Isle of Pines be omitted from the constitutional boundaries of Cuba. The article also stated that the title to the island should be settled by a future treaty. Such a treaty was signed on March 2, 1904. The United States agreed to relinquish all claims to the island, but the Senate refused to approve it. Repeated attempts were made to revive the treaty since there were no limitations as to date of ratification. In April 1907 the United States Supreme Court held that the island was at least *"de facto* Cuban territory," but in 1908 the Senate again rejected the treaty.[23]

The Cuban Government continued to administer the affairs of the Isle of Pines, but the unsettled status of the island caused much resentment among Cubans, especially since the American residents of the island continually demanded annexation by the United States. The Isle of Pines question became a major issue to Cubans, and stirred Cuban nationalism with the specter of Yankee imperialism. In March 1922 Luis Machado proposed a declaration to the Cuban Society of International Law. The declaration stated that the Isle of Pines belonged to Cuba by fact and by right, and that Cuba must never allow her territory to pass into the hands of a foreign nation. Machado concluded his speech with a ringing statement calling for the return of "our unredeemed territory: the Isle of Pines."[24] On July 28, 1922 Senator Medill McCormick sent some communications concerning the status of the Isle of Pines to Assistant Secretary of State Leland Harrison. Harrison drafted a proposed reply and sent it to Secretary Hughes for approval. The assistant secretary suggested that the reply would give the department an opportunity to express its interest in the ratification of the Treaty of 1904. "It seems to me," Harrison noted, "a very appropriate act at this particular juncture in our relations with Cuba."[25] Hughes and Harrison agreed that presidential support would be helpful, so the draft reply to Senator McCormick was sent to President Harding. The President misplaced the letter for almost two months, but on October 10, he wrote to Hughes stating his support of the treaty.[26]

Secretary Hughes had to stimulate the President's memory when Congress reconvened in November, and Hughes wrote: "May I remind you of your belief that it is desirable to dispose of this matter, and your desire to supplement my recommendation that the Treaty of March 2, 1904, be ratified by the Senate?"[27] The President then contacted Senator Lodge, and requested that the treaty be ratified in order to remove "any possible cause of friction."[28] Lodge conferred with Harding about the matter and later informed him that a meeting of the Senate Foreign Relations Committee had been called to take up the treaty and endeavor to dispose of it.[29] On December 11, 1922 the committee recommended that the treaty be ratified.[30]

The treaty ran into serious opposition, however, and was referred to committee on February 10, 1923. Very little was said or done for a year, and on February 15, 1924 the Foreign Relations Committee again recommended ratification. On June 3, 1924 the Senate decided to postpone consideration of the treaty until December 10.[31]

During 1924 the various interest groups concerned with the treaty began to take a real interest in the Senate proceedings. Most of the opposition pressure came from the states of Ohio, Michigan, and Wisconsin. This was due to the fact that most of the nonresident property owners of the Isle of Pines lived in these states.[32] The Senate Foreign Relation Committee received numerous letters, and thick bundles of signed petitions protesting against the treaty. Most of the petitions were from communities throughout Ohio.[33] In addition, some patriotic associations protested against the treaty.[34]

Most of the support for the treaty came from American business interests. The *Cuba Review*, published by the Munson Steamship Lines, took a vigorous stand in favor of the treaty.[35] The editor of this magazine wrote to President Coolidge in January 1925, and requested a statement advocating the ratification of the treaty. Such a favorable expression would have —according to the editor—"a beneficial effect in Cuba and other Latin American Countries."[36] In March 1925 the Pan American Society of the United States sent a resolution urging ratification to Senator Hiram Bingham,[37] and the American Chamber of Commerce of Cuba backed a similar set of resolutions drawn up by the National Federation of Economic Corporations.[38] The National City Bank urged the ratification of the treaty, and stressed the effect this would have on the other Latin American countries.[39]

The *Cuba Review* reflected the concern of American business interests over the Cuban resentment engendered by the prolonged Senate controversy. The magazine's Havana correspondent summed it up in these words:

> All of this may seem trivial and irrelevant, but the old-time resident, or American businessman will tell you, that on the day that Cuba's flag is lowered over the Isle of Pines . . . opportunities for successful commercial enterprises, carried on by American citizens in this Republic, will cease. Sentiment may figure but little in business in the United States, but in this, or any other Latin-American country, it is almost vital to success.[40]

The State Department was considering this situation in December 1924, and a balance sheet of American interests in Cuba and the Isle of Pines was prepared. The essential elements of this memorandum are summarized in the following chart.[41]

	Cuba	Isle of Pines
American Residents	20,000 (minimum est.)	700
American Investments	$1,360,000,000 (est.)	$15,000,000 (est.)

There could be no doubt where the preponderance of American interests lay. No actual sacrifice of American interests was involved. The American vegetable and fruit producers on the Isle of Pines would remain outside the tariff wall, but they would not lose their holdings.

The State Department furnished material for the pro-treaty Senators to use, and Secretary Hughes encourged support for the treaty whenever possible.[42] The Senate debated the treaty in January and again in March 1925. One of the most common arguments voiced in favor of the treaty was that failure to ratify would harm American economic interests in Cuba. Senator Claude Swanson stated: "Our broad trade relations, which are very important, affecting our many citizens and industries, have been prejudiced and injured by our delay and contention in this matter."[43] Senator William C. Bruce traced the extent of Cuban-American trade, and declared that the United States should be "generous" to one of its best customers.[44]

Another common argument was that failure to ratify the treaty would stir up ill will throughout Latin America, and thus harm American interests. Senator Duncan U. Fletcher inserted in the *Record* the article "Cuba's Title to the Isle of Pines," by Fernando Ortiz, which stressed the growing anti-Americanism in Cuba.[45] Senator Hiram Bingham quoted editorial comment from several South American newspapers to show that the treaty issue was really viewed as a test of American good will.[46] This argument was reiterated by Senators McCormick, Bruce, James Wadsworth, and Simeon Fess.[47]

The treaty fight came to a climax on March 11, 1925. For three days the Senate was locked in debate as Senators Frank B. Willis, Royal S. Copeland, and William Borah led the fight against it. The nature of the opposition led one senator to comment cynically that he was greatly surprised to see certain members, who had been protesting against the "militaristic" actions of the United States in the Caribbean, now maintaining that the United

States should seize the Isle of Pines.[48] On March 12, Senator
Copeland held the floor for eight consecutive hours in a minor
filibuster attempt. The debate resumed the next day, and Senator
Willis proposed an amendment which would have written the Bill
of Rights into the treaty—as pertaining to American citizens on the
Isle of Pines. This amendment was rejected, but the Borah amendment, which specifically pointed out that the Platt Ammendment
applied to the Isle of Pines, was passed. The treaty as amended
was passed on March 13, 1925 by a 63 to 13 vote—19 not voting.[49]

The ratification of the treaty was received with great rejoicing
in Cuba. A national holiday was declared, and twenty thousand
residents of Havana took part in a parade and ceremony which
was described as a great demonstration of friendship for the United States.[50] Thus, the United States made a second painless concession to Cuban nationalism.

IV

The immigration issue was not as important as the marines in
Camaguey and the Isle of Pines issue, but the arguments used
further illustrate the nature of Cuban-American relations. The
issue of restricting immigration from the countries of Latin
America arose while Congress was considering the "National
Origins" bill in 1924. The Cuban Ambassador protested to the
State Department that enactment of such legislation would "have
the effect of discouraging the commercial and business relations
between the two countries." Secretary Hughes sent the protest to the House Committee on Immigration and Naturalization.[51] Later, the Secretary informed the Cuban Ambassador that
the protested provision had been removed from the bill.[52]

The issue arose again in 1928 when legislation was introduced
to restrict Western Hemisphere immigration. Secretary of State
Frank B. Kellogg testified before the Senate Committee on Immigration, and introduced numerous letters from American businessmen in Latin America. These protested against restriction on
the grounds that such legislation would bring retaliatory action
from Latin American Governments. One of the letters was from

the American Ambassador to Cuba. This letter declared that the proposed legislation would "wound" the Cubans deeply, and closed on the ominous note that:

> I can readily foresee a campaign of intense anti-American-ism if such a measure is passed. The vast American interests here would certainly suffer to a greater or lesser degree.[53]

The Cuban immigration issue was significant because it was part of the pattern of American concessions to Cuban national-ism. While these concessions did not remove all anti-American feeling from Cuba, they did help appease Cuban resentment and made it easier for the Cuban Government to cooperate with the United States.

CHAPTER EIGHT

American Business and
the Machado Era

I

The period from 1925 to mid-1933 was characterized by the presidency of a Cuban businessman, and the active support of this administration by American business interests. Gerardo Machado appropriated all the paraphernalia of Cuban nationalism, and applied it to a pro-American policy. Thus, Machado became the very embodiment of Cuban stability to American business interests until the economic depression of the early 1930's combined with Cuban resentment over Machado's repressive policies to make him a liability. But during the heyday (1925-1930) of the Machado era American businessmen willingly boosted the "business nationalism" of Machado. As William P. Field, of the American Chamber of Commerce of Cuba, described it: "If our commerical intervention is to continue we must identify ourselves with her [Cuba's] purposes and make common cause with her in favor of her nationalistic program."[1] As long as stability and the protection of American investments was part of this program American interests could support Cuban nationalism.

American business groups interested in Cuba began to work with the forces of Cuban nationalism during the Zayas administration. This "official nationalism" was good for domestic consumption, and an aspiring presidential candidate, Gerardo Machado, proceeded to build a reputation as a foe of the Platt Amendment.[2] American businessmen knew Machado, and were not worried about his future policies.[3] Machado was connected with the public utilities business in Cuba, and had close relationships with the Electric Bond and Share Company and other American businesses.[4] Thus, after Machado's victory in the November 1924 election Colonel John H. Carroll arranged for him to make a trip to the United States to meet President Coolidge and various American businessmen.[5]

Machado conferred with the President and State Department officials, and informed them that one of the principal objects of his administration would be to increase Cuban commercial relations with the United States. In turn, the president-elect was told that the State Department hoped that investors would be treated fairly.[6] Machado then proceeded to New York where he was entertained by various business groups. Dwight Morrow addressed one of these affairs, and defended Cuban nationalism. Morrow stated that the United States should follow the Root Interpretation of the Platt Amendment, and reinforced this with the statement that:

> American businessmen who have differences with the Cuban people should first seek remedies for their alleged wrongs through the ordinary channels in Cuba. They should not look to Washington.[7]

Gerardo Machado returned to Cuba and the presidency in May 1925 with the praises of American businessmen ringing in his ears. The New York reception proved to be only a prologue to the close relations which developed after May 1925. In August 1925 the Cuban Chamber of Commerce in the United States, with the cooperation of the Cuban Government, began to make plans for a Cuban Exposition. Numerous American businessmen and firms participated in this public relations venture. The organizing committeee included Hernand Behn (President, Cuban Telephone Company), R. R. Govin (New York *Journal of Commerce*), Frank Munson (Munson Ship Lines), Gordon S. Rentschler (National City Bank), and William H. Woodin (American Car and Foundry Company).[8] The exposition was designed to advertise Cuba as a market and as a tourist attraction, and many American businesses furnished exhibits.[9]

Another example of this "helpful" policy was the hurricane

relief project of 1928. In the fall of that year Cuba was hit by a hurricane, and subsequently a relief committee was organized in New York City by American businessmen. The committee, headed by Dwight Morrow, refused to work through the Red Cross, the implication being that the Cubans should know who their friends were.[10] Over $125,000 was raised—Electric Bond and Share contributed $30,000—and the committee kept the State Department fully informed about its activities.[11]

American business groups demonstrated their support for Machado's policies on several occasions. In October 1925 a writer for the *Cuba Review* enthusiastically described one of Machado's successful "reforms." "Within the last thirty days," the correspondent wrote, "the Secretary of Government has rounded up, preferred charges, convicted, and expelled, between three and four hundred labor agitators . . . from Cuban soil." Some four hundred more were reported as being on the deportation list, and the correspondent emphatically concluded: "The red flag cannot fly in Cuba."[12]

This feeling was publicly expressed at a banquet in December 1926, given by the National Federation of Economic Corporations of Cuba—which included the American Chamber of Commerce —in honor of Machado. General Crowder called the affair a "testimony of the confidence felt by the business interests of the country in the administration." One of the officials of the Federation—Fernando Ortiz—called for an end to all political agitation so that the government could proceed with its policies.[13]

President Machado's trip to the United States in April-May 1927 gave American businessmen another opportunity to praise the situation in Cuba, and expand the suggestion made by Dr. Ortiz. Luncheons were given in honor of the Cuban president by the Chase National Bank, the Importers and Exporters Association, the Electric Bond and Share Company, J. P. Morgan and Company, the New York Chamber of Commerce, Sosthenes Behn, the National City Bank, Mayor Jimmy Walker, and others.[14] The speeches given at some of these gatherings reflected the bond between these groups and Machado. William H. Woodin —later to be the first New Deal Secretary of the Treasury—stressed the point that it was a fine thing for any country to have a businessman for president since such a situation "is greatly to our advantage."[15] At one of the bankers' luncheons Machado assured the group that American capital in Cuba would be protected "at all hazards." Thomas Lamont then rose and expressed the hope that the Cuban people would find some way to keep Machado in office "indefinitely."[16] A few days later copies of the Havana newspaper *Diario de la Marina* were confiscated because of an editorial attack on Lamont and his speech.[17] President Machado returned to Cuba assured of the support of American businessmen.

President Machado had pledged that he would serve one term, but early in his first administration he began to lay the foundation for an extension of his presidential career. In December 1925 the Cuban Congress enacted a law which provided—among other things—that the existing political parties might not be reorganized nor new ones organized except under very difficult conditions. In addition, party control was lodged in the Congressional members of the various parties.[18] In the spring and early summer of 1927 the Machado-dominated Congress passed a set of resolutions calling for certain constitutional amendments. Among the more important were: (1) the presidential term was extended from four to six years; (2) Machado's term was to be extended two years without an election; (3) the terms of senators and representatives were to be extended without an election.[19]

The State Department watched these developments with much the same attitude as the business groups. General Crowder reported in February 1927 that most Cubans favored a second term for Machado, and that the department should give the president an "informal assurance" that it was not opposed to his re-election. Crowder also stated that Machado desired the "closest possible cooperative relation with the United States," and that he had the leadership to carry out that kind of a program.[20]

Complaints about the Machado administration began to appear in 1926 and 1927. In February 1927 William Green of the American Federation of Labor protested over the alleged assassinations of labor leaders in Cuba, and charged that a "condition of virtual terrorism existed."[21] In June 1926 Senator William King (Utah) introduced a resolution calling for an investigation into certain claims of American citizens which he charged were not receiving just consideration in Cuba. The American Chamber of Commerce of Cuba protested to the State Department over the King resolution,[22] and Hugo Hartenstein told the members of the Chamber that they should read the resolution with "their commercial future in Cuba in mind." The Chamber asked the members to voice their opposition to the King resolution.[23]

In October 1927 the State Department received a confidential report on conditions in Cuba which praised Machado for his success in capitalizing on events to keep the people's minds off the economic problems. The report continued with the summary:

> Suffice it to remark that General Machado as a clever politician and . . . an energetic and capable executive can practically dictate to Congress. . . . I now feel that there is little doubt that the Constitutional Amendments will be adopted. . . . If he continues to govern as heretofore he will have ample and unfettered opportunity to accomplish for Cuba what only an intelligent executive in a position of semi-dictatorial authority can in the present stage of politics in this Island.[24]

In March 1928 Senator Henrik Shipstead (Farmer-Labor Party, Minnesota) introduced a resolution calling for an investigation into the Cuban handling of American claims, and in April the Senator proposed a longer resolution which contained a list of charges against the Machado administration.[25] Senator Alben Barkley attacked the resolutions, and stated that American investment interests had not reported any lack of protection. Barkley then read a letter from an American businessman recently returned from Cuba and an editorial from the *Philadelphia Record*. The letter praised the Machado government, and said that American resident investors were pleased with the situation.[26] The resolution died in committee, and another investigation attempt failed.

The attacks on the Machado administration increased after the presidents re-election in November 1928. Reports concerning corruption and despotism in Cuba were sent to the State Department, and some departmental officials raised the question of whether or not the United States should continue to support Machado. In April 1929 J. Reuben Clark—the Under Secretary—noted in a memorandum that he accepted many of these reports as valid. Clark stated that the department should take steps to correct any "iniquitous conditions," and that failure to do so constituted support for Machado.[27] In July 1929 an official of the National City Bank told Assistant Secretary White that Machado was becoming more dictatorial and corrupt. The official went on to say that the bank considered Ambassador Noble B. Judah a "stuffed shirt" because he had not exercised enough influence over Machado.[28] The State Department was fully informed concerning the growing opposition to Machado, but there was no change in the department's policy of supporting Machado.

One reason for this position was the continued support of the Machado administration by American business interests. A test of this friendship and its relation to policy came in September 1929. An extensive resolution charging the Machado administration with corruption and dictatorial actions was referred to the Senate Foreign Relations Committee. This resolution called for an investigation, and strongly intimated that the United States should intervene to clean up Cuba.[29] The Foreign Relations Committee acted on this resolution, and appointed a subcommittee to investigate the charges. As soon as news of the resolutions leaked out American businessmen came to the defense of Machado.

Senator George Moses called Colonel John H. Carroll, and told him about the charges in the resolution. According to Carroll the Senator said that if the resolutions were adopted it would bring about intervention. Colonel Carroll had been employed by Herbert C. Lakin to help with the sugar tariff lobbying, and also to lobby against any investigation resolution. Carroll later testified that he gave a copy of the resolutions to the *New York Times* for publication. According to Colonel Carroll's testimony, the Cuba Company wanted to sustain the Machado government because they were satisfied with its policies.[30]

A representative of the Warren Brothers Construction Company—the firm which was building the Central Highway in Cuba —rushed to the State Department and protested the threat of intervention. According to the memorandum:

> Mr. Cain said that he was very much concerned over the announcement that such a grave matter was being considered in Congress. What he was especially apprehensive of was that even if intervention should not follow the mere announcement of the consideration of such a measure might so adversely affect the credit of the Cuban Government that his company would be seriously hampered in making collections for work already performed and not yet paid for.

Manning and Thurston, of the Latin American divison, assured the representative that reports received from Cuba did not confirm the charges in the resolution or indicate a need for intervention.[31]

Protests against the resolution and the threat of intervention came from various business groups. The American Chamber of Commerce of Cuba declared that, "At no time have relations been more friendly than at present."[32] Most of the letters stressed this theme, and pointed out the close relations between the Machado administration and American business interests. Many of the protests also revealed an underlying fear that the United States might do something to upset the *status quo* in Cuba.[33]

The Senate Foreign Relations Committee received the report of the subcommittee, and announced that Secretary of State Stimson would be called to testify.[34] The State Department then announced that it had received very few reports of ill-treatment of Americans in Cuba, and Stimson emphasized publicly that the department had not originated the resolution.[35] Criticism had been expressed over the appointment of businessman Harry F. Guggenheim as Ambassador to Cuba—confirmation had been delayed by the Senate—but Stimson refused to withdraw the nomination.[36] The Secretary testified before the committee, but refused to tell reporters anything about the session. Instead, he referred them to Senator Borah, and the only thing the Senator related was that some of the claims of American citizens were valid. It was reported that Stimson had defended the Machado administration before the committee.[37] This report seems logical, since the resolution died in committee, and very little was said about it after Stimson's appearance.

Machado continued to receive enthusiastic support from American businessmen, but the "honeymoon" period of ardent enthusiasm was drawing to a close. Machado was still extolled as the businessman president,[38] and organized manifestations of good will were shown into 1930. In February 1930 the Cuban Society of America was organized and in May the Cuban Good Will Committee was formed. Both groups were interested in trade and tourists, and the latter group launched a public relations campaign to sell Americans on friendship with Cuba. One of the leading members of this committee was Machado's good friend Irenee Du Pont.[39] The Machado administration began to experience more serious native opposition during 1930, and the public manifestations of pro-Machado feeling in the United States diminished quite perceptibly.

II

Gerardo Machado had campaigned in 1924 as the "friendly" foe of the Platt Amendment. After his election Machado continued to agitate for its abrogation before the Cuban public and through diplomatic channels. Although some of Machado's statements were clearly designed for the consumption of the Cuban public, yet the president did want the Platt Amendment altered if not completely abrogated. The Cuban Ambassador, Don Orestes Ferrara, told the State Department in February 1927 that the amendment was embarrassing to Cuba since it made the republic appear to be less than independent and sovereign. The Ambassador said that Cuba did not want to eliminate it, but only to change the form so that Cuba would "look better to the world." There was some resentment in Cuba over the Guantanamo naval base, Ferrara stated, and the suggestion was made that the "status" of the base be altered.[40] President Machado broached the subject to President Coolidge during the Cuban president's

1927 visit, but Coolidge repeated the official line that there was really nothing to talk about.[41]

President Machado, however, told the Cuban people on numerous occasions that the Platt Amendment for all practical purposes no longer existed.[42] In April 1929 the State Department received information that the Cuban Congress was considering legislation which would contravene the right of American intervention. Machado was then told that such a measure would be regarded as an affront, and the measure was not passed.[43] A year later the department was informed that the Cuban Constitution was being published in official publications without the Platt Amendment.[44] The department decided that it would be "inadvisable" to raise an issue over this omission.[45]

Machado was careful, however, not to let his Platt Amendment agitation become identified with anti-American feeling. Prior to the Pan American Conference in Havana in 1928 Machado suppressed the anti-American skits which were being given in Cuban vaudeville houses.[46] On other occasions the president assured the State Department that his feelings concerning the Platt Amendment did not alter his belief that the welfare of Cuba was closely interlaced with the interests of the United States.[47]

In general, American business groups remained silent concerning the abrogation of the Platt Amendment, but there some disagreement among these interests about the need for it. Prior to Machado's visit in 1927, Henry Catlin, who represented the Electric Bond and Share Company in Cuba, planned a banquet for Machado in New York. According to the plans, invitations would be extended to the Secretaries of State and Commerce, Governor Al Smith of New York, and Mayor Jimmy Walker. The toastmaster was to make a speech praising Cuba and urging the abrogation of the Platt Amendment. This speech was to be followed by speeches from Governor Smith and Mayor Walker supporting this suggestion. Thus, Catlin and the Electric Bond and Share Company hoped to put pressure on Secretary Kellogg and Secretary Hoover. This affair did not proceed as planned, since Machado's visit was postponed, and the State Department found out the scheme before Machado arrived in April.[48]

General Crowder was apprised of this plan by Horatio Rubens, and informed the department that most of the American interests in Cuba favored the Platt Amendment. Crowder also stated that these interests shared his view that agitation of the issue would cause a downward movement for the outstanding bonds of Cuba, and seriously affect the financing of public works projects.[49]

Although some businessmen believed that the business nationalism of the "new Cuba" rendered the Platt Amendment obsolete,[50] the bankers tended to advocate its continued existence. When Gordon S. Rentschler of the National City Bank was asked if he felt that he had a right to ask for protection under the Platt Amendment if bank properties were in danger, he refused to give a definite answer. The most he would say was: "That is something we would have to decide when we came to it."[51] In September 1930, however, the vice-president of the Chase Securities Corporation reported that "any thought of revolution is curbed by a very obvious appreciation of the obligations of the United States Government under the Platt Amendment."[52] Thus, in late late 1930 some bankers, as well as other investment interests, still relied on the Platt Amendment, but the effectiveness of this guarantee had been partially dismantled by the policies of the bankers during the loan negotiations of the period from 1925 to 1930.

III

The loan cycle which extended from 1925 to 1930 was characterized by several factors: (1) the eagerness of American bankers to loan money to Cuba; (2) competition between these bankers and the resulting maneuvers for positions of influence in Cuba; (3) the tendency among most of the banks to regard article II of of the Platt Amendment and State Department action as unnecessary if not burdensome. Machado had pledged that he would not increase the foreign debt of Cuba, but as the sugar market continued to decline Machado was faced with the problem of finding funds to fulfill his public works pledges. American resident interests pointed out that road construction would do much to relieve the economic crisis, and the president was urged to accept funds from American sources.[53]

The bankers were also eager to extend funds to the Cuban Government, and the competition for the loan led the banks to adopt tactics which they hoped would make favorable impressions on Machado and his cabinet. As early as June 15, 1925 the Chase Securities Corporation was working with Henry Catlin on the formation of a syndicate for the purchase of part of Cuba's floating debt. Catlin was a former business associate and a close friend of President Machado—a fact not overlooked by the Chase group. One official wrote that: "While Mr. Catlin is close to the National City Bank . . . he states that he prefers to play with the Chase crowd." Catlin was instrumental in having Machado's son-in-law, Jose Obregon, made notarial attorney for the Chase Bank in Havana. The National City Bank had also been interested in the employment of Obregon, but Catlin claimed this prize for the "Chase crowd."[54] This loan project did not materialize, but the competition had begun.

In March 1926 the Chase Bank held several conferences with Cuban officials to discuss the possibility of a one hundred million dollar loan for road construction purposes. General Crowder found out about this plan and told a Chase official that he was going to make an immediate protest to the State Department since the loan could not be sanctioned under article II of the Platt Amendment. The Chase officials decided that it would be foolish to pretend utter lack of knowledge of the proposed public works loan, but they were not enthusiastic over Crowder's interest. As one official stated:

> It is clear that the bank should preserve cordial relations with the United States Ambassador but, while not telling him anything that would damage our interests in Cuba, to be careful not to make any statements which, he might easily learn, were contrary to facts.[55]

This loan plan did not materialize either, but the Machado administration was now definitely in the market for foreign funds.

Late in March 1926 Dwight Morrow conferred with the Cuban

Government about the three plans for financing public works which had been proposed. These plans were: (1) to pay for improvements on a cash basis from the special tax fund; (2) to pay out of the proceeds of a formal bond issue; (3) to pay with certificates of indebtedness which would be given to the contractors to be sold by them to obtain the money needed. Morrow strongly recommended the cash plan, since it would not increase the debt of Cuba. The third plan he called "the most dangerous of the three."[56] General Crowder reported that he agreed entirely with Morrow, and that most of the plans presented by American bankers were in conflict with article II of the Platt Amendment.[57] Crowder was particularly upset over the fact that some of the bankers were trying to circumvent article II through a technicality in the form of the loan. This was the plan that the Cuban Government issue certificates of indebtedness to be paid out of an extra-budgetary fund. This would not involve any formal bond issue, and would not be figured as a regular, external debt.[58] Thus, the bankers involved hoped that they could circumvent the Crowder-Morrow position on the Cuban debt and Machado could claim that he was not violating his "no indebtedness" pledge.

In November 1926 the Chase Bank submitted its final proposal to the Cuban Government. The plan involved a ten million dollar banking credit to be represented by deferred-payment public work certificates. The Cuban Government would issue these to the contractors for work performed, and the bank would buy them from the contractors. The bank would then cash the certificates as funds came into the special public works fund. General Crowder was frequently consulted during the drafting of the plan, but he told the bank's attorney that the State Department would probably want to investigate the matter. The attorney then conferred with Green H. Hackworth—the Solicitor—and Arthur N. Young, and on December 13, 1926 the bank was notified that the department had no objection to the plan.[59] The contract was signed in February 1927.

By June 1927 General Crowder had retreated from the position which he had taken in the spring of 1926. The Ambassador did want the State Department to declare that it reserved the right to object to further transactions involving certificates of indebtedness,[60] but this was a far cry from the 1926 statement that Cuba should not increase its public debt by any means.[61] The State Department was exercising very little control over loans to Cuba by 1927, and reference was seldom made to article II of the Platt Amendment. On June 23, 1927 J. P. Morgan and Company asked if the department had any objection to a nine million dollar loan for the purpose of enabling the Cuban Government to pay off certificates of indebtedness. On June 25, the department replied that it had "no objection" to the financing.[62] No protest was made under the Platt Amendment in spite of the fact that the public debt of Cuba was increasing and the finances of the government were decreasing.

In January 1928 the Chase Bank was informed by Jose Obregon that President Machado was planning to start negotiations for a new loan as soon as the Pan American Conference was over. The president's son-in-law also stated that plans were being made to hire Dr. Hernandez Cartaya, "to be our attorney in connection with any financial propositions that may arise with the Government." Cartaya was one of Machado's financial advisors.[63]

A Cuban Finance Committee, however, turned down several loan proposals, but Machado accepted the Chase offer by presidential decree. An American resident commented that this "still further convinced the public that he [Machado] is a man of action, character and correct judgment."[64] On May 22, 1928 the attorneys for the bank submitted the agreement to the State Department, and on June 20, the department notified the Chase Bank that it had "no objections" to the proposal.[65] The Cuban Government stated publicly that the department had expressed its approval, "in very strong terms," but the department assured an inquirer for Morgan and Company that the approval had been routine.[66]

Under the 1928 agreement the syndicate headed by the Chase Bank extended an additional credit of fifty million dollars to the Cuban Government. Of this total credit of sixty million dollars the bank converted twenty million dollars worth of deferred-payment work certificates into serial certificates bearing 5½ percent interest. These were in turn sold on the American security market.[67]

By the fall of 1929 the Cuban Government was again running short of funds. The sixty million dollar Chase credit was reported to be almost gone, and work on the Central Highway would have to be stopped if funds were not obtained. The Machado administration contacted the American bankers, and requested another loan. At this juncture the American Chargé d'Affaires *ad interim* reviewed the economic situation in a dispatch which clearly revealed the dilemma which plagued the department—and which would continue to do so until 1933. The Chargé suggested a series of reforms which were needed in Cuba, but admitted that it would be difficult to force these on Machado. The United States Government could not refuse to consent to a loan because the economic distress of the country would increase, and this could lead to disorders or revolution. In addition, the supervision of Cuban finances would constitute a great blow to the pride and prestige of Machado. Thus, preventive intervention or refusal to sanction a loan would weaken the Machado government, and lead to the very situation which the department wanted to prevent. Machado was viewed as the essence of Cuban stability and protection of American interests, and the substance of the Chargé's report was to the effect that the United States should try to tide Cuba over the depression while hoping for the best.[68] This remained the State Department's basic position on Cuba until the summer of 1933.

In February 1930 the syndicate headed by the Chase Bank negotiated another loan with Cuba. There was some competition for the financing, and for a time the National City Company seemed to have the "inside track."[69] The Chase group won out, however, and with little comment from the State Department negotiated an agreement. Among other things, the agreement called for the issuing of forty million dollars worth of public works bonds, and the extension of a twenty million dollar short-term credit. In addition, the Cuban Government bought at par approximately thirty-eight million dollars of serial and public work certificates from the syndicate.[70]

Thus, by the end of February 1930 the Cuban Government had incurred an eighty million dollar indebtedness through the Chase Bank and its associates. The Chase Bank kept a close watch on Cuban affairs, particularly since it held in portfolio a total of $5,415,000 par amount of bonds and serial certificates.[71] Bank officials continued to depend on Machado to keep order. In July 1930 James Bruce, of the Havana branch, wrote that Machado had "entire command" of the situation, and was the "only boss." He also noted that the loans were safe.[72]

During the closing months of 1930 the situation in Cuba degenerated rapidly. The economic picture had been deteriorating for several years, and the world-wide depression added problems to an already serious economic situation. This helped stimulate opposition to Machado, and the threats of disorder mounted in late 1930. Ambassador Guggenheim had tried to effect a compromise between Machado and the Union Nationalista—headed by Carlos Mendieta—in June 1930, but the attempt failed in July when the opposition demanded the resignation of Machado.[73] On October 2, 1930 Secretary Stimson publicly stated that the situation in Cuba was serious, but that the United States was following the Root Interpretation of the Platt Amendment. The Secretary added that he would not prophesy about the future, and that every case would be judged on its merits in determining intervention policy.[74] Guggenheim again tried to arrange a *modus vivendi* between Machado and the opposition in November.[75] This attempt failed, and the opposition began to make threats that American property would be destroyed.[76]

Late in November Guggenheim reported that the opposition had privately asked him for a preventive intervention policy to unseat Machado and place them in power. The Ambassador stated that the opposition was actively trying to promote intervention, and had threatened the lives of Americans—including Stimson and Guggenheim. The report warned, however, that the United States must avoid intervention since it would be "highly resented" both in and out of Cuba, and would, "only have the most harmful consequences for the United States."[77]

Early in 1931 the Chase Bank began to work much closer with the department. In general the State Department, Guggenheim, and the bankers agreed that Machado should be supported, but that he should be urged to reduce the budget and compromise with the opposition. In addition, the Cuban Government should not be allowed to default on the foreign debt payments if at all possible. The basic limitations to this policy were: (1) the fear that if too much pressure were put on Machado the *status quo* would be disturbed, since preventive intervention would be detrimental to the already weakened prestige of the administration; (2) the fact that additional loans to the Cuban Government were out of the question due to the depressed condition of the American security market and the Cuban economy.[78]

In January 1931 Guggenheim again urged Machado to compromise with the Menocal-Mendieta group.[79] In February James Bruce of the Chase Bank conferred with Guggenheim, and then went to see the President. Bruce told Machado that another bond issue was hardly worth considering, but that the bank would extend the twenty million dollar credit for ninety days. Machado was told that he should reduce the budget and work to re-establish political calm. The position of the bank concerning the latter point was clearly stated when Bruce told Machado that:

> This of course could only be done by making a compromise with his political enemies, and naturally the only way he could do this was to make some concessions, but the result of which would be that Cuba would present a uniform front rather than have the tourist trade disrupted and the security holders made nervous by not knowing when, if at all, the Government would be thrown out of power.

Machado replied that he realized all of this, and that in the next Congress there would not be one dissenting voice. Bruce later commented, "I suppose the two dissenting voices are already in jail."[80]

The Chase Bank was also interested in Machado's personal finances. Bruce reported that the President's personal loan was up to $130,000 with little prospect of immediate payment. In addition, the bank had loaned an unsecured $45,000 to the president's construction company, and $89,000 to his shoe factory. The latter had been reduced to $9,000, Bruce reported. The bank decided that it would be best to retain the president's son-in-law Jose Obregon, although Bruce stated: "As we know, from any business standpoint he is perfectly useless." If the bank dismissed Obregon the president would have to support him, and this would be difficult Bruce noted. The Chase Bank's stake in the Machado administration went somewhat further than the external debt of Cuba.[81]

Guggenheim and the bankers continued to urge Machado—and the opposition—to compromise, and cooperate in the reduction of the budget.[28] Open fighting broke out in August 1931, however, and the Machado administration was faced with its first real test of armed violence. The Cuban Government asked what the attitude of the State Department would be concerning the sale of arms, if needed. The department replied that the matter would be considered when the request was made—which did not happen.[83] The Cuban Government also sent a note requesting an embargo on the sale of arms to other groups. Guggenheim talked with Walter C. Thurston by phone, and then conferred with the Cuban Secretary of State. The Secretary agreed to withdraw the note, and Guggenheim concluded his summary of the meeting with the statement:

> The Cuban Secretary of State understands that shipments of arms from the United States are being prohibited as effectively as they would be under a formal proclamation of an arms embargo.[84]

Publicly, the State Deparment asserted the absolute neutrality of the United States, but in reality it was neutrality weighed in favor of Machado.[85]

By October 1931 Chase Bank officials feared that Cuba was near bankruptcy. Guggenheim told the bankers to try to work out some arrangement with Machado which would help the Cuban Government to handle its financial obligations. The Ambassador noted that the bank could handle this problem just as well as the State Department, and that it would be preferable to let the bank do so.[86] The bankers wanted to avoid complete default, but they told the department that they would accept a limited moratorium on the long-term public works indebtedness in order to convince the opposition that there would be no intervention.[87] Shepard Morgan and L. S. Rosenthall, of Chase Bank, agreed with Assistant Secretary William Castle that:

> If a plan for a moratorium on the public works amortiza-
> tion payments could be worked out, with only a *pro forma*
> protest by the bankers and no objection on our part, the
> opposition would then feel that their hope of intervention
> on our part would not be realized and that they would there-
> fore be more disposed to consider a political agreement.[88]

Guggenheim agreed with the financial aspect of this plan, but on November 13, 1931 he told the department that Machado would have to get out eventually. The Ambassador also stated that the department should give a statement to the press which would tacitly let people know that the United States was not backing Machado. Secretary Stimson thought it wiser not to issue one. As the memorandum noted:

> One element that led the Secretary to this conclusion was
> the fact that the bankers, who had a big stake in Cuba, are
> working hard on a scheme which they hope will work out
> satisfactorily, and he did not know how this statement would
> affect that program.[89]

The bankers extended the twenty million dollar credit for another six months, and the Cuban Government was able to meet its December 1931 payments. The Treasury Department sent $2,250,000 to the Chase Bank two weeks ahead of time, and one official noted that, "It is only due to our close contact and friendship with General Machado and the Secretary of the Treasury that we are receiving the above payment at so early a date." Most of the Cuban Government's employees remained un-paid, however, and Machado asked the bankers not to publicize the debt payments.[90] The bank's support for Machado continued to pay dividends—both literally and figuratively.

From late 1931 until the end of the Hoover Administration in March 1933 the State Department did virtually nothing. Ter-rorism was prevalent throughout 1932, and the repressive tactics of the Machado Government followed the same pattern. Guggen-heim wanted the department to state publicly that Machado was not being supported by the United States. One reason Guggenheim wanted such a statement was that he hoped it would shock Machado into a desire for compromise.[91] The department, however, stated that it was following a policy of "complete non-interference in Cuba's internal affairs." Menocal and Mendieta asked the United States to settle the situation, but Guggenheim had to read them the department's statement concerning the Root Interpretation of the Platt Amendment.[92]

The bankers continued to extend financial assistance to Machado during 1932. The twenty million dollar credit was extended in June and December, and in June a small group of bankers arranged an additional credit to help Cuba meet the foreign debt payments.[93] The Cuban Government began to consider the coinage of additional silver in March 1932. The banks were not too enthusiastic about the plan, but they realized that they would end up getting most of the seigniorage profit.[94]

There was some evidence late in 1932 that Machado was pushing the bankers too far. He disagreed with their request that the ten cents a bag sugar production tax be applied to the payment of a proposed advance, and told them that unless they assisted him in paying four million dollars of the December obligation he could do nothing but go into "complete and total default." In fact, the president had already informed his cabinet that the bankers had agreed because of his reputation and standing.[95] A plan was worked out in December 1932, however, to prevent a four million dollar default. The Chase Bank agreed to advance $1,650,000 to the Cuban Government, and three of the largest oil companies operating in Cuba advanced $1,835,000 against their 1933 customs duties. The Cuban Government secured the remainder from various sources—including $300,000 in newly minted silver—and passed a bill levying a tax of one cent a pound on all sugar consumed in Cuba. The proceeds of this tax, together with the 10-cent-a-bag production tax, were pledged for the repayment of the sums advanced. Guggenheim protested that these advances were in violation of article II of the Platt Amendment, but the State Department replied that the plan was a private matter between the business groups and the Cuban Government.[96]

In late October 1932 Shepard Morgan told the State Department that some form of financial intervention was the only solution to Cuba's problems. The bankers suggested that this could be accomplished under the guise of a claims commission which could supervise the budget and scale down the floating debt. The department refused to consider this proposal.[97] The Cuban financial situation continued to degenerate, and in March 1933 the Cuban Government informed the Chase officials that public clamor for a moratorium law was growing. Some public employees were reported to be starving, and many of them were eleven months behind in their salaries since the government had been taking money from the general budget to pay the public works obligations. The bankers told the Cuban Secretary of Finance that a moratorium should be avoided, but one official reported that he was "very, very disappointed," over the attitude of the Cuban Government.[98]

On January 20, 1933 Ambassador Guggenheim sent a lengthy dispatch to the department concerning the re-evaluation of the department's Cuban policy. The Ambassador recommended that the Platt Amendment be modified so as to eliminate the right of intervention. He gave two reasons why this should be done. First, the Platt Amendment actually increased the danger to American property since a "dispairing Cuban opposition" would resort to violence in order to provoke intervention. Guggenheim was convinced that this "deliberate assault" on American property would soon develop. The second reason was that such modification would increase the prestige of the United States throughout Latin America. The Ambassador added that this was a good time to consider such a move from the investor's viewpoint also. In normal times such a modification would reduce the market values of securities, but that market values could not sink much lower than they were at the time.[99] This was the twilight of the Hoover administration, and Guggenheim's recommendation was largely ignored.

Harry F. Guggenheim submitted his resignation to the new administration in late March 1933. T. M. Findlay of the Chase Bank called on the Ambassador prior to his departure to say goodbye, and Guggenheim told him that he greatly appreciated the "close cooperation" he had received from Chase during his stay in Cuba.[100] Thus, the diplomatic career of the man Cubans had labeled "Guggenado" came to a close, and all concerned awaited the appointment of the new ambassador to the simmering "Pearl of the Antilles."

IV

American policy during the Cuban crisis period of the early 1930's differed from the policy followed during the 1920-23 crisis. This was not due to any change in the basic policy of the United States, but rather to different circumstances. American business interests did not request preventive intervention or ask the department to clean up Cuba. The Chase Bank did suggest some form of "financial" intervention in the fall of 1932, but this was an isolated recommendation and was accompanied with the statement that the bankers did not want any type of direct—or forceful—intervention.[101] Horatio Rubens—the President of the Consolidated Railroads of Cuba—wrote in April 1931 that: "It cannot be ignored that an intervention in Cuba, would not only give a handle to the Democrats but would saddle on the Washington Government the entire economic and financial problem of Cuba." Rubens advised against any kind of intervention.[102]

Machado did not ask the State Department for any public statements of support, and was satisfied with the "noninterference" policy. The opposition wanted the United States to intervene in any form in order to discredit Machado. For several years the Cuban president had been telling the people that the United States had, for all practical purposes, done away with the Platt Amendment because of its confidence in Machado. American business groups had eulogized the Machado administration, and praised its business-like policies. Thus, American interests and the State Department feared that any sign of hostility toward Machado would be interpreted by the Cubans as repudiation.

Machado preserved order during the period. The uprising of 1931 was quickly suppressed, American property was protected, and payments on the foreign debt were maintained with help from the bankers. American interests believed that if Machado could be tided over until the depression ended that all would return to normal. The difficulty arose when the depression grew worse, but even in March 1933 most American interests showed no signs of wanting to unseat Machado; although there were some indications that the reservoir of business support for Machado was running dry.

In addition, American business interests had tended to oppose a rigid interpretation of the Platt Amendment during the period 1925 to 1930. Article II was circumvented by the bankers, and although the State Department continued to "supervise" the loans, the public debt of Cuba mounted as its revenue fell.[103] American interests strongly opposed any attempt to investigate the actions of the Cuban Government under article III to see if intervention was in order to protect "individual liberty." Some businessmen also stressed the Root Interpretation of the Platt Amendment. During the period 1925-30 the Platt Amendment had been practically undermined, and the noninterference tradition of the Root Interpretation had been championed by American business groups.

Another factor to be considered was the general Latin American policy of the Hoover administration. President-elect Hoover had made a good will tour to Latin America after the 1928 election. During this tour Hoover continually stressed the tie between good will and expanded trade relations; so much so that Secretary Kellogg became quite incensed over what he considered to be the repudiation of his Nicaraguan policy.[104] Hoover also wrote the first draft of his inaugural address with the intention of specifically defining the intervention policy of the administration. He devoted some three pages to intervention, and attempted to elaborate the exact limitations which he would place on the use of force. Hoover then sent the draft copy to Charles Evans Hughes with the comment:

> I want to say something that will carry confidence to the world as to the intentions of the new administration. I have also felt that it might be desirable from the point of view of South America and the business public, to give rather a closer definition of our relation to questions of intervention.

Hughes advised the president-elect to eliminate this section from the address since anything dealing with the subject was certain to be misinterpreted. Hoover accepted this advice, and did not attempt a public definition of his plans to limit intervention.[105]

Hoover and Stimson did continue the policy of terminating past intervention—which had begun under Hughes—and in May 1931 the Secretary devoted a speech to one of the major reasons for the "withdrawal" policy. Stimson linked foreign policy to domestic prosperity, and stated that trade with Latin America had been retarded by several "sore spots." These accusations of American imperialism, the Secretary declared, "have damaged our good name, our credit and our trade far beyond the apprehension of our own people." To overcome these "sore spots" the United States planned to withdraw the marines from Haiti and Nicaragua, and to apply the Root Interpretation to the Platt Amendment.[106] Thus, the Hoover administration was publicly committed to an official noninterference policy in Cuba except in case of anarchy.[107]

This "official" policy meant that the department would make no public statements for or against Machado. The bankers were asked to take the initiative in supporting Machado, since the department wanted to present a neutral front. When the uprising broke out in 1931 the department let the Cuban Government know that arms shipments to the rebels were being prohibited, and that a public declaration of an embargo was to be avoided. Stimson seems to have been convinced that Machado could ride out the storm with some help from the bankers, and that the department could avoid any definite action. In the spring of 1932 the Secretary informed Guggenheim that as far as departmental policy was concerned, Machado had been constitutionally elected to serve until 1935, and that the department had no intention of withdrawing its support from the Cuban administration.[108]

This did not mean that the State Department was contented with the growing unrest in Cuba or the repressive policies of Machado. The department, as well as the business interests, would undoubtedly have preferred an orderly Cuba with more political democracy: the harmonizing of American idealistic professions with American interests. Order was the primary concern, however, and Machado represented the *status quo* which Americans hoped to preserve.[109] The economic depression was viewed as the crucial factor by the interests concerned, and the methods used to deal with the Cuban situation were continually frustrated by the duration of the depression. Instead of improving, the Cuban problems became more complicated as the depression deepened and the price of sugar dropped to ½ cent a pound in 1932. Machado still managed to stay in power through the grace of the Cuban army and American interests. Thus, when Ambassador Guggenheim chided an official of the Chase Bank in 1933 for the "makeshift" measures pursued by the bankers in Cuba, the official replied: "We of course have to deal with facts and conditions as they are, which is rather different from the way we think they should be or might like to have them."[110] This remark could serve as a fitting epitaph for the Cuban policy of the State Department from 1930 to March 1933.

CHAPTER NINE

The Pattern of Cuban-
American Relations

I

American business interests and the State Department were closely connected in matters of Cuban-American relations. There were some disagreements over specific methods, but in general there was agreement concerning the basic goals of policy. As for example, in January 1922 Crowder and Lakin disagreed over the removal of the marines from Camaguey. Both agreed that American property should be protected, and the argument developed over the method—in this case the question of the location of the garrison. Some individual officials in the department objected to the policy advocated by these business groups interested in Cuba—such as J. Reuben Clark's advocacy of cleaning up Cuba in 1929—but the department's over-all policy was seldom swayed by these individual protests. Taken as a whole, the period from 1919–1933 was characterized by notable unanimity of views concerning motives and methods on the part of State Department officials and American businessmen.

The State Department and American business groups wanted to maintain a stable Cuban Government which would protect American economic interests—trade opportunities, and investments. Political reforms and democracy in Cuba were only stressed by the United States during times of crisis, as concessions to keep opposition groups from starting trouble. Reform was urged from 1920 to early 1923, and from 1931 into the Roosevelt period. Very little was said, however, from 1923 to 1931. It was not the policies of Machado per se that worried the State Department and businessmen after 1930, but the fact that some of these policies made compromise with the opposition more difficult—and increased the danger of revolt.

The Platt Amendment became, for all practical purposes, a stand-by organ of American policy during this period. The decision in 1921 to base reform demands on the need for a loan rather than on the Amendment; Dwight Morrow's espousal of the Root Interpretation in 1923, the circumvention of article II in regard to the loans negotiated after 1925; and the official declaration of the Root Interpretation in October 1930, were all part of the process. By January 1933 the arguments for modification of the Amendment had been formulated.[1] This development was, in part, a result of several interacting factors. Cuban nationalistic feeling grew stronger after World War I, and the rising Cuban business class became its primary exponent. The Cuban businessmen were willing to cooperate closely with the American business interests, and the latter group became firm supporters of this "business nationalism."

Colonel Jose Tarafa was a good example of this cooperative relationship. In 1923 the Colonel sponsored a bill to consolidate several of the leading railroads. The bill was pushed as a "nationalistic" measure, but it combined American and Cuban interests—under American control. The Consolidated Railroads of Cuba was a symbol of what one State Department official approvingly referred to as the "industrial technique."[2] The entente between American business groups and the "businessman-president" Machado was a logical outgrowth of this technique. This particular development was not limited to Cuba, however, and one enthusiastic writer described this "New Age" of business Pan Americanism as follows:

He who goes in to the hilt on the "bull" side of inter-American cooperation stands with Calvin Coolidge, Charles Evans Hughes, Leo S. Rowe, Victor M. Cutter, John L. Merrill, Henry Ford and a growing host of shrewd, keen, businessmen, statesmen, and diplomats. And he links hands with the Ferraras and Machados of Cuba, with the Leguias of Peru. . . .[3]

Another factor which influenced American policy was the growing belief that American actions in Cuba had a direct relationship to American trade with other Latin American countries. Isaac F. Marcosson wrote in 1930—with perhaps some exaggeration—that:

> Cuba is the key to our Latin-American relations. Our influence beyond Panama is largely regulated by our attitude toward, and our status in, the area where Columbus first set foot on land. . . . If we impair her economic growth and thereby engender resentment, it is bound to have a repercussion in the vast domain where . . . a considerable portion of our export future lies. Latin-American amity, for us, is an indispensable commercial asset.[4]

The combination of these elements became a basic factor in Cuban-American relations during the 1920's. The impact of the economic depression in the United States on the already depressed Cuban economy threatened to upset this pattern of relations which had developed prior to 1930.

Political stability, bank loans, direct investments, and trade were all mutually dependent in this pattern of Cuban-American relations. This mutual dependence was recognized by most of the American business groups interested in Cuba.[5] The basic flaw, however, in this seemingly harmonious pattern was the question of Cuban exports to the United States. The increase in the sugar tariff in 1921, 1922, and 1930 helped to decrease the Cuban share of the American sugar market, and this in turn had an adverse effect on all interests.[6] In addition, the restriction of Cuban exports of manufactured tobacco affected both the Cuban economy and the American exporters who used the parcel post system, since Cuba would not negotiate a permanent parcel post convention as long as the tobacco restrictions were maintained.

These problems involved Congressional action, and in this sphere of activity conflicting economic groups were able to influence policy. Protectionist-minded farm groups and manufacturers combined to push up the tariff, and the Republican party was caught in the dilemma of how to maintain the export trade and at the same time foster domestic production of all kinds. This was especially true in the case of sugar since influential Republican Congressmen—such as Smoot, Fordney, and Hawley—were directly connected with the beet sugar industry. This political conflict was also reflected in the executive branch. Harding was willing to lower the sugar tariff, but Coolidge refused to do so. The State Department generally desired a lower sugar tariff, but some officials—such as Arthur N. Young—discounted the effect of the tariff on American interests.

American business groups were not in complete agreement as to the effect of the 1922 tariff increase. The price of Cuban sugar increased in 1923, and some businessmen—Dwight Morrow for one—believed that the increase would not harm American economic interests. Other men, in business and government, placed their hope for continued trade expansion on loans and investments.[7] The American investment interests—represented by the American Chamber of Commerce of Cuba—and the American sugar interests in Cuba consistently maintained that political stability, investment values, and Cuban sugar exports were mutually dependent. This position was reinforced as the Cuban sugar economy declined in the latter half of the 1920's, and political unrest began to appear.

During the tariff battle of 1929–30 more export groups joined in the attempt to prevent an increase in the sugar tariff. The Republican party, however, was still caught in the basic dilemma, and the Hoover "compromise" on the sugar tariff was the result. The Cuban interests did attain one goal when the Republicans put a provision repealing the tobacco restriction statute into the tariff act.

Loans and investments postponed the time when the established pattern of Cuban-American relations would be threatened by the decline of the Cuban sugar market. By 1931, however, the depression in the United States had struck a vital blow at this pattern; no more loans could be floated, and the American consumption of sugar declined. Many American businessmen were convinced that the status quo could be maintained in Cuba, and the value of American investments protected, only if the Cubans could sell more sugar.[8]

II

The first administration of Franklin D. Roosevelt was begun amidst the increasing clamor of important business groups for measures to increase the export trade. "Foreign trade is the keystone of recovery," was a recurrent theme sounded by banking and manufacturing groups during the depression years.[9] In addition, many individuals voiced the confident belief that the new administration would take steps to stimulate trade, especially in Latin America. The revival of the Cuban market was often cited as one of the more urgent problems facing the administration, and some business sources regarded this as the testing ground for the "Good Neighbor" policy. Commenting favorably on the relationship between export markets, Cuban stability, and the price of sugar, *Business Week* magazine stated:

> Roosevelt is expected to put new stress on Latin American trade. Intervention by the United States in the affairs of any Latin American country is tremendously unpopular. Roosevelt has evidently chosen to attack the problem from another angle.[10]

After March 4, 1933 a number of men interested in Cuban-American trade wrote to various Congressmen and to the State Department calling for measures to stimulate trade with Cuba.[11] This intense interest in Cuba was further demonstrated when a number of large corporations hired Phillip Jessup to make a report on "suggestions to be incorporated in any possible new reciprocity treaty with Cuba." These suggestions were later sent to the State Department to be used in devising measures to increase the flow of exports.[12]

The Roosevelt Administration was definitely committed to a policy of stimulating exports, and this was one major factor behind the "Good Neighbor" policy. Cordell Hull was convinced that the "decline of international commerce" was one of the "most destructive factors" in the depression, and this theme was emphasized by Roosevelt, Henry A. Wallace, Adolph A. Berle, Jr., Charles W. Taussig, Sumner Welles, and other administration figures.[13] Many of these same men also stressed the link between trade and American policy toward Latin America and Cuba. Arthur S. Hillyer, of the Bureau of Foreign and Domestic Commerce, told the National Foreign Trade Convention in April 1933 that Roosevelt's "Good Neighbor" statement was evidence of the administration's interest in foreign trade.[14] Charles W. Taussig, one of the "Brain Trust," was even more specific in an address to the same group a year later. Taussig related that Roosevelt had begun to study the Cuban situation early in 1932, and "could be classed as an expert in his own right on Cuban affairs." The resulting policies, according to Taussig, had helped to increase exports to Cuba.[15] In an address in 1935, Sumner Welles described in glowing terms the increase in exports to Cuba and the revival in value of investments in Cuba, and stated: "The policy of your Government toward Cuba has been for the past 2 years, in the best sense of the word, the policy of the "good neighbor."[16] In many respects Cuba was the testing ground for the "Good Neighbor" policy, and administration officials repeatedly cited Cuban affairs as evidence of the dollars and cents value of this policy.[17]

The connection of the Roosevelt Administration with Cuba went much deeper than this, however. Three members of the "Brain Trust" were officials in the American Molasses Company—a firm with Cuban properties. Charles W. Taussig, a long-time advocate of lower sugar duties, was president of the company; Rexford Guy Tugwell served as vice-president for several years—including the period when he was Under Secretary of Agriculture; and Adolph A. Berle, Jr. was associated with the firm until 1939. The American Molasses Company controlled the Sucrest Corporation which was a sugar refining company using Cuban sugar.[18] Taussig and Berle aided Roosevelt in making his study of the Cuban situation, and both went to Cuba in December 1932 for further investigation. After returning from Cuba they reported to Roosevelt at Warm Springs, Georgia, and Taussig then began to contact the various sugar interests concerning plans for production control.[19]

Three of Roosevelt's cabinet appointees had definite connections with American business groups interested in Cuba. William H. Woodin, the Secretary of the Treasury, had a long record of economic connections with Cuba. He was on the board of directors of the Cuba Company, and was a member of the Cuban Chamber of Commerce in the United States, the Committee on the Cuban Emergency in 1921–1922, and the National Foreign Trade Council in 1931 and 1932.[20] Daniel C. Roper, the Secretary of Commerce, was a low tariff advocate who had represented several Cuban sugar companies at the February, 1933 Tariff Commission hearing.[21] Cordell Hull was also an advocate of lower duties on sugar, and had worked with the Cuban sugar lobby in 1929 and 1930. As if to put frosting on the cake of administration connections with Cuba, Thomas Walsh married Señora Mina Perez Chaumont de Truffin of Cuba in February 1933.[22]

Indeed, of this generation much was expected. American businessmen interested in Cuba wanted solutions for the related problems of the tariff and market stabilization, and the Democratic Administration gave every indication that it would work for such solutions.

CHAPTER TEN

New Deal Diplomacy and the
Cuban Settlement, 1933-1934

I

In April 1933 Sumner Welles temporarily laid aside the mantle of Assistant Secretary of State and embarked on his assignment as Ambassador Extraordinary and Plenipotentiary to the Republic of Cuba.[1] His immediate assignment was to effect a political settlement which would save the Machado Administration and to negotiate a trade agreement which would bolster the Cuban economy and stimulate the flow of American exports. The former task proved to be impossible, and the growing unrest resulted in two "revolutions." In August, Machado was ousted, but the new administration held power for only a short time. It was replaced in September by the government of Ramón Grau San Martín. During the fall of 1933 the Cuban scene was marked by violence, labor unrest, and threats that foreign properties would be expropriated. Out of this turmoil, however, there emerged a settlement which lasted for over twenty-five years. Fulgencio Batista, the Cinderella Colonel, was the political pivot in this settlement, since he became the guarantor of a Cuban government friendly to the United States and its interests. The economic aspects of the settlement were embodied in the Export-Import Bank silver loans, the Reciprocal Trade Agreement (with later changes), and the sugar marketing allotment (as embodied in the Jones-Costigan and subsequent acts). The Roosevelt Administration blended these political and economic elements into a system of Cuban-American relations which prevailed until the bearded rebels of Fidel Castro overthrew the Batista dictatorship on January 1, 1959.

Sumner Welles was a career diplomat with experience in Latin

American policy, and a well-developed concept concerning the role the United States should play in Latin America—especially in the Caribbean area. Welles expressed this concept many times in articles, official documents, and in his book, *Naboth's Vineyard*. "Friendly intervention," as Welles designated it, was a policy designed to secure stable governments, "well disposed toward the United States," in the Caribbean. Armed intervention would be used only in extreme emergencies, and the emphasis would be placed on subtle pressure applied behind the scenes. The Crowder Mission in the early 1920's was cited by Welles as a good example of this policy.[2] Welles placed a great deal of importance on economic factors. "Prosperity is the most powerful antagonist of unrest," he wrote in 1928, and trade was the vital element of prosperity.[3] In addition, the economy of the United States would prosper through the sale of its surplus products.[4] Thus, Welles linked United States prosperity and Caribbean stability with the linchpin of trade.

These views coincided with the position of the Roosevelt Administration, and both were reflected in policy statements and in Welles's official instructions.[5] The long range objective was the economic rehabilitation of Cuba—based on a reciprocal trade agreement and a fixed allotment of the United States market for Cuban sugar—with its concomitant effect, increased United States exports. Initially, however, Welles was to point out to Machado, "in the most forcible terms," the need for political reforms to conciliate the opposition political groups. Welles was to stress the necessity for a cessation of terrorism, and to offer his services as a mediator. His instructions further stated:

> You will . . . regard as your chief objective the negotiation of a definite, detailed, and binding understanding between the present Cuban government and the responsible leaders of the factions opposed to it, which will lead to a truce in the present dangerous political agitation to continue until such time as national elections can be held in Cuba. . . .[6]

After his first interview with President Machado, Welles was rather optimistic over the chances of stabilizing Cuba. He informed Secretary of State Hull that the United States should back

Machado since he was able to preserve order and commanded the loyalty of the army. If Machado were to be removed, Welles believed that chaos would result and that American property would be destroyed. The Ambassador went on to say that the negotiations leading toward a new commercial treaty would "assist in part in distracting public attention from politics." He concluded with the observation:

> Finally, the negotiation at this time of a reciprocal trade agreement with Cuba along the lines above indicated, will not only revivify Cuba, but will give us practical control of a market we have been steadily losing for the past ten years not only for our manufactured products but for our agricultural exports as well.[7]

Welles immediately contacted the opposition leaders in what was to be a lengthy attempt to arrange a settlement. At first President Machado seemed willing to negotiate a compromise, and most of the opposition groups advised Welles that they would accept his services as a mediator.[8] Negotiations on the proposed commercial treaty were also started, but Welles did not push them since he was using the treaty as a lever to force political concessions.[9] At Welles's instigation Machado abolished press censorship and submitted a general amnesty bill to Congress (where it was speedily passed).[10] Early in August, however, a general strike swept Cuba, and after consulting with opposition leaders Welles became convinced that Machado would have to go before any settlement could be worked out. On August 5, 1933 Welles handed Machado a five-point program calling for the reorganization of the cabinet and the creation of a vice-presidency, with the person chosen assuming the presidency upon his inauguration. Welles also told the President that the alternative was absolute anarchy and possible American intervention.[11] Machado stated publicly that Welles was only bluffing, and the Ambassador wired President Roosevelt requesting that he call in the Cuban Ambassador and inform him that, "absolutely no act of mine has been taken except with your full approval."[12] Roosevelt complied immediately and informed the Cuban Ambassador that the United States had no desire to intervene, "but that it was our duty to do what we could so that there should be no starvation and chaos among the Cuban people."[13]

The problem facing Welles was how to persuade Machado to "retire." This, in Welles's opinion, was the only way to end political unrest in Cuba, and prepare for economic rehabilitation. As he stated to Secretary of State Cordell Hull:

> So long as this condition continues there is no possible chance of improving economic conditions in Cuba, and there will be immense loss to the Cuban people themselves and as a natural corollary to all of the American intersts doing business in or with Cuba.[14]

Welles recommended that recognition be withdrawn from Machado if he continued to hold the presidential office. The Ambassador also stated that the removal of Machado would be easier if the Cuban President and his advisors could be convinced that United States intervention was a distinct possibility.[15] President Roosevelt tried another method, however, and informed the Cuban Ambassador that if Machado would retire on the "face saving" grounds of the economic situation the United States would send a shipload of food supplies to Cuba.[16]

President Machado remained adamant in his refusal to retire, but the situation changed completely when the ranking army officers on the night of August 11, 1933 demanded that he leave his office immediately.[17] Ambassador Welles had been working on a new plan with the opposition, and the move by the army seems to have come as a surprise to him. In spite of this, however, Welles approved of the move, and was in conference with the army leaders during the early morning hours of August 12. At 4:00 A.M. they agreed to accept the Secretary of War, General Herrera, as President *ad interim* until a new administration could be formed. This was the plan which Welles had formulated earlier. The army leaders decided, however, that General Herrera was linked too closely with the Machado regime, and at 7:00 A.M. they notified Welles that someone else should take over as President *ad interim*. Welles immediately conferred with General Herrera, and an agreement was worked out whereby the General would appoint Dr. Carlos Manuel de Céspedes

Secretary of State and then turn the presidency over to him. The army leaders agreed to this, and the necessary legislation was rushed through the Cuban Congress.[18] With the rapid "legalization" process completed, Dr. Céspedes took the oath of office as President *ad interim* on August 13, 1933. The President and Secretary of State of the United States sent a congratulatory wire to the American Ambassador, and expressed, "their appreciation of what you have done."[19]

Welles continued to advise the Cuban Government on matters dealing with the growing unrest and acts of violence. Two ships of the United States Navy were dispatched to Havana for their "moral" effect,[20] and the Cuban Secretary of War requested Welles to advise the State Department that reinforcements should be kept on hand at Key West and at Guantánamo Bay.[21] Welles did feel that the Cuban situation was under control. He also believed that he was exercising too much open control over the Cuban Government (a point which some Cubans were making), and requested recall to Washington in order to head off criticism of the new government on these grounds. This would not mean the end of American influence, as Welles pointed out:

Caffery [Jefferson Caffery, who was designated as Welles's succesor] unquestionably will obtain all of the needed influence immediately after his arrival but it will be an influence exerted behind the scenes and not apparent to the public.[22]

Welles requested permission to begin final negotiations for the new commercial treaty, as well as authorization to discuss measures to relieve the desperate financial problems of the Cuban Government.[23] Now that the political situation had changed, Welles again wanted to stress measures of economic rehabilitation. Strikes and general labor unrest were increasing, and some American businessmen in Cuba informed the Ambassador that this situation was the result of "Communist agitators under the pay of Russia."[24] Welles did not believe that a "Red menace" existed, but he was concerned over the growing demands of Cuban labor.[25] One solution he favored—as did many of the

American interests—was the regulation of the unions by the Cuban Government, with the government acting as arbitrator in disputes between foreign interests and native labor. In the last analysis, however, Welles stressed improvement of economic conditions as the key to maintaining stability and eliminating labor agitation in Cuba.[26]

Before Sumner Welles could return to the United States, the cork popped off the Cuban bottle once more. Welles had been warned by a *New York Times* correspondent that a revolt was brewing in the Cuban Army, but had "laughed" it off as an unfounded rumor.[27] On the morning of September 5, 1933 the noncommissioned officers of the Cuban Army under the leadership of Sergeant Fulgencio Batista took control of the army. The leaders of the "Sergeant's Revolt," in conjunction with other revolutionary groups (the most important being the student-faculty group from the University of Havana), then ousted the Céspedes Administration and formed a new government. Ambassador Welles surveyed the wreck of his political "solution," and promptly branded the new regime as "ultra-radical" with "frankly communistic" theories.[28]

The phase of United States–Cuban relations which began with the revolt of September 5, 1933 was characterized by manifestations of extreme Cuban nationalism and by the suspicious, if not unfriendly, attitude of the United States Government. President Roosevelt, Secretary Hull, and Ambassador Welles had to walk the thin line between protection of American interests in Cuba and the development of a "Good Neighbor" reputation among the nations of Latin America. This was a tricky game to play, but by and large the United States Government managed to play it successfully, although there were some anxious moments during the four and one-half month period.

The days following the revolution were marked by confusion and violence. Labor disorders erupted across the island, and several sugar mills were seized by the workers. The government, headed by the new President Ramón Grau San Martín, issued highly nationalistic statements which were taken at face value by the much perturbed American business interests.[29] As a result

of these factors, the United States Government briefly unveiled
a portion of the "big stick," and preparations were begun in case
the view was not sufficient. At least twenty-nine naval vessels
were ordered to proceed to Cuba or to Key West during the
early days of the September crisis. Marine air squadrons were
alerted; guns and bomb racks were mounted on the planes; and
pilots at Quantico, Virginia were ordered to pack their belong-
ings and be ready to fly south "on a moments notice."[30] Regi-
ments of Marine infantry assembled at Quantico, Virginia and at
Port Everglades, Florida.[31]

Secretary Hull and Ambassador Welles discussed the possibility of armed intervention in some detail. At first Welles wanted
to bring troops ashore to guard the Embassy and the National
Hotel, but Hull vetoed the suggestion with the exception that
troops could be called if a situation developed where they were
"absolutely indispensable" for the protection of the Embassy.[32]
The Secretary did not completely reject the prospect of armed
intervention, but he told Welles that such action would not be
taken unless "we are absolutely compelled to do so"; the point of
compulsion was not clearly defined however.[33] Hull feared
that intervention would permanently saddle the United States
with the task of governing Cuba, and he realized that such a
development would seriously hinder any efforts to woo the
rest of Latin America. In fact, several Latin American governments informed the State Department that any armed intervention would "strain, if not break" the friendly relations between
the United States and Latin America. The prospect of failure
at the forthcoming Montevideo Conference was a definite factor
in Hull's consideration of the intervention problem.[34]

Ambassador Welles, however, did make a strong plea for
intervention on September 7. He stated that he believed that
the Céspedes Government had a good chance to regain power,
provided the United States sent troops to keep order until the
government could form a new army. In the Ambassador's words:

> If the legitimate and recognized Government of Cuba
> can make an effective demonstration of its intention to re-
> establish itself, it would most decidedly appear to me to be
> in the best interest of the United States Government to afford

them immediate support. Any solution of this character is more advantageous to our interests and to our policy than full intervention and the possible necessity of an American Military Government.[35]

Hull took this message to President Roosevelt and the two agreed that troops should not be sent.[36]

The decision to avoid armed intervention was part of the delicate process of protecting American interests in Cuba, both economic and strategic, and at the same time wooing Latin American friendship. Some American interests in Cuba requested armed protection due to labor violence, but the State Department acceded to these within the limitations of its indirect intervention policy. The Bethlehem Steel Company asked for protection for its iron mines at Daiquiri, but the request was turned down since the mines were inland and troops would have to be sent.[37] On the other hand, the request of the United Fruit Company for protection of its interests at Antilla was granted due to the fact that Antilla was on the coast and a destroyer could put in an appearance and calm the situation without landing troops.[38] The State Department also received statements from representatives of the American Chamber of Commerce of Cuba and the Standard Oil Company describing their troubles with Cuban labor, and strongly hinting that the United States Government should do something to stabilize the situation in Cuba.[39]

While the policy of no armed intervention by troops complicated the protection of American interests, the United States Government did formulate a general policy designed to stabilize Cuba without overly antagonizing other Latin American countries. This policy has been called "watchful waiting," but it involved more than passive waiting. Basically it could be reduced to two points: (1) nonrecognition of any government believed to be "radical"; (2) the active encouragement of groups or individuals which might be able to form a conservative, pro-United States government. In accord with the first point, the United States Government consistently refused to recognize the Grau San Martín Government, while Welles, and later Jefferson Caffery, encouraged various Cubans to form a government which would "protect life, property, and individual liberty."

Welles and Hull frankly recognized that the key element in Cuban politics was the army, and that the new Chief of Staff, Fulgencio Batista, would be a factor in any governmental shift.[40] Early in September Batista indicated that he was willing to talk terms with other political groups, and Welles began a campaign to persuade Batista to desert the Grau San Martín Government.[41] As one American observer stated: "Batista . . . is too ambitious to have radical leanings."[42]

In conjunction with the attempts to woo Batista, Welles encouraged the leaders of the conservative parties to form a new government. Cubans such as Carlos Mendieta, Martinez Saenz, Dr. Miguel Mariano Gómez, and Mario Menocal were some of the more influential men in this group which Welles called the "political leaders." The big problem was how to formulate a working agreement between Batista and these "political leaders." The Ambassador became convinced that any change in government should be accomplished by peaceful means, and after his initial flirtation with the idea of intervention worked to discourage a violent counterrevolution.[43] Several attempts to put together a new coalition government failed, and at one time Welles pessimistically reported that:

It is also within the bounds of possibility that the social revolution which is under way cannot be checked. American properties and interests are being gravely prejudiced and the material damage to such properties will in all probability be very great.[44]

In spite of several setbacks Welles continued to work for a solution which would salvage American interests without damaging "our continental interests."[45]

The first major attempt to alter the political situation came in mid-September. Grau San Martín met several times with Welles and the political leaders, and the Ambassador arranged for Adolph A. Berle, Jr. to explain the "financial and economic picture" to Grau San Martín. Berle told the Cuban President that American companies—public utilities, importers, and sugar mills—could not and would not do business under existing conditions.[46] Welles and the political leaders also conferred with Batista, and all were confident that "a direct understanding with him is possible."[47] Batista assured the Ambassador of his opposition to "all communist propaganda and activities."[48] By September 25, however, negotiations between the political leaders and the Grau San Martín Government had broken down, and the first attempt to replace this government failed.[49]

Welles continued to meet with Batista to try to persuade him to take a more vigorous stand against Grau San Martín. Colonel Batista was playing a cautious political game. Keeping a foot in both camps, he played for time in order to see which side had the best chance of winning out. Grau San Martín had informed Welles of his distrust of Batista, and the Ambassador sought to capitalize on this division in the ranks. Batista encouraged Welles's advances, and repeatedly told the Ambassador of his desire to see a stable Cuba. Delegates of all the important business and financial interests conferred with the Colonel, and their statements seemed to "deeply impress" him. After this meeting he told Welles that a government in which business groups had confidence was an absolute necessity.[50] In addition, Batista sent troops to American sugar plantations to restore order.[51] On the other side of the fence Batista was also hard at work maintaining his position of power. In the process Batista directed military operations which cleaned out the die-hard members of the old officer corps barricaded in the National Hotel, and defeated a counterrevolutionary attempt which broke out in November. Colonel Batista was playing power politics and was in no hurry to make a final deal.

In October a second attempt was made to peacefully replace the Grau San Martín Government. Batista and Mendieta began negotiations against a background of open disagreement between Batista and the Student Directorate.[52] Grau San Martín let it be known that he was willing to accept a compromise solution with the political leaders. He would be retained as President, but the cabinet would be completely changed and an administrative commission would be created to decide financial matters. Representatives of the "commercial and financial

interests" informed Welles that they would support this arrangement, although they objected to the retention of Grau San
Martín.[53] An Organic Statute embodying the compromise was
drafted, but the Student Directorate demanded several changes.
Batista then stated that the only solution was for Mendieta to
become President.[54] The delegates of the conservative political
parties agreed to this proposal, and drew up a program "guaran-
teeing the security of Batista and the Army in general."[55] Mendieta, however, could not decide whether he wanted to be
President or not, and negotiations continued with Batista insisting
that either Mendieta or Gómez take over the presidency.[56] Ambassador Welles was quite optimistic about the outcome, but
the delay caused by Mendieta's vacillation had an adverse effect
on this attempt to work out a political solution. A counterrevolution broke out early in November and all negotiations
ended.

In December, Welles once more tried to effect a compromise
settlement. Negotiations between Batista, the political leaders,
and Grau San Martín were begun, but this attempt also failed;
this time due to Grau San Martín's refusal to compromise.[57]

Prior to this third round of negotiations, President Grau San
Martín had requested the removal of Ambassador Welles.[58]
This request was beside the point, however, since Hull and
Roosevelt had already decided to bring Welles back to Washing-
ton. Thus, on December 13, 1933 Sumner Welles departed from
Cuba.

The United States Government consistently refused to recognize the Grau San Martín Government. Sumner Welles was the
chief protagonist of this policy, and Hull and Roosevelt generally accepted the advice of the Ambassador in regard to the
recognition issue. Welles drafted two statements concerning
recognition for the State Department; one in September and the
other in November. These were slightly modified, and then
released as the official recognition policy of the United States.
The only real modification was in the substitution of "law and
order" for "life, property, and individual liberty" in describing
what the Cuban Government had to maintain in order to be
recognized.[59] Welles, however, interpreted "law and order" as

"life, property, and individual liberty," and the order of the words in the latter phrase was indicative of the Ambassador's attitude.

The State Department also followed Welles's analysis of the Grau San Martín Government, and the Ambassador constantly argued that this government did not meet the recognition criteria.[60] In his reports to the State Department the Ambassador pictured Grau San Martín as "utterly impractical and visionary"; a "figurehead" who was "under the complete domination of the worst elements in his government."[61] As far as Welles was concerned the only groups of any importance outside of the army were the upper-class political and business elements, and stability meant returning these groups to power. Concerning American interests, he reported "Our own commercial and export interests in Cuba cannot be revived under this government."[62] In addition, Welles was convinced that many decrees of the Cuban Government were "confiscatory" in nature, and damaging to American investment interests.[63] Jefferson Caffery, who replaced Welles in Cuba, also believed that the "seemingly communistic tendencies" in the Grau San Martín "regime" threatened American interests. He was especially concerned about the Workman's Compensation Law and the decrees affecting electricity rates.[64]

The situation in Cuba reached a climax during January 1934. Several factors contributed to this development. The British Government informed the United States that British interests in Cuba were bringing pressure to bear for recognition of the Grau San Martín regime.[65] There was also evidence that the incumbent regime was trying to split the political opposition by offering political appointments to members of the "Mendieta group."[66] In addition, the economic plight of Cuba was becoming increasingly serious. In the light of these developments, Fulgencio Batista decided that the time was ripe for a change. He again contacted Mendieta, but the latter wanted advance assurance of American recognition. Caffery urgently advised that such be given, since he believed that failure to effect an immediate settlement would result in a swing to the "extreme left," both by Batista and by Grau San Martín.[67] President

Roosevelt would not grant this advance guarantee to Mendieta, and Batista—in conjunction with the "Revolutionary junta"—threw his support to Carlos Hevia.[68] Thus, the Grau San Martín regime was ousted on January 15, 1934 by the army, and Carlos Hevia was installed as Provisional President. The solution which Sumner Welles had pushed since the previous September had at last been consummated. Batista had cast his lot with the conservative, pro-American political groups, and his reward was twenty-five years of power. Within four days Caffery reported that the new government met all of the recognition requirements, and on January 23, 1934 the United States extended "formal and cordial recognition" to the Government of Cuba.[69]

The new administration did not usher in an era of peace and tranquility. A wave of strikes and student riots broke out in opposition to the Mendieta Government. The administration lived up to its advance notices and instituted a series of stringent measures to protect property. Batista ordered the army to break up the student demonstrations and to arrest many of the participants. President Mendieta signed several decrees which suspended constitutional guarantees, placed the army in control of the island, strictly regulated the right to strike, and dissolved labor unions for violating the strike regulations. The army utilized these decrees to break strikes, arrest labor leaders, and to protect sugar centrals.[70] Thus, the Mendieta Government found favor in the eyes of Americans. Ambassador Caffery reported that this government was "fighting for its life against the communistic element," and the National City Bank stated that Mendieta's devotion to Cuba, "will not take the mistaken form of antagonism to the legitimate business activities and interests of foreigners in the island." As far as American officials and businessmen were concerned the political situation had been favorably resolved, and the continuing violence was the fault of communists.[71]

On May 29, 1934 the United States and Cuba signed a new treaty which modified the Platt Amendment. This Amendment, as embodied in the Treaty of Relations of May, 1903, had become a dead letter by 1933 except for the section concerning the naval base at Guantánamo Bay. The section of the 1903 Treaty concerning the naval base was retained in the 1934 Treaty. Sumner Welles later stated that he and Roosevelt had agreed in 1933 that one of the objectives of his mission would be to prepare the way for the negotiations of a new treaty. Cosme de la Torriente, the Cuban Secretary of State in 1934, believed that the Platt Amendment actually contributed to turmoil in Cuba due to the fact that certain politicians tried to provoke intervention for their own ends.[72] Harry F. Guggenheim supported this contention, as did Sumner Welles who had come to the conclusion that this was a factor which helped delay a political settlement in 1933.[73] Two additional reasons for the Treaty of 1934 have been advanced. Both of these seem to have some validity in the light of New Deal foreign policy. One suggests that the United States utilized the modification of the Platt Amendment as a means of adding prestige to a Cuban Government which protected American interests. The other view maintains that this action was part of the over-all policy of the United States of increasing export markets in Latin America through the creating of the "Good Neighbor" image.[74] The treaty was an inexpensive gesture to Cuban nationalism, and the events of the preceding months had shown that American interests could be protected by more subtle tactics.

II

Sumner Welles succinctly described American policy toward Cuba with the statement:

Cuba had fallen into a vicious circle. There was no hope for economic improvement without business confidence, which could not be reestablished until and unless some solution of the political problem was arrived at. There was no possibility of a permanent solution of the political problem so long as the Cuban people were starving and the social unrest resulting therefrom threatened to break into the flames of anarchy.[75]

The political problem was resolved to the satisfaction of the United States Government in January, 1934, and the wheels were set in motion to work out the economic solutions required. Lower duties and market stabilization were commonly regarded as the basic ingredients needed to increase exports, revive the value of United States investments, stabilize Cuba, and aid the sugar refiners using Cuban raw sugar. At the same time a compromise would be offered to placate the domestic and insular sugar producers with some form of financial *quid pro quo*.

The State Department began its approach to the tariff problem with much enthusiastic support from various business groups. The plan for reciprocal trade agreements was warmly endorsed in April 1933 by the National Foreign Trade Convention and the American Manufacturer's Export Association.[76] The Committee on Reciprocal Trade Agreements of the Committee on Inter-American Relations—a group closely connected with the National Foreign Trade Council—sent inquiries concerning reciprocal trade agreements to manufacturers, shipping concerns, and banks interested in foreign trade. The replies indicated a "definite desire" for such agreements, particularly with Latin America. In addition, more than forty chambers of commerce and trade associations endorsed the program.[77] Businessmen and government officials also stressed the relationship between reciprocal trade agreements and the value of foreign investments.[78]

The plan for a new commercial agreement with Cuba drew support, and numerous suggestions, from business groups. H. H. Pike, Jr. told the National Foreign Trade Convention in 1933 that Roosevelt would "put new life in the reciprocity treaty [with Cuba]," and this view was endorsed by various business groups in letters to the State Department and to Congressmen.[79] Welles started negotiations for a new treaty with Cuba in June, 1933, but the political situation caused the State Department to postpone further talks until February, 1934. The Congress of the United States passed the Trade Agreements Act in June, 1934, after the President had already utilized the power grant in the Tariff Act of 1930 to reduce the duty on Cuban raw sugar to 1.5 cents per pound. The new Reciprocal Trade Agreement with Cuba was signed on August 24, 1934, and further reduced this duty to .9 cents per pound.

The new treaty gave Cuba certain tariff benefits for sugar, rum, tobacco, and vegetables. In return, Cuba made six general concessions to the United States: (1) Import duties on many American goods were lowered, usually by increasing the preferential reduction. Small electric light bulbs, for example, were given a 60 percent preferential reduction; the old rate had been 25 percent. Tires received a 40 percent preferential reduction, and inner tubes a reduction of 30 percent. Both had received 20 percent reductions under the old treaty.[80] (2) Cuba agreed not to increase the existing rates of duties on a large number of American products during the life of the treaty. (3) Existing Cuban customs nomenclature was to be clarified. (4) Cuba agreed to abolish or to reduce internal taxes on many American products. (5) No quantitative restriction would be placed on any article receiving the benefit of tariff reduction in the treaty. (6) No new restrictions would be placed on the transfer and means of payment for goods.[81]

A rather pronounced concern over Japanese competition was evidenced by Americans during the negotiations, and there developed some difference of opinion as to how this problem should be handled. The American technical advisors and some business groups suggested that Cuba be requested to raise tariff rates on certain goods—with greater preferential reductions for the same American products—and impose quotas on some Japanese goods.[82] Welles and Hull decided, however, that such a direct request would be inconsistent with the policy declarations made at Montevideo, and that the United States in the treaty should rely on increased preferential reductions.[83] An understanding with the Cubans on the matter of increased tariffs was reached, and on the same day the treaty was signed the Cuban Government enacted Decree-Law No. 440 which unilaterally increased duties on more than three hundred items. Thus, the American advantage over foreign competitors was greatly increased, especially in regard to competition with Japanese yarns, copper wire, electric bulbs, and cellophane.[84]

Roosevelt and his advisors began to develop plans for an American "closed sugar area" to stabilize the market in 1932. By this time voluntary stabilization on the part of the producers had proved to be a fiasco, and important segments of the sugar industry were calling for an end to "unrestrained and

unenlightened competition."[85] Plans for dividing the domestic
market and paying bounties to beet sugar producers had been
advanced during the tariff controversy in 1930, and these same
ideas became the basis for planning in 1933. The Roosevelt Administration submitted its production control bill as an amendment to the Agriculture Adjustment Act, and the House Committee on Agriculture began hearings on the Jones-Costigan
Act in February 1934.

President Roosevelt sent a message to the committee requesting favorable action on the act.[86] To his cabinet, however,
Roosevelt stated his objections to paying a subsidy to the beet
growers, and even discussed the possibility of wiping out the
beet-sugar industry over a period of twenty years. Both of these
would be difficult, he indicated, due to the "political questions
involved."[87] Thus, the President supported the Jones-Costigan
Act as part of a general compromise scheme designed to give
something to all segments of the sugar industry; the Reciprocal
Trade Agreement and the Export-Import Bank silver loan con-
stituting the rest of the program.

During the hearing the Jones-Costigan Act received support
from a number of sources. Representatives from W. R. Grace
and Company, the Hershey Company, the Baltimore Association
of Commerce, the Revere Sugar Refining Company, and the
Department of Agriculture testified in behalf of the act. Thomas
L. Chadbourne and the National Sugar Refining Company wrote
letters urging its passage. The Hershey representative also
wanted an allotment for 600,000 tons of Cuban refined sugar—
since they produced about 50 percent of the refined sugar in
Cuba—but the American refiners demanded even more limitation
of this type of imported sugar.[88] The Farm Bureau Federation
and various beet growers' associations attacked the bill, and
declared that it was a "Wall Street" plot to destroy the domestic
industry.[89]

The Jones-Costigan Act, with the Walsh Amendment limiting
the importation of refined sugar, became law in May 1934. The
act authorized the Secretary of Agriculture to determine annually
the sugar consumption requirements of the United States. Each

producing area would then be allowed to fill a stipulated percentage of this requirement. This quota was to be established on the basis of marketings during the three-year period 1931–1933. By selecting these years Congress tended to favor domestic beet producers more than Roosevelt had originally proposed. Cuba's quota was about 28 percent or 1,866,482 short tons for 1934. Had an earlier period been selected, Cuba's quota would have been much higher. The act also limited the imports of Cuban refined sugar to 22 percent of the total Cuban allotment; this amounted to 423,000 tons in 1934. In addition, a processing tax was levied on all sugar consumed, and the receipts were used to pay subsidies to domestic producers of sugar cane and sugar beets at the rate of sixty cents per one hundred pounds of raw sugar.[90]

Thus, the Reciprocal Trade Agreement and the Jones-Costigan Act embodied the New Deal approach to reconciling the international economic interests of the country with its domestic economic interests. Earl Babst of the American Sugar Refining Company described it as, "a step in the direction of a sound Colonial Policy."[91] This approach grew out of the conflict between the various sugar interests which had become particularly acute after 1919. With these programs the sugar industry entered the era of managed capitalism characterized by regulation of competition. The United States Government assumed the role of "broker" in mediating between the various segments of the sugar industry. This was not imposed on the industry by "wild-eyed" planners, but developed in response to industry demands. The voluntary program of regulated competition, promoted by Herbert Hoover and the Trade Association movement of the 1920's, had proved unworkable when the depression placed too much pressure on the private regulation of self-interest. The sugar plan represented this tradition with the addition of the national government as administrator and supervisor of the market.[92]

The third economic element in the New Deal approach to the problem of Cuba was the Second Export-Import Bank. This agency attempted to solve two related problems: the financial

crisis of the Cuban Government, and the need for some means
of providing loans and long-term credits to other countries and
to American exporters in order to stimulate foreign trade.

Businessmen had stressed the link between foreign loans and
exports for several years, and the depression emphasized this
relationship.[93] As the flow of private capital contracted, many
bankers and exporters began to call for the national government
to devise measures to finance exports. In 1928 Franklin D.
Roosevelt organized a committee to correlate foreign loans and
foreign commerce, and this committee organized the Federal
International Corporation to do its research work.[94] The National
Foreign Trade Council, the Committee on Inter-American Relations, the American Manufacturer's Export Association, and
the American Banker's Association were also actively working
on export finance plans in conjunction with government officials.
After the creation of the Reconstruction Finance Corporation in
1932 most of the proposals concerning export financing involved
this institution.[95] The National Foreign Trade Council and the
Committee on Inter-American Relations actively campaigned
for an RFC program of export financing, and received the aid
of Commerce Department officials in this endeavor.[96] In fact
the NFTC later claimed much of the credit for the creation of the
Export-Import Bank, and continued to work closely with it.[97]
John Abbink, the chairman of the Council's committee on devising
export financing plans, enthusiastically told of the government's
initial bank announcement:

> An electrifying statement followed [the announcement of
> willingness to form a bank to finance exports], whose chief
> points appeared so completely to solve the exporter's prob-
> lems that it seemed incredible. Not only would the Govern-
> ment help, but it would do all that foreign traders asked,
> and more.[98]

While pressure was building up for governmental financing
of exports, administration officials were also beginning to advocate the need for some kind of American financial aid for the
Government of Cuba. A long range funding agreement was
worked out with the Chase Bank in June, 1933, but the Cuban

Government continued to totter on the verge of bankruptcy.[99] Welles recommended in August that the United States Government make a loan to Cuba, and suggested the RFC as a possible source.[100] This same view was embodied in the report on Cuban Financing made by Adolph A. Berle, Jr., John G. Laylin, J. H. Edwards, and A. F. Nufer. This commission recommended a loan of four million dollars to be used for the purchase of silver.[101] The use of the RFC became a persistent note in policy memorandums, but officials in the Treasury Department were cool to the idea.[102]

The pressure from these two convergent sources had its effect. On March 9, 1934 the Second Export-Import Bank was created by an executive order for the purpose of loaning money to Cuba. The capital of the bank was $2,750,000, of which $250,000 was common stock held by the Secretaries of State and Commerce, and $2,500,000 was preferred stock held by the RFC. The bank lost no time in extending financial aid to Cuba. Two loans were made in 1934: the first in March for approximately $3,774,724, and the second in December for approximately $4,359,095.[103] With these funds the Cuban Government purchased a surplus "commodity"—silver. Thus, the Roosevelt Administration utilized the Export-Import Bank to help stabilize Cuba, to improve trade, and to subsidize a very vocal minority within the party. The silverites, led by Senator Key Pittman, were demanding aid for this Western industry, and some individuals suggested that the silver purchasing scheme was also designed to allay the opposition of the beet-producing Western States to the Jones-Costigan Bill.[104]

The Reciprocity Treaty, the Jones-Costigan Act, and Export-Import Bank's silver loans were designed to meet the needs of a complex mixture of economic interests, and to solve the problem of Cuban stability. This grand compromise did not completely satisfy all the various interests involved, but some were rather enthusiastic about it. The National Foreign Trade Convention officially "commended" the Latin American policy of the Roosevelt Administration, and the President of the Guaranty Trust Company, speaking for the National Foreign Trade Council, commended Secretary Hull in these terms:

We would like him to have realized that, businessmen as we are, makes us completely sympathetic with the broad and statesmanlike view which he has always given in Congress and out . . . to the problems of this nation. We do think that there is no man in public life who merits so much today the confidence and the esteem of the political factors, the cultural factors and business factors of this country, as does the President's highly distinguished Secretary of State (applause).[105]

American business interests were generally satisfied with the New Deal's political and economic solutions of the Cuban problem, and these solutions would provide the substance of Cuban-American relations from 1934 to 1959.

CHAPTER ELEVEN

From Batista to Castro: The Twenty-Five-Year Honeymoon

I

For twenty-five years American relations with Cuba followed the pattern established in 1934. A few modifications were made in some of the economic arrangements, but the basic programs remained the same. The period from 1934 to 1959 was relatively free of problems in the area of United States–Cuban relations. An occasional disturbance might arise, as when several sailors desecrated the Martí Monument in Havana, but such did little to disturb the existing pattern of relations. Beneath the surface, however, there were unsolved problems in the economic, political, and social life of Cuba which were either given superficial attention or were ignored entirely. These had helped to produce the eruption in 1933, and would come to the surface again in 1959. During the intervening period the United States Government and American businessmen expressed satisfaction over the situation in Cuba. As a 1956 publication of the Commerce Department stated:

> This intimate economic relationship is so much the outgrowth of mutually helpful association that many of the problems that have plagued less close relationships in other areas have largely been avoided in Cuba.[1]

American exports to Cuba increased steadily after 1934. By 1937 the State Department could report:

> The rate of recovery in the trade between the United States and Cuba during the agreement [Reciprocal Trade

Agreement of 1934] has been in operation has been much
more pronounced than the increase in the commerce of
either country with the world generally.[2]

The total value of these exports increased from $22.7 million in
1933, to an average of $147.1 million for the period 1941–1945.
This trade continued to increase after 1945, reaching a peak in
1951 of $539.8 million. A general decline set in between 1951 and
1956, but then the amount increased to $617.9 million in 1957.
Another decline began in 1958.[3] The United States supplied 54.0
percent of all Cuban imports in 1933. This percentage increased
to 64.4 percent in 1936, and to 80.7 percent for the period
1946–1950. In 1955 the figure was 73.4 percent.[4]

American imports from Cuba followed the same general
pattern in terms of rising and declining value. Cuba, however,
has been slightly lessening its dependence on the United States
market since 1945. This trend reached something of a peak in
1951 when Cuba sold 54.6 percent of its exports to the United
States. Since then the United States has purchased a greater
share of Cuban exports, and the figure was up to 68.9 percent
in 1955.[5]

American direct investments in Cuba declined between 1929
and 1946; from $919 million to $553 million. This decline in
value, "resulted primarily from revaluation of assets and reorganization of overexpanded corporate activities."[6] Much of the
total loss came in sugar properties which had been overcapitalized in the period 1921–1929. The reorganization process in the
sugar industry reduced the amount of preferred stock from $55
million to about $25 million, and the amount of bonds and other
issues from $125 million to $55 million.[7] After 1946 a slow increase in sugar investments began, and by 1956 investment in
this area totaled $285 million. The Cuban share of the quantity
of sugar produced rose from 22.4 percent in 1939 to 58.7 percent
in 1955. By the latter date American interests produced about
40 percent of the raw sugar of the country.[8]

The value of direct investments in manufacturing and other
enterprises also declined after 1929. The upturn in manufacturing investments began prior to 1946, and had increased to

$65 million by 1956.[9] Investments in the petroleum industry declined between 1929 and 1936—from $9 million to $6 million—but these increased after the latter date to $51 million by 1956.[10]

Public utilities investments, however, increased in value between 1929 and 1940, and by 1956 these represented the largest American stake in Cuba—$316 million. This constituted control over 90 percent of the public utilities in Cuba.[11] American capital also controlled about 50 percent of the public service railways, and American branch banks held almost 25 percent of all bank deposits.[12]

By 1957 American direct investments totaled $850 million, and portfolio investments amounted to $210.9 million. These are the only foreign investments of any importance. British holdings have been practically eliminated since 1945, and Canadian investments are placed at $9.4 million. There are still some Spanish holdings—often families of mixed Cuban-Spanish nationality—but most of these date from the colonial period. Cuba ranked third in Latin America in the value of United States direct investments in 1956, in spite of the fact that the rate of increase in investments since 1946 has been the lowest of any of the major Latin American countries. This was due to several factors. One of the most important was the fact that since 1946 about one-third of United States investments have gone into oil holdings, and Cuba has not received much of this capital.[13]

Since 1934 the Reciprocal Trade Agreement and the sugar marketing plan have been modified, but the basic ideas have been developed in more detail. During this period the tariff on raw sugar imports from Cuba has been steadily lowered—except for the period from September 12 to December 27, 1939. On September 12 President Roosevelt suspended the quotas on sugar, and the tariff on Cuban raw sugar automatically increased to 1.5 cents per pound. A supplementary trade agreement was negotiated in December 1939, and when Roosevelt reimposed quotas on December 27 the tariff reverted to .9 cents per pound.[14] The supplemental trade agreement negotiated in 1941 further reduced the duty on Cuban raw sugar to .75 cents per pound. Both of these agreements gave additional tariff advantages to the exports of the United States.[15]

In 1948 the General Agreement on Tariffs and Trade (GATT) was negotiated by twenty-three nations at Geneva, Switzerland. Cuba displayed great reluctance in giving its assent to this plan, since the United States had agreed during the discussions to a policy which would generally reduce and possibly even eliminate the Cuban preferential system. Cuba joined GATT, and signed an exclusive agreement with the United States supplementing the General Agreement. As a result, the duty on Cuban raw sugar was lowered to .5 cents per pound, and significant reductions were made on other items. In return Cuba lowered the duty on 128 items imported from the United States, and bound the duty on 330 others. At the 1950 GATT meeting in Torquay, England, Cuba obtained substantial modifications on tariff concessions previously enjoyed by the United States, and increases on a variety of Cuban products. Compensating concessions on other United States exports were granted by Cuba. These provisions were embodied in the Torquay Trade Agreement of 1951.[16]

The system of sugar controls ran into trouble in 1936 when the United States Supreme Court handed down a decision in the Hoosac Mills case. Congress, however, promptly passed the Soil Conservation Act—which continued payments to farmers—and a joint resolution which continued the quota system. The Sugar Act of 1937 embodied many provisions of the Jones-Costigan Act but with changes in tactics to meet the objections of the Supreme Court. An excise tax was substituted for the processing tax, and "conditional payments" were made to domestic sugar growers at the rate of 60 cents per 100 pounds of raw sugar produced. In addition, a fixed quota system was created which allotted Cuba 28.6 percent of the total consumption requirements of the United States. All quotas were suspended between April 1942, and December 1947.[17]

The Sugar Act of 1948 changed the method of quota allocation. Domestic beet and sugar cane producers, and the insular producers—Hawaii, Puerto Rico, and the Virgin Islands—received fixed annual quotas rather than percentage quotas. The quota for the Philippines had been given a definite tonnage figure by the Philippine Trade Act of 1946. Cuba, and other producing areas, received percentage quotas to be applied to the remainder of the annual consumption requirement after deduction of the fixed quotas. Cuba was then allowed to supply 98.64 percent of the remainder, and this could not fall below 28.6 percent of the total consumption requirement. The rate for conditional payments was fixed at 80 cents per hundred pounds of raw sugar. In addition, domestic producers could receive subsidy payments because of the abandonment of planted acreage or because of a crop deficiency.[18] This was the basic system which was renewed by Congress in 1952 and in 1956. The sugar marketing act came up for Congressional consideration again in 1960, and President Dwight Eisenhower requested several changes. The President asked for power to cut the quota of any foreign producer—except the Philippines—and for changes in the quota allotment. Under this executive proposal the domestic producers would receive an additional allotment of 200,000 tons. The domestic producers, however, would lose the right to supply the deficit in the Puerto Rican quota—currently about 200,000 tons per year. This deficit would be alloted to Cuba and other nations, with Cuba receiving the right to supply 96 percent of this deficit. This would contribute to the future instability of the Cuban sugar producers, since Cuba's ability to make up for the reduced quota would be tied to Puerto Rican production. Initially, however, Cuba would continue to supply about the same amount of sugar to the United States as in the past.[19]

The sugar industry continues to be one of the most tightly controlled in the country. The American consumers in effect pay the excise tax—about five cents on a ten-pound bag—as well as the tariff. An industry publication has estimated that twenty-eight cents out of every consumer dollar spent for sugar goes to the government for subsidy payments.[20] Sugar beet and sugar cane acreage in the United States is rigidly controlled, and it is practically impossible for new farmers to break into this "producer's circle."[21] This was the system which Under Secretary of Agriculture True D. Morse defended before the Senate Committee on Finance in 1956. The Senators chuckled over what the housewife had to unknowingly pay to keep it running.[22]

The Export-Import Bank made three additional silver loans

to Cuba—the last being made in July 1938—and all were listed as repaid by 1940. In 1941 the Export-Import Bank granted a loan of $25 million for purposes of agricultural diversification, and another loan of $11 million to grind additional sugar.[23] Since then the Bank has extended credits to various business groups for purposes of trade or plant expansion. In the three-year period 1955–1957 the Bank authorized nine new credits totaling $19.7 million. Much of this went to American companies.[24]

From 1934 to 1959 Colonel Fulgencio Batista was—with apologies to Graham Greene—"Our man in Havana." For six years he exercised his power as Chief of Staff of the Army. He served as President from 1940 to 1944, and under his leadership Cuba was one of the first Latin American nations to declare war on the Axis powers. In 1944 the Colonel retired to Miami, Florida, a wealthy man, and Ramón Grau San Martín served as President until 1948.[25] Dr. Carlos Prío Socarrás then became Chief Executive until Batista staged another "barracks-revolt" on March 10, 1952.[26] This established the dictatorship which was finally overthrown by Fidel Castro on January 1, 1959. During the eight-year interlude between 1944 and 1952 Batista still retained much influence in Cuba. His supporters retained control of Congress in 1944, and he was elected Senator—in absentia—in 1948.[27] Although Grau San Martín had tried to remove Batista's henchmen from the top military positions, the army did not forget the man who had raised the soldier's pay and built the modern brick barracks. This loyalty was demonstrated in March 1952.

Batista was the symbol of stability to many Americans. In spite of some nationalistic utterances and labor reforms he could be counted on to defend American interests. The United States Government helped Batista build his military forces by supplying arms and advisors.[28] One American Ambassador, Arthur Gardner, was so enthusiastic in his support that it even embarrassed Batista.[29] American businessmen also supported Batista. Mrs. R. Hart Phillips, the *New York Times* correspondent, reported that this group criticized her for sending reports on the Castro rebellion since they wanted Batista to crush the rebels.[30] As late as November 1958, Senator Allen J. Ellender of Louisiana told reporters in Havana that he was in favor of selling arms to Batista.[31] The United States Government fully realized that military aid to Batista was essentially for the purpose of keeping order—"internal stability" as it was called.[32] As under Machado, stability covered a multitude of sins.

The experience of the 1920's and the handling of the crisis of 1933 proved to the State Department that American interests in Cuba could be protected by a combination of factors. Support for a strong political figure who had military power, coupled with economic pressure were the ingredients of the new "big stick" in a velvet glove policy. Commenting on Roosevelt's boast that the administration had not had to use troops to settle controversies, Harold L. Ickes noted in 1936:

> I do not like the situation in Cuba. I think that this Government is interfering altogether too much in the internal affairs of Cuba, but it is being done through diplomatic channels.[33]

This was vividly illustrated in 1938 and 1939 when the State Department put pressure on Cuba to begin payments on the defaulted public works bonds. This unresolved problem grew out of the vast bond issues floated by the Machado regime, and the financial plight of the Cuban Government during the 1930's.[34] In 1933 and 1934 Cuba defaulted on these issues, and a Public Works Obligation Commission in 1934 ruled that most of the bonds had been illegally issued. The violation of the Platt Amendment was cited as one reason for the illegality.[35] The State Department protested this ruling informally, but did not press the issue at the time.[36] The financial position of the Cuban Government was extremely precarious, and the State Department did not pressure for a settlement until the Cuban economy was in better condition. The Supreme Court of Cuba later reversed the decision of the commission.

A committee of bondholders was formed in 1933 to work for a settlement. The members of this committee were Senator Gerald P. Nye, chairman, A. F. Coyle, T. H. Healy, J. Fred Rippy, Max Winkler, and Burton K. Wheeler. In December 1937 a new plan for resumption of payments on most of the defaulted bonds was negotiated, and this was approved by the Cuban Congress in February 1938.[37] The bonds held by Warren Brothers Company and Purdy and Henderson were not included in this settlement. The State Department then began to pressure the Cuban Government for a settlement of these remaining claims. The Cuban Government was particularly anxious to revise the 1934 Trade Agreement, but the State Department refused to take any action until the claims were settled. Sumner Welles stated the situation to the Cuban Ambassador in October 1938:

> I told him I felt his Government should know that if this Government were to continue the policy of intimate and close cooperation with the Cuban Government . . . it must have concrete evidence from the Cuban Government that it was prepared to cooperate in the same effective and practical manner which the Government of the United States had pursued.

The "practical evidence" which Welles requested the Cuban Government to provide was a settlement with the American creditors, as well as the modification of several internal economic measures then being considered by the Cuban Congress.[38]

The United States Ambassador to Cuba, J. Butler Wright, and the Chargé in Cuba, Williard Beaulac, worked with Colonel Batista to try to arrange the desired settlement. The cooperation of the Chief of Staff of the Army was considered to be of primary importance in any negotiations.[39] The Colonel attended many of the conferences held by the United States Ambassador and the President of Cuba, and on occasion issues were discussed with him prior to these meetings. The Cuban Ambassador to the United States also worked to promote a settlement, and Batista promised him that he would be rewarded by being retained as ambassador.[40] Batista had some difficulty with the Cuban Congress due to the unpopularity and the expense of the proposed "Obligaciones" settlement. In addition, the Colonel was not above playing for time in order to obtain a cheaper resolution of the issue.

The "Obligaciones" bill was introduced in the Cuban Congress late in 1938. It was debated and shelved—a process which was repeated several times in 1939. The State Department continued its policy of cajoling, then threatening. The Department discussed the settlement problem with Colonel Batista during his official visit to the Armistice Day ceremonies in November 1938. A "Ten Point" plan, involving various concessions to Cuba, was worked out, but in April 1939 the Cuban Government was warned that these concessions hinged on the settlement of the Public Works indebtedness.[41] The Cuban Government also wanted another loan from the Export-Import Bank, but this was refused on the same grounds.[42]

On July 20, 1939 the State Department issued an economic ultimatum to Cuba. This note stated that negotiations on the supplemental trade agreement would be "indefinitely suspended" unless the Cuban Government provided satisfactory settlements for several problems. The settlement of the public works bonds was listed first. The credit moratorium and the Revaluation Bill were the other outstanding problems. The latter required exporters in Cuba to exchange a certain percentage of the dollars earned for pesos at par, and the State Department wanted assurances that this would not constitute exchange relations.[43]

At the request of the Cuban Government the State Department postponed the public announcement of the suspension of negotiations. By late August the American Ambassador believed that the Cubans were "thoroughly frightened," and ready to settle the claims of the American creditors. The internal economic legislation had been generally modified—with the exception of the credit moratorium—and additional changes were promised by President Federico Laredo Bru.[44]

On September 11, 1939 President Roosevelt announced that on the following day all sugar quotas would be suspended. According to the Reciprocal Trade Agreement of 1934, this meant that the duty on Cuban raw sugar would automatically increase to 1.5 cents per pound. The Cuban Government saw this as a move to force payment of the bonds, although there is no evidence that Roosevelt had this in mind.[45] Ambassador Wright, however, was not averse to using the opportunity at hand, and he stated that the Cubans were "in a negotiating mood."[46]

The Cuban Senate continued to postpone action on the "Obligaciones" Bill, but the State Department slightly modified its former position and renewed negotiations on the supplementary tariff. The economic plight of Cuba and the advent of World War II in Europe were the factors behind this shift. The State Department had no intention of giving any of the concessions which had been discussed earlier in the year, but the Department did see the need to restore the tariff to the 1934 treaty rate when quotas were reimposed. Without a supplementary agreement the rate would remain at 1.5 cents, and Ambassador Wright feared that "economic disaster" would be the result if the tariff were not restored to its former rate.[47]

The war in Europe also presented difficulties. As Wright noted in August:

> In case of a European war ... Cuba would obtain a higher and practically limitless market for her sugar which might change certain aspects of the situation entirely .... a friendly Cuba—perhaps achieved by reasonable elasticity in this matter, might be of greater value to us than an antipathetic Cuba—possibly brought about by insistence upon the letter of the agreement [July 20, 1939 note].[48]

The possibilty existed that Cuba might try to take advantage of the war to raise sugar prices and find new markets, and the Cuban Secretary of State did hint at the former. He also threatened to reduce the tariff benefits enjoyed by the United States.[49] In addition, the German Government had been discussing a barter agreement with the Cubans. The specter of German competition, coupled with the possibility of greater Cuban economic independence, undoubtedly helped to soften the State Department's approach.[50]

The supplementary trade agreement signed in December 1939 was a stopgap measure designed to restore the tariff to .9 cents per pound when quotas were reimposed. This was effected on December 27, 1939. The United States obtained several new concessions, but Cuba's desire for an even lower tariff on sugar was not realized.

On September 16, 1940 the Cuban Congress finally passed the bill to settle the outstanding public works bonds by the floating of a new issue and the use of the remainder of the 1937 issue.[51] The new Constitution of 1940 also lifted the credit moratorium. During the next two years the United States granted the concessions promised in 1939. The Export-Import Bank credit of $25 million in 1941, and the supplementary trade agreement signed in January 1942—reducing the sugar tariff to .75 cents per pound —completed this episode.

In spite of the generally improved condition of the national economy, many of the basic problems of Cuba remained unsolved. Urban labor retained many of the reforms enacted in 1933, and the Constitution of 1940 embodied these—and subsequent—measures. Between 1952 and 1959, however, the Cuban Government modified some of these to meet business objections.[52] The problem of illiteracy continued to plague Cuba, especially in the rural areas. No gain in literacy was made between 1931 and 1943. The 1953 census revealed a higher illiteracy rate among the 10- to 14-year age group than among the population as a whole. This indicates a possible increase in illiteracy.[53]

The entire Cuban economy remained under the domination of "king sugar" and the United States market. In 1951 sugar accounted for 88.1 percent of all Cuban exports. This declined to 79.8 percent in 1955.[54] In 1959 and 1960 Cuba exported about one-half of its sugar to the United States.[55] About 40 percent of the profits from sugar exports went to American-owned companies, and this further complicated the economic problems of Cuba.

The most glaring problem of all was, and is, the extreme poverty of the masses. This has been especially true in the rural areas where the pattern of landholding has changed little since the early days of the Spanish Empire. In 1945, 7.9 percent of the "farms" occupied 71.1 percent of the land, while on the other end of the scale 69.6 percent of the farms occupied only 11.2 percent of the total farm land.[56] There are more than 200,000 families with no land at all. These agricultural laborers rarely work more than three months out of a year.[57] "The land is very rich, but the people are very poor," is an accurate summary of the situation in Cuba.

Thus, Cubans have lived in a country where most of the re-

sources are controlled by a small minority, and part of this
latter group are citizens of the United States. The power of the
United States is an ever present element in Cuba. The naval
base at Guantánamo Bay, and the frequent visits of naval vessels
to Cuban ports give concrete evidence of this power. These
factors have produced anti-United States feelings in Cuba, and
many Cubans feel that their island is an "economic satellite"
of the United States.[58]

All of these factors worked together to produce the victory
of the "26th of July" Revolutionary movement. The roots of this
movement go back to 1953 when a young lawyer, Dr. Fidel Castro, led an abortive revolution. Castro was sentenced to prison
after a spectacular trial highlighted by his denunciation of the
Batista regime, and by the elaboration of his proposed reforms.
Released from prison in 1955, Castro put together an army which
finally drove Batista from power on January 1, 1959.

The United States promptly recognized the new government,
and prepared to do business with it. As the year progressed,
however, it became increasingly apparent that this had not been
a typical political revolution of the standard Caribbean variety.
Instead, Castro's Government was proclaiming a social revolution.
During 1959 the Cuban Government completed ten hospitals,
constructed several hundred miles of highways, built several
thousand low-cost dwellings, and erected numerous schools. The
infamous Camp Columbia and other military barracks were also
converted into schools. A striking degree of honesty has prevailed in the new administration. This stands in vivid contrast
to past situations where the older parties have traditionally
elbowed their way to the "public trough." In addition, gambling
has been rigidly controlled, and the large cities of Cuba have
been subjected to something of a clean-up campaign. A CBS
reporter stated in February 1960 that Havana was a much safer
city for tourists than it had been two years earlier.[59]

The most controversial aspect of the new administration,
however, was its policies of business and agrarian reforms.
Castro had generally tempered these themes during the dark
days in 1957 and 1958, but once in power he began to formulate
plans to meet the chronic problems of the Cuban masses. At

first the American businessmen and the "rich, powerful and normally cynical Cubans"—as *Fortune* magazine described them —believed that Castro was bluffing. As *Fortune* stated:

> Some prominent citizens thought that the new hero was merely making appropriate noble noises, and that when the excitement subsided, he would give them the cordial and cooperative government they liked.[60]

By June 1959, however, it was evident that Fidel Castro intended to make Cuba less dependent on the United States, and that a sweeping program of land reform was on the way.

In the first reform wave the Cuban Government moved to eliminate various abuses. Thousands of government positions were eliminated, home and apartment rentals were lowered 30 to 50 percent, mortgage rates were reduced, and urban property owners were compelled to build on their vacant lots or put them up for sale. Tax laws were revised to simplify an elaborate system riddled with loopholes.[61] Prior to this companies could avoid the excess profits tax by declaring an artificial capitalization "at least 10 times greater than the anticipated profits." Such a procedure eliminated the excess profits, and was recommended by the United States Department of Commerce.[62]

The Cuban Government installed "interventors" to oversee the affairs of several American-owned companies—including the Cuban Telephone Company, the Compañía Cubana de Electricidad, and the Otis Elevator Company. Utility rates were lowered, and wages were increased in most cases. Controls have been imposed on the movement of currency and on imports. As a result Cuban imports have dropped almost 30 percent.[63]

In June 1959 the Agrarian Reform Law was promulgated, but prior to this the distribution of idle government land had already begun. The Reform Law invoked the long neglected section of the Constitution of 1940 which forbade the holding of more than a thousand acres in a single property. The 1959 law, however, provided exceptions for land used in rice and cattle production. These holdings could be 3,316 acres.[64] The Cuban Government then began expropriation proceedings and the holdings of Castro's family were among the first to be taken.[65]

Part of the 33,500 acre King ranch has been expropriated and 30,000 acres of the United Fruit Company's pasture land has been "intervened." In April 1960 the Agrarian Reform Institute (I.N.R.A.) started formal expropriation proceedings against nearly all of the 272,000 acres owned by United Fruit Company. This did not include the company's sugar mills and the lands they occupy. Under the law the company will be allowed to retain about 1,700 additional acres. The 1.9 million acres owned by other American sugar companies has also been earmarked for expropriation after the 1960 harvest.[66]

By early March 1960 the State Department estimated that $5 to $6 million in American-owned property had been expropriated. Under the Reform Law expropriations are to be paid for with twenty-year government bonds bearing 4½ percent interest. The payments will be based on the assessed valuation of the property for tax purposes. This adds an ironic note to the expropriation proceedings, since American real property has been assessed at only a fraction of its value. Castro requested the American owners to reassess their property for taxes, but they gave the same low figures.[67] As a result it is difficult for these owners to publicly protest too much, since this would be an admission of past tax evasion.[68]

The I.N.R.A. has distributed some land to landless peasants, but much of the expropriated holdings will be farmed as co-operatives. Some of these cooperative farms have already been formed, and these are experimenting with programs of diversified agriculture. For the time being, however, sugar will remain the basic cash crop, and the cooperative approach is based on the fact that sugar is a crop most profitably produced on an extensive basis. Rice and cattle production fit into the same category. These cooperative farms, however, are designed to have functions other than production alone. They are supposed to provide low-cost housing and meals, schools for children and adults, playgrounds, and cultural facilities. In addition, I.N.R.A. is setting up other types of cooperative enterprises such as petroleum refining, sale of consumer goods, and auxiliary services—to provide farm machinery, credit, and technical assistance.[69]

For the first time in Cuban history something is being done

for the common people. It is possible to argue that Castro has gone too far, too fast. But to a people who have lived in poverty while the few have enjoyed the riches of the land, gradualism has little meaning. Americans must realize that the economic situation in Cuba is quite different from that in the United States. Land reform has been postponed much too long, and now that the "worm has turned" the repressed resentment produced by centuries of exploitation has erupted into a sweeping reform program.

Relations between the United States and Cuba have deteriorated a great deal since the early days of 1959. The reasons for this deterioration are varied, and groups in Cuba and the United States must share the blame.

The American press, with certain exceptions, has contributed its share through its propensity to find fault and pass judgment on the basis of hasty observations. One of the best examples of this attitude was the reporting of the trials of the Batista supporters. These were generally characterized as "barbaric orgies," but the press overlooked the fact that Castro's army had actually prevented the riots, looting, and street slaughters which have characterized many revolutions—including the Cuban outbreaks in 1933.[70] Instead, trials were held, and then only some of the former officials were executed. These trials may not have conformed to ideal American standards, but a CBS reporter stated that the evidence submitted would have convicted the accused in any respectable American court.[71] The Cuban people demanded retribution for the crimes committed—crimes which the American press generally ignored. As a Cuban Catholic priest explained:

> To the people who had had their fingernails ripped off, their eyes gouged out . . . who had seen their sons and fathers and husbands tortured and beaten until they died, this was merely just retribution for the crimes the Batistianos had committed.[72]

These trials undoubtedly prevented widespread, indiscriminate vengeance, and American failure to understand this fact antagonized the Cubans.[73]

American businessmen have generally opposed much of the
Cuban reform program, and have conveyed their feelings to the
United States Government. One official of the United Fruit
Company stated:

> The U. S. Government should work more closely with the
> U. S. companies doing business in Cuba and should be more
> concerned about what is happening to them.[74]

Businessmen, however, have been divided over what action
should be taken. A State Department official was reported to
have estimated that 75 percent of the business "leaders" who
contacted the Department concerning Cuban problems want
some form of "get tough" policy. Most have advocated cutting
the Cuban sugar quota or freezing Cuban assets in the United
States. About 15 percent, according to this official, urge the
government to give aid and moral support to Castro. Caution,
and the need to reach a *modus vivendi* with Cuba, have been
stressed by many of those contacting the State Department.[75]

The Government of the United States followed a rather cautious, indeterminate policy toward Cuba until July 1960. Officials generally opposed the agrarian reforms, but the government did little except protest until the President cut the Cuban
sugar quota.[76] This policy of hesitation was due, in part, to
conflicting views of the situation and the general feeling that
caution was necessary. This latter feeling was expressed by
various groups whose interests were at stake, or which sought
to preserve the Cuban market for American exports. The fear
of antagonizing other Latin American countries has also been
an important factor. The opposition of American sugar producers to any policy which would upset the sugar marketing
system was another element which influenced policy. Eisenhower's request for power to cut foreign quotas drew fire from
these domestic producers. An Idaho beet farmer wrote to the
Wall Street Journal:

> For well over a quarter of a century the Sugar Act has
> been widely considered one of the best . . . pieces of farm
> legislation ever devised in this country. . . . It just does not

make sense now, because we are frustrated over what to do about Fidel Castro, to start tearing down something it has taken us years to build up.[77]

The acceleration of the Cuban expropriation program and the increasingly friendly relations between Cuba and the Communist bloc provided the pressure which enabled President Eisenhower to obtain the power to slash the Cuban sugar quota. In addition, pressure from certain farm interests may have helped to override Congressional opposition to the Eisenhower sugar bill. Farm groups in New Mexico, Texas, and other states saw the potential Cuban reduction as an opportunity to break into the rigid sugar system and obtain a share of the beet sugar market. This pressure on Democratic Congressmen may have helped to override Representative Harold Cooley's opposition to the President's request for quota-cutting authority.[78]

The policy of the United States, before and after the revolution, played into the hands of Cuban extremists. Support for Batista and the role of American capital in the Cuban economy— with its political implications—provided an initial residue of suspicion. The failure of the United States Government to give at least a measure of positive support to the Castro Government, at a time when moderate elements were still in control, gave the extremists another argument to cite as proof of American hostility to the revolution. The unfavorable reaction of the United States Government to the agrarian and business reforms—as in the demand for immediate cash compensation for property taken —provided additional fuel for the fires of anti-United States sentiment. Thus, the extremists in the movement skillfully utilized the actions—and lack of actions—of the United States to undermine the moderates and convince Fidel Castro of the need to draw closer to the Communist bloc in order to save the revolution.[79]

The Communists have had a foothold in Cuba for years, and Batista had working agreements with them at various times in his career.[80] Fidel Castro came to power without their support, however, since the Communist union leaders refused to support his call for a general strike in 1958.[81] The Communists quickly

rallied behind his movement on the eve of victory, and began
their campaign to convince the more extreme members of the
26th of July Movement that the nationalistic goals of the movement would be opposed by the United States. The United States
policy of watchful waiting played into their hands, and between
November 1959 and March 1960 the moderates in the Castro
movement were ousted by the extremists led by Raúl Castro
and "Che" Guevara. Although Fidel Castro is not a Communist,
this latter group has influenced his decision to work with the
Communist bloc. Theodore Draper has summarized this situation
as follows:

> Thus it is a mistake to think of Castro as merely a Com-
> munist stalking-horse or a Soviet puppet. His ambitions
> go far beyond these modest roles. In his own mind, he is
> using the local Communists and playing off the Russians
> against the Americans. Just who is using whom remains to
> be seen.[82]

The Castro Government must also share the blame for deteriorating Cuban-American relations. Castro won against heavy
odds, and this led to a mood of "friendless and reckless defiance"
on the part of his movement.[83] Fidel is a fanatical idealist who
has never counted the costs of his actions. He gave up a promising
career to become a hunted revolutionist, and he is blindly dedicated to a vision of the new Cuba. This messianic self-righteous-
ness produces an extremely hostile reaction to any hint of
criticism or even neutralism. As a result he has heaped abuse on
the United States and on Americans in Cuba which has provided ammunition for those Americans who look with disfavor
on revolutions. In addition, Castro's drift toward the Communist bloc has raised legitimate fears in the United States that
the Russians will try to use Cuba as a base of operations in the
hemisphere. Thus, he has greatly hindered the acceptance of his
reforms by many in the United States. A more realistic understanding of the United States, and a dash of moderation in his
handling of American interests would have contributed to the
maintenance of good-will between the two countries.[84]

This cross-fertilization of antagonisms has produced a serious situation in Cuban-American relations which the Soviet Union is trying to exploit. An elderly Cuban asked an American:

> And why can't we have our social revolution and still be able to do business with you Americans as we have always done? What is wrong with all this?[85]

The answer to his question will have to come from both the United States and Cuba. The United States must accept the realistic necessity of economic reform, and the Cubans must change their attitude which condemned the favorable sugar quota as colonialism and then charged economic aggression when the quota was slashed.

Some Americans have called for armed intervention, and some have advocated intervention by the Organization of American States.[86] The era of direct, armed intervention came to an end prior to 1933, and there is little chance of its being revived. A policy of hostility and coercion could drive Cuba further into the arms of the Soviet Union, and alienate other nations in Latin America. The elimination of Fidel Castro may not necessarily be the best answer to this problem. As in the parable of the demise of the one unclean spirit, seven others may enter, "and the last state of that man becomes worse than the first."[87]

II

In the long-range perspective of United States policy the emphasis has been placed on order, stability, and the protection of American interests. This has meant that the United States has generally opposed sweeping economic reforms, and Cuban nationalism—except that of the Machado and Batista variety. From the 1890's to the present the United States has supported the conservative upper classes and their American allies. The history of Cuban-American relations testifies to the consistency of this policy.

This is only one segment of American foreign policy. The United States stress on order and the protection of American interests has been part of a larger world-view held by statesmen in the twentieth century. This world-view—while opposing large, closed empires—has often insisted that the nations of the world protect American interests. We have particularly stressed this view in our dealings with the so-called "backward" countries of Latin America, Asia, and Africa. The flag may no longer follow the dollar, but the power and prestige of the United States certainly does. The editor of *The Reporter* magazine recently stated: "it is obvious that the development of business abroad is just about as important to us as was our western advance across the continent."[88] There is nothing wrong with doing business abroad, but in our push into "new frontiers" we have all too often believed that our interests were synonymous with what was best for other countries. This helps to explain why the United States has in many cases been rather unsympathetic to the nationalistic programs of underdeveloped nations. Their attempts to solve their peculiar problems have often conflicted with our definition of correct economic and political practices. Thus, the United States has tended to oppose change when it seemed to threaten some alteration in American economic interests. Stability has meant the status quo, even if we have had to include a few dictators in our definition of "freedom-loving peoples."

The emphasis on stability above all else explains why the United States has supported a Machado and a Batista in Cuba, a Trujillo in the Dominican Republic, and a Franco in Spain. This is not to argue that the United States should set out to overthrow all dictators. But there is a difference between neutral acceptance and enthusiastic support. Franklin D. Roosevelt once said of Trujillo: "He may be an S.O.B., but he is our S.O.B."[89] The late John Foster Dulles, in a similar vein, told a Senate Committee about Venezuela under the dictator Pérez Jiménez:

> Venezuela is a country which has adopted the kind of policies which we think that the other countries of South America should adopt. Namely, they have adopted policies which provide in Venezuela a climate which is attractive to foreign capital to come in.

He concluded by saying that if all Latin American countries followed the example of Venezuela, the danger of Communism and social disorder would disappear.[90]

The United States has to deal with various governments which do not conform to a republican pattern, since the necessary elements for such a system do not exist in many areas. We should be sensitive to the aspirations of the common people in these countries, however, and not give our enthusiastic support to every government which seems to protect our interests. Calling the Dominican Republic a "bulwark against communism," and at the same time directing democratic homilies at Cuba is pure inconsistency.[91]

Today the United States faces a rapidly changing world. Countries formerly dominated by European nations are proclaiming nationalistic programs of political and economic independence. In the process some of the interests of the United States have suffered. We may not agree with all the tactics employed, and the solutions these countries devise may not be identical to those employed in this country. Yet it is necessary that we adhere to our stated ideal of national self-determination. To adhere to our traditional definition of order, stability, and protection of American interests, and to demand that these struggling nations conform to our policy is to court disaster in the cold war. Former Ambassador Chester Bowles has succinctly stated the present situation:

> We can adjust ourselves in advance to the certainty that reason will not always prevail, that injustices will almost surely occur, and that the short-term price paid for long-term stability will often appear exorbitant.
>
> Above all, let us not lose sight of the essential issue. The real choice in Latin America, as in Asia and Africa, is citizenship or serfdom, hope or dispair, orderly political growth or bloody upheaval. Our failure to understand this choice, or to support the vital new elements which are striving to assert leadership, would be catastrophic.[84]

Today the United States must choose which path it will follow in regard to Cuba. We can blindly follow the traditional policy and try to force the Cubans back into line—under another Batista—or we can work with the Cubans as they try to meet their chronic problems.

We have gone through such an experience with Mexico during the period 1910–1940. Many of the same charges used against Cuba were also employed against Mexico. The Mexican Revolution ran its course without undue interference from the United States, and today the two countries enjoy excellent relations. Cuba today is an important testing-ground for American policy toward the struggling nations of former colonial areas. We can prove the sincerity of our national ideals, or we can add to the lingering suspicions that we are just another empire trying to run the world by our own rules.

Appendix

TARIFFS ON RAW SUGAR FROM CUBA SINCE 1897

July 24, 1897; Dingley tariff	1.6850
Dec. 27, 1903; Reciprocity Treaty effective	1.3480
Aug. 5, 1909; Payne-Aldrich tariff	1.3480
Mar. 1, 1914; Underwood-Simmons tariff	1.0048*
May 27, 1921; Emergency tariff	1.6000
Sept. 22, 1922; Fordney-McCumber tariff	1.7648
June 18, 1930; Hawley-Smoot tariff	2.000
June 8, 1934; Presidential Proclamation	1.5000
Sept. 3, 1934; Cuban Trade Agreement	.9000
Sept. 12, 1939; Suspension of Sugar Act Quotas	1.5000
Dec. 27, 1939; Reimposition of Sugar Act Quotas	.9000
Jan. 5, 1942; Trade Agreement with Cuba	.7500
Jan. 1, 1948; Geneva Trade Agreement	.5000
June 6, 1951; Torquay Trade Agreement	.5000

* The act of 1913 provided that sugar should be placed on the free list on May 1, 1916. This provision was repealed April 27, 1916.

U. S., Senate, Committee on Finance, *Hearings on Sugar Act Extension*, 84th Cong., 2nd Sess., 1956, 279.

THE PLATT AMENDMENT

That in fulfilment of the declaration contained in the joint resolution approved April twentieth, eighteen hundred and ninety-eight, entitled "For the recognition of the independence of the people of Cuba, demanding that the Government of Spain relinquish its authority and government in the island of Cuba, and to withdraw its land and naval reserve forces from Cuba and Cuban waters, and directing the President of the United States to use the land and naval forces of the United States to carry these resolutions into effect," the President is hereby authorized to "leave the government and control of the island of Cuba to its people" so soon as a government shall have been established in said island under a constitution which, either as a part thereof or in an ordinance appended thereto, shall define the future relations of the United States with Cuba, substantially as follows:

I. That the government of Cuba shall never enter into any treaty or other compact with any foreign power or powers which will impair or tend to impair the independence of Cuba, nor in any manner authorize or permit any foreign power or powers to obtain by colonization or, for military or naval purposes or otherwise, lodgment in or control over any portion of said island.

II. That said government shall not assume or contract any public debt, to pay the interest upon which, and to make reasonable sinking fund provision for the ultimate discharge of which, the ordinary revenues of the island, after defraying the current expenses of government shall be inadequate.

III. That the government of Cuba consents that the United States may exercise the right to intervene for the preservation of Cuban independence, the maintenance of a government adequate for the protection of life, property, and individual liberty, and for discharging the obligations with respect to Cuba imposed by the Treaty of Paris on the United States, now to be assumed and undertaken by the government of Cuba.

IV. That all Acts of the United States in Cuba during its military occupancy thereof are ratified and validated, and all lawful rights acquired thereunder shall be maintained and protected.

V. That the government of Cuba will execute and as far as necessary extend, the plans already devised or other plans to be mutually agreed upon, for the sanitation of the cities of the island, to the end that a recurrence of epidemic and infectious diseases may be prevented, thereby assuring protection to the people and commerce of Cuba, as well as to the commerce of the southern ports of the United States and of the people residing therein.

VI. That the Isle of Pines shall be omitted from the proposed constitutional boundaries of Cuba, the title thereto being left to future adjustment by treaty.

VII. That to enable the United States to maintain the independence of Cuba, and to protect the people thereof, as well as for its own defence, the government of Cuba will sell or lease to the United States land necessary for coaling or naval stations at certain specified points, to be agreed upon with the President of the United States.

VIII. That by way of further assurance the government of Cuba will embody the foregoing provisions in a permanent treaty with the United States.

Notes

1. National Archives: General Records of the Department of State—Record Group 59; Miscellaneous Memos and Data Containing Material on which Secretary Stimson's Speech of February 6, 1931 was based, January 12, 1930, 710.11/1518. Original documents used in the National Archives will be cited hereafter by the letters NA, followed by the file number of the documents. If the document has been printed in *Foreign Relations* this will be indicated after the file number as follows: (FR, date, volume, page on which document begins).

2. A few of the more recent examples: John Foster Dulles (Sullivan and Cromwell, international law firm); Laurence A. Crosby (Sullivan and Cromwell, also counsel for the United States Sugar Institute); Douglas Dillon (Dillon-Read investment bankers).

3. Herbert Hoover, *The Memoirs of Herbert Hoover* (3 Vols., New York, 1952), II, 90-91.

4. Vice Admiral H. G. Rickover, "Where Do We Go From Here?" *Saturday Evening Post* (July 30, 1960), 68. The need for a Latin American Marshall Plan is discussed in A. A. Berle, Jr., "The Communist Invasion of Latin America," *The Reporter* (July 7, 1960), 23-25.

NOTES FOR CHAPTER ONE

1. "Memorandum and Arguments Relating to Constructive Steps Which Should be Taken in Central America before the Close of the European War," February 15, 1918, NA 711.13/55. For a similar statement of the relationship of stability, trade, and investments see Chester Lloyd Jones, *Caribbean Interests of the United States* (New York, 1919), 94; Jones's book was written in 1916 and represents the view of a former member of the State Department.

2. Lansing to Gonzales, February 18, 1917, NA 837.00/1106a (FR, 1917-1:363). Wilfrid H. Callcott, *The Caribbean Policy of the United States 1890-1920* (Baltimore, 1942), 471-472. A list of the various landings can be found in, U. S., Department of State, *Right to Protect Citizens in Foreign Countries by Landing Forces* (3rd revised ed., with supplemental appendix: Washington, 1934), 101-107. The State Department files contain numerous requests for protection from American business groups, and time after time Gonzales was instructed to "demand" that the Cuban Government protect American properties.

3. Callcott, *Caribbean Policy of the United States,* 471-472.

4. Memorandum: Stabler (Latin American Division) to Secretary of State, June 4, 1917, NA 837.00/1395.

5. Gonzales to Secretary of State, July 14, 1917, NA 837.00/1395.

6. *Ibid.*

7. Lansing to American Legation (Habana), August 17, 1917, NA 837.00/1407.

8. Gonzales to Lansing, August 16, 1917, NA 837.00/1407.

9. Gonzales to Lansing, August 14, 1917, NA 837.00/1406.

10. Lansing to American Legation (Habana), August 17, 1917, NA 837.00/1407.

11. Numerous such reports are in the Archives and were read by the author. They reported the areas covered by the patrols and activity encountered.

12. Guantanamo, Cuba to Opnav, Washington, July 17, 1917, NA 837.00/1395.

13. Frank L. Polk to the Secretary of War, July 18, 1917, NA 837.00/1395. Polk to Wilson (President), July 18, 1917, NA 837.00/1395. Polk did not mention the "German threat" to the Secretary of War and told Wilson that "this movement [revolution] may be backed by Germans."

14. Memorandum by General Richards, December 10, 1921; NA 837.00/2183 [?].

15. H. C. Lakin (President of the Cuba Railroad) to Charles Evans Hughes, August 29, 1921, NA 837.00/2155. Marines were camped on the property of the railroad. Lakin, in stating the reason for the intervention in 1917, cited the Bolshevist menace, not the German.

16. Lansing to McAdoo, August 13, 1917, in *Foreign Relations of the United States, 1918* (Washington, 1930), 298.

17. Leland Jenks once described this concession as "the most grandiose attempt at plunder in the history of Cuba." Leland Jenks, *Our Cuban Colony* (New York, 1928), 119. Norman H. Davis was associated with the Morgan Bank and was a leading Democrat. In 1917 he was financial adviser to the Treasury Department in charge of loans to the allies. In this capacity he helped to handle the Cuban loan.

18. Memorandum by John Foster Dulles (Special Counselor, Latin American Division), August 29, 1917, in *Foreign Relations,* 1918, 301.

19. Gonzales to Lansing, July 18, 1918, *Ibid.,* 331. The Cuba Railroad ended up getting over three million dollars, and they continued to ask for more.

20. Jenks, *Cuban Colony,* 125-126.

21. *Ibid.,* 197-198.

22. U. S., Department of State, *The World War* (Vol. I), Supplement 2 of *Foreign Relations of the United States, 1917* (Washington, 1932), 655.

23. Gonzales to Lansing, December 16, 1917, in *Foreign Relations, 1918,* 350-353.

24. *Ibid.,* 347.

25. Herbert Hoover to Woodrow Wilson, *Ibid.,* 349.

26. Gonzales to Lansing, December 16, 1917, *Ibid.,* 350-353.

27. U. S., Senate, Subcommittee of the Committee on Manufactures, *Hearings, Shortage of Sugar,* 65th Cong., 2nd Sess., 1918, 1028-1029. (Hereafter cited as *Shortage of Sugar.*)

28. Cespedes to Lansing, January 18, 1918, in *Foreign Relations 1918*, 353-354.

29. Jenks quotes a telegram from Lansing to Gonzales (source given was the newspaper *El Mundo*, January 14, 1918), which, if it is accurate, definitely states that imports into Cuba were stopped in order to convince the Cubans that they should "cooperate" with the United States. Jenks, *Cuban Colony*, 199.

30. Senate, *Shortage of Sugar*, 205. Officials of other refineries testified that the American Sugar Refining Company was favored by the International Committee and profited from the price set for Cuban sugar.

31. For the views of businessmen on this matter see, Edwin F. Atkins, *Sixty Years in Cuba* (Cambridge, 1926), 212-215, 237; Robert P. Porter, *Report on the Commercial and Industrial Condition of the Island of Cuba* (Treasury Department Document No. 2072, Washington, 1898); this publication contains numerous interviews with and letters from businessmen interested in Cuba. The opinions of Secretaries of State Richard Olney and John Sherman, Fitzhugh Lee (the American Consul in Cuba), and Stewart L. Woodford (American Minister to Spain) can be found in Jenks, *Cuban Colony*, 43-44, and Callcott, *Caribbean Policy of the United States*, 83-84. Some newspaper views on this concern can be found in George W. Auxier, "Middle Western Newspapers and the Spanish-American War," *The Mississippi Valley Historical Review* (March 1940), 523-534.

32. See Julius W. Pratt, *Expansionists of 1898* (Baltimore, 1936) for an elaboration of the thesis that business had little or nothing to do with the decision to declare war.

33. Phillip G. Wright, *The Cuban Situation and Our Treaty Relations* (Washington, D. C., 1931), 20.

34. American interests in Cuba did not want the insurgents to take power. Edwin F. Atkins had been working against such a step since 1896. Atkins, *Sixty Years in Cuba*, 209, 288, 306. Senator Henry Teller later repudiated the "self denying" amendment, and his biographer states that the Senator never intended for Cuba to have much more than local self-government. Elmer Ellis, *Henry Moore Teller* (Caldwell, Idaho, 1941), 343.

35. Russell H. Fitzgibbon, *Cuba and the United States* (Menasha, Wis., 1935), Chaps. 2, 3.

36. Charles Morris, *Our Island Empire* (Philadelphia, 1899), 162-164.

37. Edwin F. Atkins stated that a reciprocity treaty was needed to protect investments and provide political stability; he was satisfied with the Platt Amendment but believed that such a treaty was just as vital. Atkins, *Sixty Years in Cuba*, 323, 347. For a similar view see Robert P. Porter, *Industrial Cuba* (New York, 1899), 7; Porter was Special Commissioner for the United States to Cuba and Puerto Rico. This book represents the conclusions he reached during the compilation of the *Report on the Commercial and Industrial Conditions of the Island of Cuba*.

38. U. S. Tariff Commission, *The Effects of the Cuban Reciprocity Treaty of 1902* (Miscellaneous Series No. 22, Washington, 1929), 376-378.

39. *Ibid.*, 377. President McKinley stated the need for Cuban reciprocity in his annual messages of 1899 and 1900.

40. *Ibid.*

41. *Ibid.*, 387.

42. *Ibid.*, 388.

43. *Messages and Papers of the Presidents* (Vol. XIV, New York, n. d.), 6717.

44. Tariff Commission, *Effects of the Cuban Reciprocity Treaty of 1902*, 386-418.

45. Wright, *Cuban Situation*, 26-30.

46. H. C. Prinsen Geerligs and R. J. Prinsen Geerligs, *Cane Sugar Production, 1912-1937* (London, 1938), 99. Tariff Commission, *Effects of the Cuban Reciprocity Treaty of 1902*, 66. Jones, *Caribbean Interests of the United States*, 90-91.

47. *Ibid.*, 88. The 1897 value represented a sharp decline from the 1894 value.

48. U. S. Department of Commerce, *Investment in Cuba, Basic Information for United States Businessmen* (Washington, 1956), 9; Gustavo Gutierrez, *El Desarrollo Economico de Cuba* (Habana, 1952), 229.

49. *Ibid.*, and Julian Alienes Y Urosa, *Caracteristicas Fundamentales de la Economia Cubana* (Habana, 1950), 201.

50. Jenks, *Cuban Colony*, 166-174.

51. Enoch Crowder to Henry P. Fletcher, October 29, 1921 (Private and Confidential), NA 837.51/632½.

52. Fitzgibbon, *Cuba and the United States*, 119-120.

53. Jenks, *Cuban Colony*, 91-92; prints letters from Steinhart to the United States Government.

54. President Roosevelt offered to appoint Steinhart Deputy Governor. Jenks, *Cuban Colony*, 97.

55. State Department, *Right to Protect Citizens in Foreign Countries by Landing Forces*, 98-99.

56. National Foreign Trade Council, *South American Handbook* (New York, 1915), ix, x. Among those appointed were Robert Dollar, James A. Farrell, J. P. Grace, Willard Straight, Robert H. Patchin, and E. P. Thomas.

57. *The Commercial and Financial Chronicle* (June 26, 1915), 2132. The American section of this body was composed of leading businessmen; its task was to clear the way for American exports by removing legal barriers to trade.

58. National Foreign Trade Council, *South American Handbook*, xix.

59. [H. J. Dreher,] "American Banking Possibilities And Foreign Trade Development," *The Commercial and Financial Chronicle* (September 11, 1915), 814; "Pan-Americanism and its Bearing on Development of the Central West," *The Commercial and Financial Chronicle* (June 3, 1916), 2037.

60. National Association of Manufacturers, *Proceedings of the Twenty-First Annual Convention of the National Association of Manufacturers* (New York, 1916), 320.

61. "Willard Straight on Foreign Relations and Overseas Trade," *The Commercial and Financial Chronicle*, (May 8, 1915), 1547. The Webb-Pomerene Act and the Edge Act were examples of this cooperation.

62. National Association of Manufacturers, *Proceedings of the International Trade Conference, 1915* (New York, 1915), 40. For other expressions of Latin American feeling see Samuel Guy Inman, *Problems in Pan Americanism* (New York, 1921), 136-137.

63. Francis H. Sisson, *America's Foreign Trade* (New York, 1917), 4-5;

a Guaranty Trust Company pamphlet reprint of a speech given by the vice-president of the bank. See also, Harry Levy, "Using Motion Pictures to Get South American Trade," *American Industries* (September, 1919), 42. Isaac F. Marcosson, *The War After the War* (New York, 1916). A. Hyatt Verrill, *Getting Together with Latin America* (New York, 1918).

64. W. S. Kies, *After the War Business Problems* ([New York], 1918), 12-13; author was the vice-president of the American International Corporation. Francis Sisson, *America's Foreign Trade,* 5.

65. Stephen H. Voorhees, *The War and Its Effect on World Trade* (New York, 1918), 13. Pamphlet printed by the National City Bank. Francis H. Sisson, *America's Foreign Trade,* 4-5. A. Hyatt Verrill, *South and Central American Trade Conditions of Today* (New York, 1914), 6. W. S. Kies, *A Permanent Foreign Trade and Its Problems* (New York, 1916), 15-16.

66. NA 711.13/55.

67. Jenks, *Cuban Colony,* 309.

NOTES FOR CHAPTER TWO

1. Max Winkler, *Investments of United States Capital in Latin America* (World Peace Foundation Pamphlet Vol. XI, No. 6, Boston, 1928), 182. In 1928 sugar comprised over 80 percent of Cuba's exports, and tobacco comprised about 12 percent. Alienes y Urosa, *Caracteristicas Fundamentales de la Economia Cubana,* 105.

2. Winkler, *Investments of United States Capital in Latin America,* 1; quote from the *New York Times* (November 25, 1928). See also, Gutierrez, *El Desarrollo Economico de Cuba,* 89.

3. Winkler, *Investments of United States Capital in Latin America,* 275.

4. *Ibid.,* 278. Gutierrez, *El Desarrollo Economico de Cuba,* 90.

5. The National City Bank of New York, *Cuba, Review of Commercial, Industrial and Economic Conditions in 1919,* (New York, 1919), 5. Jenks, *Cuban Colony,* 281.

6. *Ibid.,* 284. Gutierrez, *El Dessarrollo Economico de Cuba,* 234. Gutierrez estimates that American control averaged 63 percent for the decade.

7. Jenks, *Cuban Colony,* 220. In 1915 Manuel Rionda (of the Czarnikow-Rionda Company) and several associates formed the syndicate known as the Cuba Cane Sugar Corporation. J. and W. Seligman were the principal bankers for the group. The group began to buy up sugar mills in 1916 and became the largest permanent investment of American capital in Cuba. *Ibid.,* 179-180.

8. "Many Changes in Ownership of Cuban Mills," *The Cuba Review* (October, 1920), 32-33. *The Cuba Review* was published in New York by the Munson Steamship Lines.

9. *The Cuba Review* (December, 1924), 33.

10. *Ibid.* (February, 1927), 27-28.

11. *Ibid.* (October, 1920), 32-33. Jenks, *Cuban Colony,* 219-220. The Coca-Cola Company and five other bottling concerns introduced the

Norit process into their plants and began to utilize raw sugar direct from the Cuban mills.

12. Jenks, *Cuban Colony*, 281.

13. U. S. Congress, Senate, Subcommittee of the Committee on the Judiciary, *Hearings, Lobby Investigation*, Part 3, 71st Cong., 1st Sess., 1929, 1320-1327. (Cited hereafter as *Lobby Investigation.*) The General Sugars Company was a holding company whose stock was held by the National City Company (the stock of this corporation was held by the National City Bank). The National City Bank denied being in the sugar business since the bank held no direct shares in the sugar company.

14. Robert W. Dunn, *American Foreign Investments* (New York, 1926), 122-123.

15. Senate, *Lobby Investigation*, Part 3, 1328. This reflects the importance of sugar to the National City Bank.

16. U. S., Congress, Senate, Committee on Finance, *Hearings, Sale of Foreign Bonds or Securities in the United States*, Part 1, 72nd Cong., 1st Sess., 1931, 162 f. (Cited hereafter as *Sale of Foreign Bonds.*)

17. Gutierrez, *El Desarrollo Economico de Cuba*, 233.

18. Atkins, *Sixty Years in Cuba*, 31.

19. Jenks, *Cuban Colony*, 287-288.

20. Winkler, *Investments of United States Capital in Latin America*, 189-190. Gutierrez, *El Desarrollo Economico de Cuba*, 234.

21. Department of Commerce, *Investment in Cuba*, 108. Dunn, *American Foreign Investments*, 127-128. The board of directors of the Cuba Company included Percy A. Rockefeller, W. H. Woodin, Horatio Rubens, and Herbert C. Lakin. W. A. Harriman & Company was also represented.

22. W. A. Howell (Chargé d'Affaires in Cuba) to Secretary of State, September 4, 1923, NA 837.00/2344.

23. Senate, *Sale of Foreign Bonds*, Part 1, 162 f.

24. U. S., Congress, Senate, Committee on Banking and Currency, *Hearings, Stock Exchange Practices*, Part 6, 73rd Cong., 2nd Sess., 1933 & 1934, 2796. (Cited hereafter as *Stock Exchange Practices.*)

25. Wright, *The Cuban Situation*, 144.

26. Raymond L. Buell *et al.*, *Problems of the New Cuba*, Report of the Commission on Cuban Affairs of the Foreign Policy Association (New York, 1935), 59.

27. U. S., Department of Commerce, Bureau of Foreign and Domestic Commerce, *Cuban Readjustment to Current Economic Forces* (Trade Information Bulletin No. 725, Washington, 1930), 12. The United States supplied about the same percentage of Cuban imports in 1929 as it did in 1914, but the 1929 value was much higher. In 1931 the percentages remained about the same, but the 1931 value was somewhat lower than the 1914 value.

28. Buell, *Problems of the New Cuba*, 60; Britain and Spain increased their share of the Cuban import trade between 1925 and 1933.

29. Winkler, *Investments of United States Capital in Latin America*, 182. Viriato Gutierrez, *The World Sugar Problem, 1926-1935* (London, 1935), 46.

30. Wright, *The Cuban Situation*, 75.

31. United States Cuban Sugar Council, *Sugar—Facts and Figures*, 1952

(Washington, 1952), 37. Phillippine sugar exports to the United States steadily increased in quantity from 1926 to 1934.

32. Buell, *Problems of the New Cuba*, 60, 236. Department of Commerce, *Cuban Readjustment to Current Economic Forces*, 12.

33. Gutierrez, *The World Sugar Problem*, 31.

34. Buell, *Problems of the New Cuba*, 60. *Sugar-Facts and Figures*, *1952*, 106.

35. *Ibid.*, 37, 106, 116. Gutierrez, *El Desarrollo Economico de Cuba*, 74 f.

36. Wright, *The Cuban Situation*, 160-162.

37. Department of Commerce, *Investment in Cuba*, 9-10. Gutierrez, *El Desarrollo Economico de Cuba*, 91.

38. *Ibid.*, 89-92, 233. Department of Commerce, *Investment in Cuba*, 9-10; and Gutierrez, *El Desarrollo Economico de Cuba*, 91.

39. Buell, *Problems of the New Cuba*, 227-229. The Cuba Cane group was sold at auction in February 1934 to a banking group headed by the Central Hanover Bank and Trust Co. for four million dollars and accrued interest. In 1930 the group was valued on their books at over sixty-four million dollars. For bond values see a pamphlet of the National City Co. entitled *Foreign Dollar Bonds*, inserted in Senate, *Sale of Foreign Bonds*, Part 4, 2095-2096.

40. O. K. Davis, "The Activities of the National Foreign Trade Council," *American Consular Bulletin* (February, 1924), 40-41.

41. *Commerce Monthly* (August, 1919), 21-22.

42. James M. Curley, "Welcome Address," *Official Report of the Eleventh National Foreign Trade Convention* (New York, 1924), 7. See also *ibid.*, V. The Final Declaration of the 1924 Foreign Trade Convention; Walter Parker, "The Trade Promise of the New World," *Mississippi Valley Magazine* (March-April, 1928), 8-9; *Iron Age* (January 27, 1921), 274.

43. See speech by Dwight Morrow in *The Commercial and Financial Chronicle* (January 21, 1922), 244; J. T. Holdsworth, "A Foreign Loan Policy that will Enable Our Factories to Get to Work," *Official Report of the Ninth National Foreign Trade Convention* (New York, 1922), 11.

44. *Ibid.*, 14; James S. Alexander, "Our Foreign Trade and Our Foreign Investment Policy," *Official Report of the Fourteenth National Trade Convention* (New York, 1927), 27.

45. See *Textiles* (December, 1919), a Boston publication, as quoted in the *Congressional Record*, 66th Cong., 2nd Sess., 1919, Vol. 59, Part 1, 631. The Committee on Foreign Trade of the National Association of Manufacturers recommended use of surplus funds to aid trade. *Proceedings of the Thirtieth Annual Convention of the National Association of Manufacturers* (New York, 1925), 107.

46. Frank O'Malley, *Our South American Trade and its Financing* (National City Bank Pamphlet, Foreign Commerce Series No. 3, New York, 1920), 1-2. See also, Walter Parker, "A New Vision in Business for the Americas," *Mississippi Valley Magazine* (November-December, 1929), 13; Walter Parker, "The Trade Promise of the New World," *Mississippi Valley Magazine* (March-April, 1928), 9.

47. Paul J. Kruesi, "Building Foreign Trade Through Foreign Loans,"

Official Report of the Thirteenth National Foreign Trade Convention (New York, 1926), 418.

48. Franklin Remington, "Foreign Loans a Trade Builder," *Official Report of the Eleventh National Foreign Trade Convention* (New York, 1924), 169-170. See also, G. Butler Sherwell, "Our Investments in Latin American Government Securities," *American Banker's Association Journal* (July, 1926).

49. *London Times* (January 9, 1920). *The Commercial and Financial Chronicle* (July 3, 1920), 23-24.

50. "South America as a Buyer of Steel," *Iron Age* (May 12, 1921), 1255. See also, Herbert H. Rice, "Executive Aid in Foreign Trade," *Official Report of the Thirteenth National Foreign Trade Convention* (New York, 1926), 227.

51. Nuno Pinheiro, "Pan-Americanism and the Commercial Expansion of the United States," *The Pan-American Magazine* (July, 1920), 107. This magazine was a good example of this business Pan-Americanism. "American Business Builds a New Pan-Americanism," *Business Week* (January 18, 1930), 40. "Golden Ties of the Americas," *Commerce and Finance* (January 25, 1928), 224.

52. *The Cuba Review* (November, 1920), 21. For the interest of the American Manufacturers' Export Association, see *ibid.* (July, 1919), 25.

53. "Our Opportunity," *Mississippi Valley Magazine* (October 1923), 6, editorial.

54. National City Bank, *Cuba, Review of Commercial, Industrial and Economic Conditions in 1919*, 3-6.

55. "Market Demands and Selling Methods in Cuba," *The Cuba Review* (April, 1919), 20; *ibid.* (November, 1920), 21.

56. July 21, 1919, NA 637.11171/Orig.; *The Cuba Review* (August, 1919), 20. Frank Steinhart was appointed temporary chairman; among the other members of the organization committee were Sosthenes Behn (Cuba Telephone Co.), John M. Draper (Borden & Co.), William H. Smith (Ward Line), William Field (Field & Co.), William M. Whitner (Trust Company of Cuba), Lawrence B. Ross (Ford Motor Co.).

57. Julius Klein, "Cuban Markets for American Goods," *The Cuba Review* (August, 1925), 19.

58. Memorandum of a Conversation between Walter C. Thurston (Latin American Division) and Mr. Carl Byoir, May 6, 1929, NA 711.37/130.

59. Palmer E. Pierce, "American Business and Latin America," *Official Report of the Seventeenth National Foreign Trade Convention* (New York, 1930), 77. Some of the executive committee members were Palmer Pierce (Standard Oil of N. J.), George D. Buckley (National City Bank), James S. Carson (American and Foreign Power Co.), James D. Mooney (General Motors Export Corp.), and Eugene P. Thomas (U. S. Steel Corp.).

60. National Foreign Trade Council, *Official Report of the Twentieth National Foreign Trade Convention* (New York, 1933), 92. Palmer Pierce, "American Business and Its Latin American Relations," *The Pan American Magazine* (September 1930), 174.

61. "These Americas—Way to Prosperity," *World's Work* (July 1932). Statement by Victor Cutter to the annual meeting of the United Fruit Co. in February 1931, printed in, *Congressional Record*, 71st Cong., 3rd. Sess., 1931, Vol. 74. Part 7, 7066-7067.

62. J. Walter Drake, "Government Service to Foreign Trade," *Official Report of the Eighth National Foreign Trade Convention* (New York, 1921), 213.

63. Allen Walker to Herbert Hoover, April 19, 1921, NA 600.1115/280.

64. Herbert Hoover to Henry P. Fletcher, April 21, 1921, NA 600.1115/280.

65. Percival Farquar to Charles Evans Hughes, April 14, 1921, NA 600.1115/296.

66. Memorandum: W. W. Cumberland to Dearing, May 13, 1921, NA 600.1115/296.

67. *New York Times* (May 21, 1921), 23:2.

68. *Ibid.* (May 27, 1921), 1:8.

69. *Ibid.* (May 28, 1921), 1:6. It was noted that the government would give support to overseas investment and there were no further letters in the file (600.1115) concerning the subject of Farquar's letter; i.e., a statement to let the public know that the government supported foreign investments.

70. *Messages and Papers of the Presidents,* Vol. XVI, 7955; from a speech in 1915.

71. National Association of Manufacturers, *Proceedings of the Twentieth Annual Convention of the National Association of Manufacturers* (New York, 1915), 298; speech by Warren Harding.

72. Charles Evans Hughes, *Some Aspects of the Work of the Department of State* (67th Cong., 2nd Sess., Senate Document No. 206, Washington, 1922), 10; see also, *International Telephone Review* (April, 1928), 30, for speech given by Hughes at a Chamber of Commerce dinner in Havana, Cuba. Charles Evans Hughes, *Foreign Relations* (Republican National Committee Pamphlet, NP, 1924), 53.

73. *Congressional Record,* 71st Cong., 2nd Sess., 1930, Vol. 72, Part 7, 7107-7108.

74. Joseph C. Grew, *Turbulent Era* (2 vols., Boston, 1952), I: 410. Entry for January 18, 1920.

75. J. Butler Wright, "The Department of State and American Enterprise Abroad," *Official Report of the Twelfth National Foreign Trade Convention* (New York, 1925), 163, 170-171. See also, U. S., Department of the Interior, Bureau of Education, *Practices and Objectives in Training for Foreign Service* (Bulletin No. 21, Washington, 1924), 20.

76. U. S., Department of Commerce, *Annual Report of the Secretary of Commerce: 1928* (Washington, 1928), 93-94. See also, Julius Klein, *Frontiers of Trade* (New York, 1929), 9-10.

77. U. S., Department of the Navy, Office of Naval Intelligence, *The United States Navy as an Industrial Asset* (Washington, 1923), 1; *Information Concerning the United States Navy and Other Navies* (Washington, 1925), 12; *Some of the Unusual Peacetime Activities of the United States Navy* (Washington, 1923). *The United States Navy in Peace Time* (Washington, 1931).

78. *Congressional Record,* 68th Cong., 2nd Sess., 1925, Vol. 66, Part 3, 2377. For examples of speeches concerning the necessity for trade with Latin America, see *ibid.,* 67th Cong., 1st Sess., 1921, Vol. 61, Part 5, 4451-4455; *ibid.,* 68th Cong., 1st Sess., 1924, Vol. 65, Part 6, 5928.

79. *Ibid.,* 68th Cong., 1st Sess., 1924, Vol. 65, Part 8, 7573. For examples

of what Senator Connally was referring to, see *ibid.*, 7562 and 7571 (speeches by Representatives John J. Rogers and Milton Shreve). As early as May 1921 the National Foreign Trade Council and the American Manufacturers' Export Association informed the Departments of State and Commerce that they would like to see the Foreign Service reorganized. Ogden H. Hammond to Henry P. Fletcher, May 21, 1921, NA 600.1115/353.

80. Joseph Grew, "Speech by Mr. Grew," *American Consular Bulletin* (September, 1924), 313. William R. Castle, Jr., "The Department of State and American Enterprises Abroad," *Official Report of the Fifteenth National Foreign Trade Convention* (New York, 1928), 193-194. Castle—an Assistant Secretary of State—stressed the theme that one of the chief duties of the department was to keep the highways of commerce open and in good repair, especially in Latin America. The State Department had the Council print four hundred copies of this speech, and these were sent to diplomats in the field "as an explanation of United States policy"; Nelson T. Johnson to Gardiner L. Harding, July 17, 1928, NA 111/329.

81. Grosvenor Jones, "The Latin American Frontier," *Pocket Bulletin* (November, 1927), 18-20.

82. U. S., Department of Commerce, *Annual Report of the Secretary of Commerce: 1924* (Washington, 1924), 132. Statement of Klein before the House Appropriations Committee quoted in, *Congressional Record*, 68th Cong., 2nd Sess., 1925, Vol. 66, Part 3, 2392.

83. For additional examples, see speech by Charles Evans Hughes as quoted in *Congressional Record*, 70th Cong., 1st Sess., 1928, Vol. 69, Part 2, 1844; speech by Representative Edith Rogers, *ibid.*, 1269; Clayton S. Cooper, *Foreign Trade, Markets and Methods* (New York, 1922), 404.

84. Speech to the Motion Picture Producers and Distributors of America as printed in, *Mississippi Valley Magazine* (March-April, 1927), 20. See also, Alexander de Conde, *Herbert Hoover's Latin American Policy* (Stanford, 1951), 6.

NOTES FOR CHAPTER THREE

1. James R. Connor, "National Farm Organizations and United States Tariff Policy in the 1920's," *Agricultural History* (January, 1958), 37.

2. Philip G. Wright, *Sugar in Relation to the Tariff* (New York, 1924), 59. F. W. Taussig, *The Tariff History of the United States* (8th ed., New York, 1931), 451-452, 457.

3. Wright, *Sugar in Relation to the Tariff*, 204-205.

4. U. S., Congress, House Committee on Ways and Means, *Hearings, General Tariff Revision*, 66th Cong., 3rd Sess., 1921, Part 2, 1356-1358, 1387. Arbuckle Brothers Refinery submitted a brief also. (Cited hereafter as *General Tariff Revision*, 1921.)

5. *Ibid.*, 1356-1358.

6. *The Cuba Review* (August 1921), 31-32.

7. *Wall Street Journal* (August 2, 1921), 1.

8. *The Cuba Review* (October 1921), 10.

9. R. P. Spooner (American Abrasive Metals Co.) to Senator Joseph Frelinghuysen, August 25, 1921, NA 611.3731/113. See also, G. F. Bauer (National Automobile Chamber of Commerce) to Office of the Trade Advisor, August 31, 1921, NA 611.3731/109; L. L. Ransom (John R. Proctor Inc.) to Joseph Frelinghuysen, August 15, 1921, NA 611.3731/104.

10. M. A. Oudin to Fred M. Dearing (Assistant Secretary of State), September 8, 1921, NA 611.3731/110; Dearing to Oudin, September 13, 1921, NA 611.3731/110.

11. October 11, 1921, NA 611.3731/115.

12. October 12, 1921, NA 611.373 Sugar/24.

13. Fenton R. McCreery (International Rotary Clubs) to Henry P. Fletcher, October 8, 1921, NA 611.373 Sugar/23; George W. Jones (Evans & Howard Fire Brick Co.) to Charles Evans Hughes, November 23, 1921, NA 611.373 Sugar/27; letter from the Casey-Hedges Co. to Representative Ewin Davis, *Congressional Record*, 67th Cong., 1st Sess., 1921, Vol. 61, Part 7, 6762-6763. *The Cuba Review* (October, 1921), 10, editorial support of the Cuban proposal.

14. *The Cuba Review* (October 1921), 11; *ibid.* (November 1921), 34-35, extracts from the Cuban Commission's memorandum.

15. *Ibid.* (October, 1921), 11. Horatio Rubens was chairman; some other names on the list were Edwin F. Atkins, Herbert C. Lakin, W. H. Woodin, and Frank Lowry.

16. November 1, 1921, NA 611.373 Sugar/26. On December 18, 1921 the Chamber, and the American Club, participated in a Havana protest parade against the Fordney Bill; Chargé d'Affaires *ad interim* to Secretary of State, December 19, 1921, NA 611.373 Sugar/35.

17. Senator Smoot told Señor Portuondo that the preferential was a "refiner's" gimmick and that he would fight it as long as he had the power to do so. *Congressional Record*, 67th Cong., 2nd Sess., 1922, Vol. 62, Part 11, 11010.

18. U. S., Congress, Senate, Committee on Finance, *Hearings, The Proposed Tariff Act of 1921*, 67th Cong., 2nd Sess., 1922, 2349. (Cited hereafter as *Tariff Act of 1921*.)

19. See Memorandum: W. R. Manning to Sumner Welles, January 25, 1922, NA 611.373 Sugar/40, quotes from a bulletin of this organization which is much the same as Shattuck's brief before the committee.

20. Senate, *Tariff Act of 1921*.

21. *Ibid.* The arguments can be found as follows: Atkins, 2173-2179; Shattuck, 2210-2215; Rubens, 2215-2237; Craycraft, 2241.

22. Jenks, *Cuban Colony*, 225-226. Attitude of Smoot expressed in, *Congressional Records*, 67th Cong., 2nd Sess., 1922, Vol. 62, Part 11, 11010.

23. *Monthly Bank Letter* (June 1922); official publication of the National City Bank of New York.

24. Chester Lloyd Jones (Acting Commercial Attaché) to Julius Klein, December 5, 1921, Chester Lloyd Jones Papers (University of Wisconsin Library, Madison). (Cited hereafter as Jones Mss.)

25. Crowder to Hughes, November 12, 1921, in, *Foreign Relations, 1921*, 804.

26. NA 611.373 Sugar/82. All of the documents numbered 82 were sent to the State Department, by Morrow, on September 5, 1923.

27. Dwight Morrow to Senator Reed Smoot, October 9, 1922, NA 611.373 Sugar/82.

28. Memorandum: Conversation between Henry P. Fletcher and Herbert C. Lakin, December 28, 1921, NA 837.51/1027.

29. *New York Times* (December 31, 1921), 17:3. All of these were either refining companies or sugar companies with refining connections.

30. *Ibid.* The Federal, Arbuckle Brothers, and Warner refineries refused to enter the pool; the first two had no Cuban connections.

31. *Ibid.* (January 7, 1922), 21:1. By October 7, 1922 the corporation had disposed of most of the sugar. *Ibid.,* (October 7, 1922), 24:4.

32. Moody's Investors Service, *Industrial Investments,* Part II, *Moody's Analysis of Investments* (New York, 1920), 324. In 1920 this company was interested in 30 of the 101 beet sugar factories in the U. S. Wright, *Sugar in Relation to the Tariff,* 59, 76. The negotiations of Havemeyer and the other Cuban sugar interests with the beet sugar people is traced in the *Economic Bulletin of Cuba* (September, 1922), as reprinted in *Congressional Record,* 67th Cong., 2nd Sess., Vol. 62, Part 12, 13124-13125.

33. Smoot's letter printed in, *Congressional Record,* 67th Cong., 2nd Sess., 1922, Vol. 62, Part 11, 11011. See also Dwight Morrow to Dana G. Munro, September 5, 1923, NA 611.373 Sugar/82; Morrow wrote that Crowder had shown Zayas both of the letters, but had not urged restriction at all. (Crowder had been accused of taking the side of the beet sugar interests.)

34. *Congressional Record,* 67th Cong., 2nd Sess., 1922, Vol. 62, Part 11, 11569-11573.

35. *Ibid.,* 11010-11011.

36. Wright, *The Cuban Situation,* 75.

37. *Congressional Record,* 67th Cong., 2nd Sess., 1922, Vol. 62, Part 11, 11010-11011. Smoot singled out Morrow for special attack and Morrow wrote to Smoot denying the charges, October 9, 1922, NA 611.373 Sugar/82.

38. H. O. Neville, "Looking Backward Over the Past Year in Cuba's Sugar Industry," *The Cuba Review* (March, 1923), 13.

39. Memorandum: Dr. Manning (Latin American Division) to Francis White, March 20, 1925, NA 611.3731/167. Manning noted the arguments of Rubens, and the hope of involving the Department in the tariff controversy.

40. U. S., Congress, Senate, Select Committee on Investigation of the Tariff Commission, *Hearings, Investigation of the Tariff Commission,* 69th Cong., 1st Sess., 1926, 278. Harding stated that he would cut the tariff if the Commission so recommended.

41. *Ibid.,* 93.

42. *The Cuba Review* (July, 1925), 30-33. Coolidge told the Commission not to publish the majority report, Senate, *Investigation of the Tariff Commission,* 372.

43. *The Cuba Review* (July, 1925), 30. Column written by the firm of Willett & Gray.

44. Memorandum: "Suggested Modification of Commercial Treaty With Cuba," by Arthur N. Young, February 25, 1927, NA 611.3731/230.

45. Manning to White, May 13, 1926, NA 611.3731/200.

46. Hugo Hartenstein to Frank Kellogg, May 21, 1926, NA 611.3731/201.

47. February 21, 1927, NA 611.3731/234.

48. *Ibid.* Also, Manning to White, April 22, 1927, NA 611.3731/232; Note, McClure to Manning, April 22, 1927, NA 611.3731/232.

49. Conversation between Ferrara and Morgan, February 21, 1927, NA 611.3731/234; "Suggested Modification of Commercial Treaty With Cuba," by Arthur N. Young, February 25, 1927, NA 611.3731/230; McClure to Manning, April 22, 1927, NA 611.3731/232.

50. Memorandum: Manning to Morgan and White, June 29, 1927, NA 711.37/107.

51. Harold L. Williamson (Chargé d'Affaires *ad interim*) to the Secretary of State, September 29, 1927, NA 611.3731/239.

52. "Summary of Cuban Proposals for Revision of Reciprocity Treaty," by Office of the Economic Advisor, January 10, 1928, NA 611.3731/267.

53. Memorandum: "Preliminary Comment on Cuban Proposals for Revision of Reciprocity Treaty," January 11, 1928, NA 611.3731/268.

54. Guy Wellman (Associate General Counsel for the Standard Oil Company of New Jersey) to the Secretary of State, June 10, 1926, NA 611.3731/206.

55. Manning to McClure, June 15, 1926, NA 611.3731/220.

56. McClure (Office of the Economic Advisor) to the Latin American Division, June 17, 1926, NA 611.3731/219.

57. Orestes Ferrara, "Cuba's Foreign Trade," *Official Report of the Fifteenth National Foreign Trade Convention* (New York, 1928), 170-172.

58. National City Bank, *Cuba, Review of Commercial, Industrial and Economic Conditions in 1919*, 3-4.

59. Theodore H. Price, "Cuba's Defense of Sugar," *Commerce and Finance* (March 10, 1926), 512.

60. *Monthly Bank Letter* (September, 1928), 146.

61. The *Monthly Bank Letter* hardly mentioned the tariff until 1929.

62. Jenks, *Cuban Colony*, 262-263.

63. Roy D. Chapin to Senator Reed Smoot, March 21, 1927, NA 611.373 Sugar/91. In 1921 the Chamber had supported the Cuban proposal for increasing the preferential, G. F. Bauer to Office of the Trade Advisor, August 31, 1921, NA 611.3731/109.

64. See, Philip B. Deane, "The Where in Profitable Exporting," *Official Report of the Thirteenth National Foreign Trade Convention* (New York, 1926), 351.

65. National City Bank, *Cuba, Review of Commercial, Industrial and Economic Conditions in 1919*, 5-6.

66. The Department generally knew what was going on, although Morrow filled them in on some of the details in September 1923 (Morrow to Munro, NA 611.373 Sugar/82) but it took little action.

67. Memorandum: Arthur N. Young, January 11, 1928, NA 611.3731/268. Young stressed the factors of proximity and investments as being the key to Cuban trade.

68. Atkins, *Sixty Years in Cuba*, 345, 347.

69. *The Cuba Review*, (December, 1928), 13.

NOTES FOR CHAPTER FOUR

1. Wright, *The Cuban Situation*, 86.

2. Buell, *Problems of the New Cuba*, 236. The term Insular Areas refers to the Philippine Islands, Puerto Rico, and Hawaii. Sugar was admitted duty free from these areas.

3. Senate, *Lobby Investigation*, Part 1, 375-401. The Cuba Company did own some sugar mills, but this was not its major business.

4. Members included the Cuba Cane Sugar Corporation, Cuban-American, Cuban-Dominican, Czarnikow-Rionda, Fidelity, General, Lowry, Manati, Punta Alegre, Tuinucu, and the Atlantic Fruit and Sugar Companies.

5. The association was composed of both Cubans and Americans. The Chadbourne Brothers were members of this group.

6. Senate, *Lobby Investigation*, Part 4, 1769-1770. Coca-Cola and Hershey furnished the bulk of the money for this group. H. H. Pike collected it and then disbursed it to Junior Owens of the Bottler's and William Baldwin, a professional lobbyist.

7. The only seaboard refining companies with Cuban holdings which worked with this group were Revere and Pennsylvania.

8. Senate, *Lobby Investigation*, Part 1, 375-401 (Lakin). The Lobby Investigation turned up much valuable material on this subject. The correspondence files of the lobbies were subpoenaed and many complete letters were printed in the record of the hearings. Information taken from letters will be cited the same as correspondence in a collection, while information taken from the testimony will be regularly cited with the name of the person testifying indicated in parenthesis after the page number.

9. *Ibid.;* and *ibid.*, Part 4, 1503.

10. *Ibid.*, Part 2, 1216. Shattuck had worked for several sugar companies during the tariff hearings of 1921-22. $10,000 contributors were the Cuba Company, Czarnikow-Rionda, United Fruit Company, Royal Bank of Canada, General Sugar Company (money supplied by the National City Bank), Cuban-American Sugar Company, Cuba Cane Sugar Corporation, and the Punta Alegre Sugar Company.

11. U. S., Congress, House, Committee on Ways and Means, *Hearings, Tariff Readjustment—1929*, 70th Cong., 2nd Sess., 1929, 3041. (Cited hereafter as *Tariff Hearings—1929*).

12. *Ibid.*, 3106 (Cannon Mills), 3126-3128 (Frank L. Allen Company), 3189 (Lakin and Shattuck).

13. *Ibid.*, 3171-3172, 3216.

14. Lakin to Shattuck, January 28, 1929, Senate, *Lobby Investigation*, Part 4, 1671.

15. Lakin to Crowder, January 29, 1929, *ibid.*, 1510.

16. *Ibid.*, 1724-1728 (Shattuck).

17. *Ibid.*, 1552 (Lakin); Lakin to Tarafa, February 1, 1929, *ibid.*, 1566; Lakin to Aballi, February 27, 1929, *ibid.*, 1540-1541.

18. Lakin to Tarafa, *ibid.*, 1566.

19. Lakin to The Secretary of Communications (Havana), February 19, 1929, *ibid.*, 1559-1560.

20. Lakin to the Czarnikow-Rionda Company, December 1928, *ibid.*, 1505.

21. Lakin to Machado, January 26, 1929, *ibid.*, 1507.

22. Lakin to Shattuck, February 9, 1929, *ibid.*, 1572; Machado to Lakin, March 1, 1929, *ibid.*, 1578-1579.

23. Lakin to Hayden (National City Bank), February 9, 1929, *ibid.*, 1571.

24. Lakin to Shattuck, February 9, 1929, *ibid.*, 1572.

25. Lakin to Machado, March 15, 1929, *ibid.*, 1583-1586; *ibid.*, 1552 (Lakin).

26. *Ibid.*; and, Lakin to Aballi, March 15, 1929, *ibid.*, 1598.

27. Crowder to Lakin, March 22, 1929, *ibid.*, 1607.

28. Noble to Lakin, February 18, 1929, *ibid.*, 1573-1574. The agency would engage in a form of cooperative marketing.

29. *New York Times* (April 18, 1929), 2:2; and (April 21, 1929), 6:1.

30. Crowder to Lakin, April 10, 1929, Senate, *Lobby Investigation*, 1691.

31. Tarafa to Lakin, April 20, 1929, *ibid.*, 1703.

32. Lakin to Tarafa, April 27, 1929, *ibid.*, 1704. Raymond L. Buell, *Problems of the New Cuba*, 243-244.

33. Lakin to Tarafa, May 15, 1929, Senate, *Lobby Investigation*, 1742. It was reported that Herbert Hoover had the Tariff Commission working on the sliding scale also.

34. Lakin to Shattuck, March 2, 1929, *ibid.*, 1683.

35. This was the Bottler's of Carbonated Beverages, the Hershey Corporation, and the H. H. Pike Company group. The efforts of this lobby were directed solely toward keeping down the tariff.

36. Lakin to Shattuck, February 7, 1929, Senate, *Lobby Investigation*, 1685.

37. *Ibid.*, 1697 (Lakin). Lakin was very evasive when questioned on this point, but finally admitted that Hull was the member.

38. Crowder to Lakin, April 10, 1929, *ibid.*, 1691. Frear to Lakin, April 4, 1929, *ibid.*, 1688. Frear asked Lakin to visit him since he had some matters to discuss with Lakin.

39. *New York Times* (April 18, 1929), 2:2.

40. Lakin to Mason B. Starring (California and Pittsburgh Utilities Corporation), April 16, 1929, Senate, *Lobby Investigation*, 1695. Bacharach was from New Jersey, and the other two were from Pennsylvania.

41. *Ibid.*, 1778-1780 (Owens). The telegrams from Lakin to these men were printed in the record, *ibid.*, 1692. Early in April Lakin requested Dr. Machado to use his DuPont connections to influence the Congressmen from Deleware. Machado sent Lakin a copy of the letter he had sent to Irenee DuPont, *ibid.*, 1688.

42. *New York Times* (May 9, 1929), 1:1.

43. *Ibid.*

44. *Ibid.*, (May 10, 1929), 2:3.

45. Owens to Pike, April 25, 1929, Senate, *Lobby Investigation*, 1779-1780.

46. *New York Times* (May 18, 1929), 4:4.

47. *Ibid.* (May 21, 1929), 1:5. Senate, *Lobby Investigation*, Part 5,

1957-1958. A copy of Mrs. Pratt's speech was in Mrs. Jones's files with the heading "Ruth's speech."

48. *New York Times* (May 23, 1929), 1:5.

49. Austin to Col. Gallagher (Continental Sugar Company), June 3, 1929, Senate, *Lobby Investigation*, Part 4, 1759-1760. Petriken testified that he called on Herbert Hoover and told him that the beet producers were not too enthused with the sliding scale idea; Petriken was the president of the Great Western Sugar Company.

50. *Ibid.* See also, *New York Times* (May 23, 1929), 1:5.

51. Senate, *Lobby Investigation*, Part 4, 1604-1605 (Lakin).

52. Baldwin to Pike, April 9, April 22, May 23, and June 4, 1929, *ibid.*, Part 5, 1822-1832. *New York Times* (June 7, 1929), 44:6.

53. Baldwin to Pike, April 22, May 23, and June 4, 1929, *ibid.*, Part 5, 1825, 1830, 1831.

54. *Ibid.*, 1822-1832.

55. *Ibid.*, April 22, 1929, 1826.

56. Staples to Pike, March 27, 1929, *ibid.*, 1821.

57. Lakin to Staples, April 24, 1929, *ibid.*, Part 4, 1700.

58. Memorandum: Conversation between Walter C. Thurston and Carl Byoir, May 6, 1929, NA 711.37/130.

59. NA 611.003/1916 (FR, 1929-I:998).

60. Memorandum by H. H. Pike, Jr., May 1929, Senate, *Lobby Investigation*, Part 5, 1871-1872. This businessman's opinion of lawmakers makes revealing reading; for example, "Shortridge . . . likely to speak for California interests. Whatever they'll want he'll want. C. & H. [California and Hawaiian Sugar Co.] will certainly tell Shortridge what to do."

61. *Ibid.*, 1872.

62. Pike to Hershey, June 19, 1929, *ibid.*, 1872.

63. U. S., Congress, Senate, Committee on Finance, *Hearings, The Tariff Act of 1929*, 71st Cong., 1st Sess., 1929, 19.

64. *Ibid.*, 190-220, 233, 181-187.

65. Elmer E. Schattschneider, *Politics, Pressures and the Tariff* (New York, 1935), 39, 99. The general course of the hearings is traced on pp. 32-34. Lakin later complained to Machado that "There is not much sentiment for American investments in Cuba. The Senators think that the investors are only a few bloated men of money." August 21, 1929, Senate, *Lobby Investigation*, Part 4, 1750.

66. Lakin to Machado, August 21, 1929, *ibid.*, Part 4, 1745. The Hawaiian interests had already rejected the sliding scale idea. *New York Times* (June 25, 1929), 4:2.

67. *Ibid.* (July 2, 1929), 1:8. *Monthly Bank Letter* (August 1929), 114. The Single Sales Agency went into effect on July 26, 1929, but it did not provide for production controls. Buell, *Problems of the New Cuba*, 243-244.

68. *The Cuba Review* (September 1929), 37.

69. *New York Times* (August 8, 1929), 30:1.

70. *Ibid.* Lakin to Machado, August 21, 1929, Senate, *Lobby Investigation*, Part 4, 1745.

71. *Ibid.*, 1747.

72. *Ibid.*, 1747-1748.

73. *The Cuba Review* (November 1929), 35.

74. *New York Times* (January 3, 1930), 13:4; and (January 18, 1930), 1:2.

75. *Ibid.* (January 17, 1930), 1:7.

76. *Congressional Record*, 71st Cong., 2nd Sess., 1930, Vol. 72, Part 2, 1932.

77. *Ibid.*, 1568-1569.

78. *Ibid.*, 1366-1367. The National City Bank did state at one time that the beet sugar industry did not need to be fostered if it required a high tariff to protect it, *Monthly Bank Letter* (August 1929), 114. There was no evidence of the plot mentioned.

79. *New York Times* (March 6, 1930), 1:2. *The Cuba Review* (April 1930), 34-35.

80. *Ibid.* (June 1930), 35-36.

81. Paul Y. Anderson, "Old Joe's Senate," *Nation* (March 26, 1930). One of the sugar lobbyists said that the *Nation* was a medium through which they could give their "most drastic opinions." Gladys Moon Jones to Shattuck, June 24, 1929, Senate, *Lobby Investigation*, Part 5, 1946.

82. Harry F. Guggenheim, *The United States and Cuba* (New York, 1934), 139.

83. *New York Times* (January 17, 1930), 22:1.

84. *Ibid.* (August 8, 1929), 30:1.

85. Connor, "National Farm Organizations and United States Tariff Policy in the 1920's," 41.

86. Mermey to Baldwin, September 17, October 2, October 22, 1929; Senate, *Lobby Investigation*, Part 5, 1834-1837.

87. House, *Tariff Hearings—1929*, 3126-3128.

88. *Monthly Bank Letter* (June 1929). *Congressional Record*, 71st Cong., 2nd Sess., 1930, Vol. 72, Part 2, 1369. Senate, *Tariff Hearings—1929*, 187. *The Cuba Review* (July 1929), 26-28.

89. The State Department files contained numerous examples of such Latin American editorials. Some of these were brought to the attention of President Hoover. Lakin to Shattuck, August 24, 1929, Senate, *Lobby Investigation*, Part 4, 1744.

90. The National City Bank was the best example of this due to its direct interest in the General Sugar Company.

91. Many of the refiners continued to oppose Cuban controls of any kind. See The American Sugar Refining Company, *Annual Report, 1929* (New York, 1930), 2; and *Annual Report, 1930* (New York, 1931), 2-6.

92. *The Cuba Review* (September 1930), 33-35. Thomas L. Chadbourne invested over two million dollars in the Cuban sugar industry after the deflation of 1920-21.

93. Wright, *The Cuban Situation*, 91-92. Gutierrez maintained that a "gentleman's agreement" had been made, and that the American domestic and insular producers did not honor it. Gutierrez, *The World Sugar Problem*, 85.

94. *Ibid.* "Mr. Chadbourne Makes a Plan," *Fortune* (July 1931), 23.

95. Buell, *Problems of the New Cuba*, 236.

96. Pan American Union, *Fourth Pan American Commercial Conference Proceedings* (3 vols., Washington, 1931), 1:71. Speech by Thomas L. Chadbourne.

97. NA 637.11171/8. The Cuban Chamber of Commerce in the United

States was described as "an American organization representing manu-
facturers, ship lines, and investors." Similar views were expressed in:
The Cuba Review (July 1930), 16; remarks of Henry Lauten to the
Textile Export Association of the United States, National Foreign Trade
Council, *Official Report of the Eighteenth National Foreign Trade Con-
vention* (New York, 1931), 104.

98. Thomas L. Chadbourne, *Cuba and Sugar Stabilization* (NP, 1931), 5,
13-16.

99. Pan American Union, *Fourth Pan American Commercial Conference
Proceedings*, 3:36-37. On November 6, 1931 Shepard Morgan, of the Chase
National Bank, told the Assistant Secretary of State that the sugar tariff
should be reduced, since sugar was the fundamental problem in the
Cuban economy. Memorandum, NA 837.51/1484.

100. Milo H. Woolman to Senator Royal S. Copeland, June 9, 1932,
NA 611.373 Sugar/157. Woolman was director of the Acme Garment
Cutting School.

101. *New York Times* (October 8, 1932), 25:2. After the signing of the
Ottawa Agreement A. D. Hutcheson stated that the United States must
revise the reciprocity treaty in order to compete with Britain; *ibid.*, (August
26, 1932), 6:8. See also, Howard Mingos, "Sugar and the Tariff," *Commerce and Finance* (November 2, 1932), 1313-1314.

102. H. H. Pike, Jr., "Our Trade With Cuba: An Examination of Our
Only Reciprocity Treaty," *Official Report of the Twentieth National Foreign
Trade Convention* (New York, 1933), 129-134.

103. The American Sugar Refining Company, *Annual Report, 1933* (New
York, 1934), 9-10.

104. *Ibid.*, 35-37; see also *Annual Reports* for 1931 and 1932.

NOTES FOR CHAPTER FIVE

1. *The Cuba Review* (November 1920), 21.

2. For example, see C. D. Snow (Chamber of Commerce of the United
States) to the Department of State, December 17, 1923, NA 811.71537/36.
The Cuba Review (September 1923), 28.

3. *Ibid.* This law was first passed on July 26, 1866, and the provisions
were repeated in the Tariff Act of August 1894.

4. NA 811.71537/42.

5. Dispatch, "U.S.–Cuban Postal Conference," February 20, 1925, NA
811.71537/45. The time limit was raised to eighteen months in the final
draft.

6. Rochester, New York, Chamber of Commerce to Frank B. Kellogg,
June 11, 1925, NA 811.71537/46.

7. Julius Klein, "Cuban Markets for American Goods," *The Cuba
Review* (August 1925), 19.

8. National Foreign Trade Council, *Official Report of the Twelfth
National Foreign Trade Convention* (New York, 1925), ix.

9. W. Irving Glover (Second Assistant Postmaster General) to the
Secretary of State, October 31, 1925, NA 811.71537/50.

10. Dr. William Manning to Francis White, October 27, 1925, NA 811.71537/51.

11. Manning to Stokely W. Morgan and White, September 24, 1925, NA 811.71537/49.

12. William R. Vallance to Joseph Grew, March 3, 1926, NA 811.71537/58.

13. *Ibid.*

14. Vallance to Grew, March 11, 1926, NA 811.71537/58.

15. Enoch Crowder to the Secretary of State, May 7, 1926, NA 811.71537/65.

16. Document File Note, Crowder to the Secretary of State, June 3, 1926, NA 811.71537/70.

17. Vallance to Grew, April 17, 1926, NA 811.71537/58.

18. National Foreign Trade Council, *Official Report of the Thirteenth National Foreign Trade Convention* (New York, 1926), ix.

19. Resolution, Chamber of Commerce of the State of New York, May 6, 1926, NA 811.71537/66. Resolution, Chamber of Commerce of the United States, May 27, 1926, NA 811.71537/69.

20. Vallance to Grew, April 17, 1926, NA 811.71537/58; Memorandum, Manning to Jordan Stabler, August 17, 1926, NA 811.71537/71.

21. O. K. Davis to Arthur N. Young, NA 811.71537/73. This, and other material, was sent to General Crowder by the department, Jordan Stabler to Enoch Crowder, November 8, 1926, NA 811.71537/74a.

22. "U.S.–Cuban Parcel Post Propaganda," NA 811.71537/71. Clipping from August 17, 1926 issue included with memorandum by Manning of the same date.

23. Article sent to the department by the National Foreign Trade Council, September 25, 1926, NA 811.71537/72.

24. Press release from the Chamber of Commerce Press Service, sent to the department, February 17, 1927, NA 811.71537/87.

25. Lloyd Blair to Stokely Morgan, March 28, 1927, NA 811.71537/81.

26. U. S., Congress, House, Committee on Ways and Means, *Act to Amend Sections 2804 and 3402 of the Revised Statutes of the United States,* 69th Cong., 2nd Sess., 1927, H. Rept. 1816 to accompany H. R. 8997. (Cited hereafter as *H. Rept. 1816, 1927.*)

27. U. S., Congress, House, Committee on Ways and Means, *Act to Amend Sections 2804 and 3402 of the Revised Statutes of the United States,* 70th Cong., 1st Sess., 1928, H. Rept. 636, to accompany H. R. 9195. (Cited hereafter as *H. Rept. 636, 1928.*) The modus vivendi is printed on pp. 11-12.

28. National Foreign Trade Council, *Official Report of the Fourteenth National Foreign Trade Convention* (New York, 1927), ix.

29. J. Butler Wright to O. K. Davis, April 21, 1926, NA 811.71537/60.

30. John W. O'Leary (President of the Chamber of Commerce of the United States) to Frank B. Kellogg, May 27, 1926. Note attached to same letter, Manning to Morgan and William Beck, June 3, 1926, NA 811.71537/69.

31. Memorandum: Manning to White, April 22, 1927, NA 611.3731/232.

32. NA 811.71537/91.

33. National Archives: Senate Records; General Files (Finance Com-

mittee files on the Parcel Post Convention, 70th Cong., 1st Sess., 1927-28). Record Group No. 46.

34. See, for example, Philadelphia Board of Trade to the President of the United States, January 18, 1928, NA 811.71537/97. This letter said that there were over ninety merchants and manufacturers in the area availing themselves "extensively" of the parcel post service with Cuba. They would lose out to European competitors if the service were terminated.

35. House, *H. Rept. 636, 1928,* 1.

36. NA 811.71537/93.

37. Memorandum: Manning to Morgan, "Introduction of proposed legislation to remove restrictions on the entry of Cuban cigars desired before the President's arrival at Habana," January 11, 1928, NA 811.71537/74.

38. O. K. Davis to Arthur N. Young, January 13, 1928, NA 811.71537/96.

39. House, *H. Rept. 636, 1928,* 1.

40. O. K. Davis to Jordan Stabler, February 18, 1928, NA 811.71537/101.

41. Memorandum: Arthur N. Young to Manning, February 25, 1928, NA 811.71537/103. A treaty was under "hasty consideration" just prior to the termination of the convention. Memorandum: Manning to Barnes, June 14, 1928, NA 811.71537/110.

42. *Congressional Record,* 70th Cong., 1st Sess., 1928, Vol. 69, Part 5, 5316-5319.

43. Clarke and Courts (Manufacturing Stationers, Galveston, Texas) to Clay S. Briggs (Representative, Texas), March 6, 1928, NA 811.71537/104; Alexis Caswell (Manufacturers' Association of Minneapolis) to Senator Thomas D. Schall, March 10, 1928, NA 811.71537/105.

44. National Foreign Trade Council, *Official Report of the Fifteenth National Foreign Trade Convention* (New York, 1928), x.

45. Memorandum: Manning to Charles M. Barnes (Treaty Division), June 14, 1928, NA 811.71537/110. This was one of the last items in the file.

46. *The Cuba Review* (October 1928), 24.

47. *Congressional Record,* 70th Cong., 2nd Sess., 1929, Vol. 70, Part 2, 1874-1875.

48. The repeal provision was not mentioned in the hearings. The tariff act was written by the majority party (see Schattschneider, *Politics, Pressures and the Tariff,* 32-34, for details), and at least two of the Republican members of the committee (Henry Watson and Carl Chindblom) were advocates of the repeal provision. Thus, it is a reasonable assumption that they were instrumental in writing the provision into the act (paragraph 4, section 647).

49. *New York Times* (May 8, 1929), 22:3, 4.

50. Senate, *Tariff Hearings–1929,* Vol. XVII, 159, 612, 170.

51. National Foreign Trade Council, *Official Report of the Seventeenth National Foreign Trade Convention* (New York, 1930), ix.

52. U. S., Congress, House, Committee on Ways and Means, *Hearings, Limiting the Importation Packages of Cigars,* 70th Cong., 2nd Sess., 1930, 5, 24-25.

53. *Ibid.,* 24-25, 15-24.

54. *Ibid.*, 5.

55. For statements of approval, see *The Cuba Review* (August 1930), 11; and, the Resolution of the Middle West Foreign Trade Conference of October 1930, in, *Congressional Record*, 71st Cong., 3rd Sess., 1931, Vol. 74, Part 5, 5152.

NOTES FOR CHAPTER SIX

1. Memorandum: "The Outlook for Cuban Sugar," Chester Lloyd Jones to General Crowder, November 10, 1921, Chester Lloyd Jones Mss. See also, Memorandum: Boaz Long to Robert Lansing February 15, 1918, NA 711.13/55. This memorandum, discussed in Chapter I, has similar arguments.

2. *The Cuba Review* (April 1919), 11.

3. William E. Gonzales to the Secretary of State, May 29, 1919, NA 837.00/1554.

4. William Phillips to the American Legation (Habana), October 20, 1919, NA 837.00/1581a.

5. Long to Secretary of State, Attention Norman H. Davis, NA 837.00/1761 (FR, 1920-II:22).

6. September 23, 1920, NA 837.00/1761 (FR, 1920-II:23).

7. September 25, 1920, NA 837.00/1769 (FR, 1920-II:23).

8. Long to Colby, October 1, 1920, NA 837.00/1791 (FR, 1920-II:24).

9. Long to Colby, October 5, 1920, NA 837.00/1797 (FR, 1920-II:25).

10. Woodrow Wilson to Norman H. Davis (Under Secretary of State), October 18, 1920, *Confidential*, NA 837.00/2117. Colby to Long, October 20, 1920, NA 837.00/1809 (FR, 1920-II:29).

11. Chauncey D. Snow (Chamber of Commerce of the United States), to Wesley Frost (Acting Foreign Trade Advisor), December 13, 1920, NA 837.51/386.

12. Frost to Snow, December 14, 1920, NA 837.51/386.

13. Davis to Long, January 4, 1921, NA 837.516/55a (FR, 1921-I:773).

14. Long to the Secretary of State, January 20, 1921, NA 837.516/61 (FR, 1921-I:774).

15. April 13, 1921, NA 837.516/64 (FR, 1921-I:789).

16. J. P. Morgan & Company to the Secretary of State (Attention, Sumner Welles), November 8, 1920, NA 837.51/362.

17. Long to the Secretary of State, November 18, 1920, NA 837.51/367. Long recommended that a financial expert be sent. He stated: "We owe a certain element of protection to Americans who now have so much at stake in Cuba."

18. Colby to Long, November 26, 1920, NA 837.51/371.

19. Long to Colby, November 18, 1920, NA 837.51/367.

20. Long to the Secretary of State, December 21, 1920, NA 837.51/399.

21. Davis and Wilson—with, possibly, some help from Welles—were formulating Cuban policy during 1920 and early 1921. This is evident from the confidential correspondence which passed between them. Davis

continued to hold a financial interest in Cuba (The Trust Company of Cuba) during this period.

22. Davis to Crowder, NA 837.00/1952b (FR, 1920-II:41).

23. Crowder to the Secretary of State, January 27, 1921, NA 837.00/1972 (FR, 1921-I:674).

24. Memorandum by Sumner Welles, March 1, 1921, NA 837.00/2216.

25. Jenks, *Cuban Colony*, 241. These bills were passed by January 31, 1921.

26. Frank Steinhart to Charles Evans Hughes, April 28, 1921, NA 837.00/2102. President of the Pressed Steel Car Company to Charles Evans Hughes, May 2, 1921, NA 837.00/2102. Edward McConnell & Sons to the Foreign Trade Advisor, March 21, 1921, NA 837.51/466.

27. Crowder to Hughes, July 1, 1921, NA 837.51/504 (FR, 1921-I:703).

28. J. P. Morgan & Company to the Secretary of State, July 13, 1921, NA 837.51/515 (FR, 1921-I:705).

29. Hughes to J. P. Morgan & Co., July 9, 1921, NA 837.51/515a; Hughes to Crowder, July 15, 1921, NA 837.51/504 (FR, 1921-I:706).

30. Crowder to Hughes, July 3, 1921, NA 837.51/508.

31. Memorandum: "Cuban Financial Situation," Welles to Hughes, July 28, 1921, NA 837.51/743 (FR, 1921-I:711).

32. Hughes to Crowder, September 24, 1921, NA 837.51/594a (FR, 1921-I:733).

33. Dwight W. Morrow to the President of Cuba, October 7, 1921, NA 837.51/624.

34. Alfredo Zayas to Dwight W. Morrow, October 8, 1921, NA 837.51/624.

35. Morrow to Zayas, October 11, 1921, NA 837.51/624.

36. Crowder to Hughes, October 9, 1921, NA 837.51/610 (FR, 1921-I:737).

37. J. P. Morgan & Co. to the Secretary of State, October 17, 1921, Hughes to J. P. Morgan & Co., October 20, 1921, NA 837.51/624; Hughes to Crowder, October 20, 1921, NA 837.51/610 (FR, 1921-I:759).

38. J. P. Morgan & Company to the Secretary of State, October 25, 1921, and, Charles Evans Hughes to J. P. Morgan & Company, November 1, 1921, NA 837.51/626.

39. Crowder to Hughes, November 16, 1921, NA 837.51/643 (FR, 1921-I:757); Crowder to Hughes, November 27, 1921, NA 837.51/652 (FR, 1921-I:652).

40. George Rahmann & Company to the Secretary of State, August 10, 1921, NA 837.51/545; letter and resolution, C. E. Dodson (Southern Lumber Exporter's Association) to George B. Christian (Secretary to the President), September 24, 1921, NA 837.51/595; G. M. Milam (New Orleans Board of Trade) to Warren Harding, October 20, 1921, NA 837. 51/625; letter and resolution, Malcolm Stewart (Cincinnati Chamber of Commerce Foreign Trade Association) to the Secretary of State, November 23, 1921, NA 837.51/651; *The Cuba Review* (November 1921), 10.

41. Memorandum: Conversation between Henry P. Fletcher and Herbert C. Lakin (Cuba Company), December 28, 1921, NA 837.51/1027; Lawrence Turnure & Company to the Secretary of State, September 19, 1921, NA 837.51/590; Frank Robins (Frank Robins Company, Havana)

to Herbert Hoover, January 23, 1922, and, Frank Robins to Charles Evans Hughes, January 11, 1922, NA 837.00P81/20.

42. Frank Robins to General Enoch Crowder, January 21, 1922, NA 837.00P81/20.

43. Charles Evans Hughes to President Warren Harding, December 28, 1921, NA 837.51/672 (FR, 1921-I:772). This position was taken by Dwight Morrow in the memorandum (Sugar Restriction in Cuba) which he sent to Hoover on December 11, 1921, NA 611.373 Sugar/82.

44. Hughes to Harding, December 28, 1921, NA 837.51/672 (FR, 1921-I:772).

45. A. Shaler Williams (Havana) to the Secretary of State, April 7, 1921, NA 837.00P81/21; Frank Robins to Charles Evans Hughes, January 11, 1922, NA 837.00P81/20.

46. Nicholson, *Dwight Morrow*, 265. Morrow became convinced that Cuba needed a small loan to preserve her credit as a result of his trip to Cuba in October 1921, Morrow to Zayas, October 7, 1921, NA 837.51/624.

47. Robins to Hoover, January 23, 1922, NA 837.00P81/20. Robins complained about the attitude of nonresident interests which would loan money without strict supervision (that is, to make sure that the Cuban Government paid its resident creditors such as Robins).

48. Henry P. Fletcher to Dwight Morrow, January 11, 1922, NA 837.51/682a. Personal and Confidential.

49. Hughes to Crowder, January 21, 1922, NA 837.51/696a (FR, 1922-I:1006). This was the official beginning of the "moralization" program. David A. Lockmiller states that he has examined "authentic copies of the original memoranda" in the Crowder Papers, and that numbers one through fourteen were delivered between February 24, 1922 and July 21, 1922. The last one was delivered on July 15, 1923. David A. Lockmiller, *Enoch H. Crowder, Soldier, Lawyer and Statesman* (Columbia, Missouri, 1955), 233.

50. Morrow to Zayas, October 7, 1921, and, J. P. Morgan & Company to the Secretary of State, October 17, 1921, NA 837.51/624.

51. Crowder to Hughes, March 25, 1922, NA 837.51/746 (FR, 1922-I:1016). These were Memoranda nos. 6 and 7. Crowder told the Cubans to reduce the budget to fifty-five million dollars, the same figure specified by Morrow in October 1921 (NA 837.51/624).

52. Memorandum: Dana Munro to the Secretary of State, April 10, 1922, NA 837.51/756 (FR, 1922-I:1022).

53. Hughes to Crowder, April 11, 1922, NA 837.51/749 (FR, 1922-I:1023).

54. Elliot C. Bacon (J. P. Morgan & Co.) to General Crowder, January 22, 1923, NA 837.51/931. This was a general review of the 1922 talks between the bankers and Crowder.

55. Crowder to Hughes, June 14, 1922, NA 837.51/793 (FR, 1922-I:1033).

56. *The Cuba Review* (December 1922), 13. The protest was submitted on July 3, 1922.

57. *Ibid.*, 10.

58. Phillips to Crowder, September 14, 1922, NA 837.51/842 (FR, 1922-I:1042).

59. Memorandum: Munro to White, December 18, 1922, NA 837.51/945. The stock comments, adopted after the loan announcement of March 1922, were, "Offers no objection," and, "unable to view . . . with favor at this time"; see, Herbert Feis, *The Diplomacy of the Dollar* (Baltimore, 1950), 10-12.

60. Memorandum: White to Hughes, December 21, 1922, NA 837.51/944.

61. Morrow to Hughes, December 28, 1922, Charles Evans Hughes Papers (Library of Congress, Washington, D. C.). (Cited hereafter as Hughes Mss.)

62. Hughes to Morrow, January 3, 1923, Hughes Mss.

63. The bonds carried an interest rate of 5½ percent, and gave the syndicate a profit of $55,087.41. The syndicate was composed of Morgan & Co., Guaranty Co., Harris, Forbes & Co., Kuhn, Loeb & Co., J. & W. Seligman, The National City Co., Banker's Trust Co. of New York, Dillon, Read. Senate *Sale of Foreign Bonds*, Part 1, 162, 280-281.

64. Memorandum: telephone call, Morrow to Hughes, January 13, 1923, NA 837.51/924.

65. Senate, *Sale of Foreign Bonds*, 280-283.

66. September 19, 1921, NA 837.00/2166.

67. September 28, 1921, NA 837.00/2166.

68. August 2, 1922, NA 837.00/2242.

69. Note: Phillips (Under Secretary) to Hughes, December 5, 1922, NA 837.00/2281. Crowder thought that the post should be raised to Embassy level.

70. Morrow to Hughes, Hughes Mss.

71. December 28, 1922, NA 837.00/2290.

72. John A. Campbell (Trenton Potteries Co.) to Senator Walter E. Edge, January 8, 1923, NA 837.00/2290; Wiley Blair (Southwest National Bank of Dallas, Texas) to Senator Charles A. Culberson, January 10, 1923, NA 837.00/2296; George Meyercord (American Manufacturers Foreign Credit Insurance Exchange) to the State Department, January 9, 1923, NA 837.00/2291; Theodore Solter (M. Werk Co.) to Senator Frank B. Willis, January 10, 1923, NA 837.00/2291; B. F. Geyer (Wayne Tank and Pump Co.) to Congressman Louis Fairfield, January 15, 1923, NA 837.00/2297.

73. Senator Walter E. Edge (New Jersey) to Charles Evans Hughes, January 9, 1923, NA 837.00/2290; Senator Charles A. Culberson (Texas) to the President of the United States, January 15, 1923, NA 837.00/2296; Senator Joseph E. Ransdell (Louisiana) to Hughes, January 15, 1923, NA 837.00/2295; Note for Secretary Hughes *in re* visit of Senator Claude Swanson (Virginia), January 15, 1923, NA 837.00/2298.

74. Hughes to Morrow, January 3, 1923, Hughes Mss.

75. *The Cuba Review* (October 1921), 15.

76. Lockmiller, *Enoch Crowder*, 237-238.

77. Crowder to Hughes, May 5, 1923, NA 837.51637/2 (FR, 1923-I:862).

78. Hughes to Crowder, June 29, 1923, NA 837.51637/07a (FR, 1923-I:865).

79. Letter from Crowder to Hughes, July 15, 1923, quoted in Lockmiller, *Enoch Crowder*, 244.

80. Memorandum: to Under Secretary Phillips, conversation between John M. Draper and Francis White, October 3, 1923, NA 837.00/2373.

81. Memorandum: conversation between Secretary Hughes and the Cuban Ambassador (Torriente), November 15, 1923, NA 711.37/73½ (FR, 1923-I:850).

82. Fitzgibbon, *Cuba and the United States*, 184.

83. Some people even accused Zayas of staging the revolt in order to gain prestige in American eyes for putting it down.

84. Jenks, *Cuban Colony*, 265; Fitzgibbon, *Cuba and the United States*, 180; Lockmiller, *Enoch Crowder*, 244.

85. Robert Lansing to William G. McAdoo, August 13, 1917, *Foreign Relations 1918*, 298.

86. Memorandum: Dana Munro to Sumner Welles, February 28, 1922, NA 711.13/59.

87. Memorandum: Sumner Welles and others, "Summary of Questions Pending Between the United States and the Republics of Latin America," February 27, 1922, NA 710.11/568.

88. Crowder to Hughes, September 11, 1921, NA 837.51/584.

89. Memorandum: Sumner Welles, March 1, 1921, NA 837.00/2216.

90. Memorandum: Welles to Hughes, July 28, 1921, NA 837.51/743.

91. Memorandum: Dana Munro, April 10, 1922, NA 837.51/756.

92. Crowder to Henry P. Fletcher, October 29, 1921, NA 837.51/632½; Nicholson, *Dwight Morrow*, 264; Steinhart to Hughes, April 28, 1921, NA 837.00/2102. Steinhart was writing on behalf of the American Chamber of Commerce of Cuba. *The Cuba Review* (August 1921), 32.

93. Crowder to Hughes, September 7, 1921, NA 837.51/538; see also, Memorandum: Welles to Hughes, July 28, 1921, NA 837.51/743.

94. *El Mundo* (August 30, 1923), as quoted in Jenks, *Cuban Colony*, 263-264.

95. NA 837.51/931.

96. Zayas to Crowder, February 1, 1923, NA 837.51/931.

97. Chapman, *History of the Cuban Republic*, 504.

98. For examples, see *The Cuba Review* (June 1924), 12; and speech by Dwight Morrow to a luncheon in honor of President Gerardo Machado, *New York Times* (April 23, 1925), 20:8.

99. Memorandum: conversation between Secretary Hughes and the Cuban Ambassador, November 15, 1923, NA 711.37/73½.

100. Memorandum: "Our Central American Policy," Francis White to Joseph Grew (Under Secretary), November 7, 1924, NA 711.13/65.

NOTES FOR CHAPTER SEVEN

1. *New York Times* (June 22, 1922), 3:6. Examples of this resentment can be found in: Luis Machado, "El Derecho De Intervention," *Cuba Contemporánea* (August 1922), 337-350; Enrique Jose Varona, "Una Carta y su Comentario," *Cuba Contemporánea* (May 1922), 5-10; Raul Cardenas, "La Preponderancia De Los Estados Unidos En El Mar Caribe," *Cuba Contemporánea* (March 1921), 221-237.

2. Anita S. Carter, "Our Shadow in Cuba," *New York Times* (July 16, 1922), VI, 4:1.

3. Fitzgibbon, *Cuba and the United States,* 177. See also, Emilio Roig de Leuchsenring, "La Enmienda Platt, su Interpretación Primativa y sus Aplicaciones Posteriores," *Cuba Contemporánea* (August 1922), 305-336. The Root interpretation was elaborated in a wire from Secretary of War Root to General Leonard Wood in 1901. The heart of it stated: "The intervention described in the third clause of the Platt Amendment is not synonymous with intermeddling or interference with the affairs of the Cuban Government. . . ."

4. The files of the State Department contain numerous clippings and cartoons from Cuban newspapers since the department desired to be kept informed about public opinion in Cuba (the same thing applied to all of Latin America). The department also questioned visitors from Cuba, or people who were informed about the island, about the feelings of Cubans and any anti-American activities; see for example, Memorandum: Conversation of Henry P. Fletcher with Herbert C. Lakin, December 28, 1921, NA 837.51/1027.

5. *New York Times* (May 25, 1921), 19:2.

6. *Ibid.* (January 27, 1922), 6:2, (January 31, 1922), 24:4.

7. Nicholson, *Dwight Morrow,* 264; see also, *The Cuba Review,* (August 1921), 32.

8. See, for example, Elliot Bacon to General Crowder, January 22, 1923, NA 837.51/931 (FR, 1923-I:839). The term "Bolshevist" with all its connotations was often applied to strikers or to agitators of any kind.

9. Lakin to Hughes, August 18, 1921, NA 837.00/2155.

10. Albert B. Fall to Henry P. Fletcher, April 20, 1921, NA 837.00/2202.

11. Lakin to Hughes, April 23, 1921, NA 837.00/2116. Edwin Denby to Hughes, June 17, 1921, NA 837.00/2140.

12. *Ibid.*

13. Hughes to Denby, July 6, 1921, NA 837.00/2140.

14. Lakin to Hughes, August 18, 1921, NA 837.00/2155.

15. Hughes to Lakin, August 29, 1921, NA 837.00/2155.

16. Memorandum: "Withdrawal of Marine Garrison from Camaguey," Crowder to Hughes, December 12, 1921, NA 837.00/2183.

17. Memorandum: Conversation between Lakin and Fletcher, December 28, 1921, NA 837.51/1027.

18. Lakin to Crowder, January 3, 1922, enclosed in, Lakin to Fletcher, January 3, 1922, NA 837.00/2194.

19. Memorandum: "Withdrawal of Marines from Camaguey," Welles to Hughes, January 23, 1922, NA 837.00/2199.

20. Hughes to Denby, January 24, 1922, NA 837.00/2184 (FR, 1922-I:1052); Denby to Hughes, January 26, 1922, NA 837.00/2195 (FR, 1922-I:1053).

21. Lakin to Hughes, August 2, 1922, NA 837.00/2242. The Cuba Company was the only American group to complain about the removal of the marines.

22. *New York Times* (January 26, 1922), 1:7. The Cuban Minister sent a strong protest to the department on January 25.

23. Janet D. Frost, "Cuban-American Relations Concerning the Isle

of Pines," *Hispanic American Historical Review* (August 1931), 336. The court case was *Percy v. Stranahan.*

24. Luis Machado, "La Isla De Pinos, De Hecho y De Derecho, Es Territorio Cubano," *Cuba Contemporánea* (April 1922), 253-263. Aurelio Hevia, "Los Derechos De Cuba Sobre La Isla De Pinos," *Cuba Contemporánea* (March 1924), 177-203, (April 1924), 285-303.

25. Memorandum: Harrison to Hughes, August 11, 1922, NA 837.014P/171.

26. Harding to Hughes, October 9, 1922, NA 837.014P/167.

27. Hughes to Harding, November 18, 1922, NA 837.014P/167.

28. Harding to Lodge, November 28, 1922; George B. Christian, Jr. (Secretary to the President) to Hughes, November 28, 1922, NA 837.014P/169.

29. Lodge to Harding, November 29, 1922; Harding to Hughes, December 1, 1922, NA 837.014P/170.

30. U. S., Congress, Senate, Committee on Foreign Relations, *Adjustment of Title to Isle of Pines,* 67th Cong., 4th Sess., 1922, S. Rept. 1.

31. U. S., Congress, Senate, *Papers Relating to the Adjustment of Title to the Ownership of the Isle of Pines,* 68th Cong., 2nd Sess., 1924, S. Document 166.

32. According to official estimates 10,000 Americans owned 90 percent of the property on the island, but only 700 were residents. U. S., Congress, Senate, *American Property Interests in the Isle of Pines,* 67th Cong., 4th Sess., 1923, S. Document 295.

33. National Archives: Senate Records; General Files (Foreign Relations Committee files on the Isle of Pines Treaty, 68th Cong., 2nd Sess., 1924-25). Record Group number 46.

34. Francis H. Knauff (New Jersey Dept., United Spanish War Veterans) to President Coolidge, November 28, 1924, NA 837.014P/300.

35. Capt. Eldridge Colby (U.S.A.), "The Isle of Pines Controversy," *The Cuba Review* (October 1924), 22; Fernando Ortiz, "Cuba's Title to the Isle of Pines," *The Cuba Review* (December 1924), 14-20.

36. January 21, 1925, NA 837.014P/337. The President decided not to send a statement.

37. *Congressional Record,* 69th Cong., 1st Sess., 1925, Vol. 67, Part 1, 188. The Pan American Society was composed of leading American businessmen (Minor C. Keith, John L. Merrill were two examples).

38. *The Cuba Review* (February 1925), 13.

39. *Monthly Bulletin* (January 1925 [?]), as printed in, *Congressional Record,* 68th Cong., 2nd Sess., Vol. 66, Part 4, 1925, 3603.

40. *The Cuba Review* (February 1925), 13.

41. Memorandum: "Population of Cuba and Isle of Pines and United States Investments Therein," December 1924, based in part on a telephone conversation with the Commerce Department concerning American investments in Cuba, December 10, 1924, NA 837.014P/313.

42. Hughes to Cosme de la Torriente (Cuban Ambassador), December 3, 1924, NA 837.014P/301; Hughes to Senator Joseph T. Robinson, January 2, 1925, NA 837.014P/324 (FR, 1925-II:1).

43. *Congressional Record,* 68th Cong., 2nd Sess., 1925, Vol. 66, Part 3, 1864-1865.

44. *Congressional Record*, 69th Cong., 1st Sess., 1925, Vol. 67, Part 1, 190.

45. *Ibid.*, 142-144.

46. *Ibid.*, 141-142.

47. *Ibid.*, 137, 139, 190. The Senators in the above paragraph were from (starting with Fletcher) Florida, Connecticut, Illinois, Maryland, New York, and Ohio.

48. *Ibid.*, 139, statement by Senator Wadsworth. The three opposition Senators mentioned were from Ohio, New York, and Idaho.

49. *Ibid.*, 206. The opposition group was a heterogeneous assortment with such men as Bob LaFollette (Wisconsin), Henrik Shipstead (Minnesota), Lynn J. Frazier (North Dakota), Cole Blease (South Carolina), and Tom Heflin (Alabama). Most of the opposition was based on three factors: (1) the protests of the nonresident property owners; (2) the fear that American residents would not be treated justly by Cuba; (3) the nationalistic desire to hold on to territory.

50. *The Cuba Review* (April 1925), 12.

51. U. S., Congress, House, Committee on Immigration and Naturalization, *Hearings, The Restriction of Immigration*, 68th Cong., 1st Sess., 1924, 1097-1098.

52. Hughes to Torriente, February 21, 1924, NA 150.01/806 Supplemental (FR, 1924-I:224).

53. U. S., Congress, Senate, Committee on Immigration, *Hearings, Restriction of Western Hemisphere Immigration*, 70th Cong., 1st Sess., 1928, 164.

NOTES FOR CHAPTER EIGHT

1. Quoted in, Jenks, *Cuban Colony*, 340.

2. An article by Machado in *El Dia* (May 9, 1922) was one of the first steps in this campaign; quoted in *ibid.*, 270.

3. *The Cuba Review* (December 1924), 12, a report extolling the virtues of Machado. Shutan (Military Attaché) to the Adjutant General, October 18, 1923, NA 837.00/2419, reports that Machado called Frank Steinhart to request that the United States take preventive action against the Veterans movement.

4. Memorandum: Conversation between R. L. Clarkson and Karl A. Panthen (Chase Securities Corporation), June 15, 1925, Senate, *Stock Exchange Practices*, Pt. 5, 2654-2655. The Senate hearings on Stock Exchange Practices and the Sale of Foreign Bonds were similar to the Lobby Investigation. The material will be cited in the same manner as the Lobby hearing.

5. Senate, *Lobby Investigation*, Pt. 3, 1264-1266, 1278. Carroll was a representative of six railroads, The United Fruit Company, The Cuba Company, Royal Dutch Shell, and legal advisor for the Cuban Embassy.

6. White to Crowder, April 23, 1925, NA 033.3711/32a; White stated that Machado created a "favorable impression" on the department.

7. *New York Times* (April 23, 1925), 20:8. See also, *The Cuba Review* (May 1925), 33.

8. *The Cuba Review* (August 1925), 9.

9. *Ibid.* (October 1925), 10.

10. Kellogg to Crowder, October 26, 1926, NA 837.48/29.

11. Martin Egan (Morgan and Co.) to Joseph Grew, November 3, 1926, NA 837.48/68.

12. *The Cuba Review* (October 1925), 16. Machado was reported to have boasted, in the United States, that no strike in Cuba lasted longer than twenty-four hours. Erna Fergusson, *Cuba* (New York, 1946), 254.

13. Crowder to Secretary of State, December 6, 1926, NA 837.00/2623.

14. *Commerce and Finance* (May 4, 1927), 903-904. *The Cuba Review* (May 1927), 19-20.

15. *New York Times* (April 28, 1927), 22.

16. *Ibid.* (April 29, 1927), 20:8.

17. *Ibid.* (May 6, 1927), 2:5.

18. Fitzgibbon, *Cuba and the United States*, 187.

19. Raymond L. Buell, "Cuba and the Platt Amendment," *Foreign Policy Association Information Service* (April 17, 1929), 39-40. Wright, *Cuban Situation*, 43.

20. Crowder to Kellogg, February 14, 1927, Personal & Confidential, NA 837.00/2627.

21. Buell, "Cuba and the Platt Amendment," 42-43.

22. J. B. Frisbie to Kellogg, June 26, 1926, NA 437.11/17.

23. Hartenstein to Members of the American Chamber of Commerce of Cuba, June 17, 1926, NA 437.11/16. See also A. H. Lamborn, "Cuba Asserts Herself," *Commerce and Finance* (January 26, 1927), 230-231. The editor of the magazine attacked the idea of intervention. Three sets of claims were involved: Charles J. Harrah, Capt. Walter F. Smith, and Joseph E. Barlow. The Barlow claim caused the most controversy, and Harry Guggenheim wrote that a Cuban junta used the "claims racket" to try to turn Americans against Machado. Guggenheim, *The United States and Cuba*, 180.

24. Harold Williamson (Chargé d'Affaires *ad interim*) to Kellogg, October 5, 1927, NA 711.37/109; marked "Strictly Confidential."

25. *Congressional Record*, 70th Cong., 1st Sess., 1928, Vol. 69, Part 5, 4738; Part 6, 6591.

26. *Ibid.*, Part 7, 7193-7194.

27. April 26, 1929, NA 837.00/2749. The 1929 convention of the AFL adopted a resolution calling for an investigation of conditions in Cuba. Buell, *Problems of the New Cuba*, 187.

28. Conversation between Francis White and W. W. Lancaster, July 25, 1929, NA 837.00/2755.

29. *New York Times* (September 20, 1929), 1:6, 6:3, resolution printed in full.

30. Senate, *Lobby Investigation*, Part 2, 1217 (Lakin); Part 3, 1264-1266, 1278 (Carroll).

31. September 20, 1929, NA 837.00/2761.

32. Matthew V. Molanphy (President) to Stimson, September 21, 1929, NA 837.00/2759.

33. R. A. Anderson (American Club of Havana) to Stimson, September 23, 1929, NA 837.00/2760. Gustavo Lobo (Cuban Chamber of Commerce in the United States) to Stimson, September 24, 1929, NA 837.00/2762.

Frederick Snare (Frederick Snare Corporation, Engineers) to Hoover, September 26, 1929, NA 837.00/2765. American Steel Corporation of Cuba to Stimson, September 27, 1929, NA 837.00/2767. Robert Carr (Dearborn Chemical Co.) to Stimson, September 27, 1929, NA 837.00/2763. J. Paul Jones (Contracting Engineers) to Stimson, October 3, 1929, NA 837.00/2770. *New York Times* (September 22, 1929) 2:5, several letters made public by the Cuban Embassy. Senate, *Lobby Investigation*, Part 2, 1220-1221 (Shattuck), testimony concerning intervention and stability.

34. *New York Times* (September 19, 1929), 2:5, and (September 20, 1929), 1:6, 6:3.

35. *Ibid.*, and (September 21, 1929), 3:1.

36. *Ibid.*

37. *Ibid.* (September 26, 1929), 3:3. The hearings were not made public.

38. John V. Noel, "Cuba—A Country on the Rise," *The Pan American Magazine* (January 1930), 255, an example of this type of opinion.

39. *The Cuba Review* (February 1930), 14, (May 1930), 12. *New York Times* (June 12, 1929), 2:5, reports the visit of Du Pont to Machado.

40. Memorandum: Conversation between Orestes Ferrara and Stokeley W. Morgan, February 21, 1927, NA 611.3731/234.

41. Memorandum: Conversation between President Coolidge and President Machado, April 23, 1927, NA 033.3711/73 (FR, 1927-II:525). Machado must have been expecting some action on the Platt Amendment (possibly the Catlin plan) since he told an Isle of Pines audience early in April that the United States would end the Amendment "on a not distant date," Crowder to Kellogg, April 18, 1927, NA 711.37/98.

42. C. B. Curtis (Chargé d'Affaires *ad interim*) to Kellogg, October 17, 1928, NA 711.37/122; reports three such speeches. Judah to Kellogg, January 7, 1929, NA 711.37/125.

43. Stimson to Judah, April 23, 1929, NA 837.00/2730 (FR, 1929-II:894).

44. Guggenheim to Stimson, April 4, 1930, NA 711.37/137.

45. Memorandum: State Department Solicitor's Office, April 10, 1930, NA 837.011/44.

46. Speech: "The Pan American Conference at Habana," given by Chester Lloyd Jones at the Park Hotel, Madison, Wisconsin, October 15, 1928, Chester Lloyd Jones Mss.

47. Harold Williamson (Chargé d'Affaires *ad interim*) to Kellogg, October 5, 1927, NA 711.37/109. Marked "Strictly Confidential."

48. Memorandum: Conversation between the Assistant Secretary and John H. Edwards, March 24, 1927, NA 033.3711/58. Crowder to Kellogg, February 17, 1927, NA 711.37/126.

49. *Ibid.* Crowder contacted Catlin, and had an extended argument with him.

50. See, for example, Isaac F. Marcosson, "Cuba Libre: New Edition," *Saturday Evening Post* (April 23, 1927), 14. Marcosson was the author of numerous articles and books on business and relations with Latin America.

51. Senate, *Lobby Investigation*, Part 3, 1346-1348 (Rentschler).

52. William H. Eddy (Vice-president, Chase Securities Corp.) to Hal-

sted G. Freeman (President, Chase Securities Corp.) September 23, 1930, Senate, *Stock Exchange Practices*, Part 6, 2770.

53. *The Cuba Review* (January 1926), 10-11. Machado's loan pledge reported in, White to Crowder, April 23, 1925, NA 033.3711/32a.

54. Memorandum of a conversation between R. L. Clarkson and Karl A. Panthen (Chase Securities Corp.), June 15, 1925, Senate, *Stock Exchange Practices*, Part 5, 2654-2655.

55. Memorandum: Graves to Tinker, March 22, 1926, *ibid.*, 2608-2609. Shepard Morgan testified that the Chase group felt that Crowder was too friendly with the Morgan interests, 2556-2557.

56. Dwight Morrow to Carlos Miguel de Cespedes (Sec. of Public Works), March 31, 1926, NA 837.51/1155.

57. Crowder to Kellogg, April 6, 1926, NA 837.51/1155.

58. Crowder to Kellogg, April 5, 1926, NA 837.51/1154. Senate, *Sale of Foreign Bonds*, Part 2, 739-742 (Grosvenor M. Jones).

59. Senate, *Stock Exchange Practices*, Part 5, 2614-2617 (Alfred E. Mudge of the law firm of Rushmore, Bisbee and Stern).

60. Memorandum: Morgan to White, June 24, 1927, NA 837.51/1210.

61. Crowder to Kellogg, April 6, 1926, NA 837.51/1155.

62. J. P. Morgan & Company to State Department, June 23, 1927, and, Francis White to J. P. Morgan & Company, June 25, 1927, NA 837.51/1210.

63. J. E. Obregon to Sherrill Smith, January 6, 1928, Senate, *Stock Exchange Practices*, Part 5, 2642.

64. *The Cuba Review* (July 1928), 13.

65. Francis White to the Chase National Bank, June 20, 1928, NA 837.51 Chase Natl. Bank/7 (FR, 1928-II:652).

66. Robert E. Olds (Sullivan & Cromwell) to Kellogg, July 5, 1928, NA 837.51 Chase Natl. Bank/16. Kellogg to Olds, July 7, 1928, NA 837.51 Chase Natl. Bank/17.

67. Senate, *Sale of Foreign Bonds*, Part 2, 739-742 (Grosvenor M. Jones): 425.

68. Charles B. Curtis (Chargé d'Affaires *ad interim*) to Secretary of State, October 25, 1929, NA 837.51/1360. Curtis was commended for the "timeliness and lucidity" of his report, White to Curtis, November 8, 1929, NA 837.51/1360.

69. Senate, *Sale of Foreign Bonds*, Part 2, 739-742 (Grosvenor M. Jones).

70. *Ibid.*, and, 425. The syndicate also had the right to issue another forty million dollars in bonds, but this right was not exercised.

71. *Ibid.*, Part 4, 1945-1947 (Carl J. Schmidlapp, Vice-president of Chase National Bank).

72. James Bruce to Freeman, Callahan, Batchelder, and Panthen, July 17, 1930, Senate, *Stock Exchange Practices*, Part 5, 2764-2765.

73. Guggenheim to Stimson, June 23, 1930, NA 837.00/2809 (FR, 1930-II:649), July 15, 1930, NA 837.00/2815 (FR, 1930-II:650).

74. Memorandum of Conference by the Secretary of State with the Press, October 2, 1930, NA 837.00/2844½ (FR, 1930-II:666). Guggenheim had asked the Secretary for a declaration of policy, and had suggested the Root Interpretation; Guggenheim, *United States and Cuba*, 230-232.

75. Guggenheim to Stimson, November 14, 1930, NA 837.00/2887 (FR, 1930-II:671).

76. Guggenheim to Stimson, November 16, 1930, NA 837.00/2891 (FR, 1930-II:672).

77. November 24, 1930, NA 837.00/2912 (FR, 1930-II:673).

78. Guggenheim to Stimson, December 12, 1930, NA 837.00/2922 (FR, 1930-II:678), and, January 20, 1931, NA 837.00/2961 (FR, 1931-II:44). James Bruce to Joseph Rovensky, February 23, 1931, Senate, *Stock Exchange Practices*, Part 5, 2632-2633.

79. Guggenheim to Stimson, January 20, 1931, NA 837.00/2961 (FR, 1931-II:44).

80. James Bruce to Joseph Rovensky, February 23, 1931, Senate, *Stock Exchange Practices*, Part 5, 2631-2633.

81. *Ibid.*, 2630.

82. Memorandum: W. H. Eddy (Chase Bank), June 12, 1931, *ibid.*, Part 6, 2772. Memorandum: Guggenheim to Machado, April 23, 1931, NA 837.00/3056 (FR, 1931-II:56).

83. Guggenheim to Acting Secretary of State, August 11, 1931, NA 837.00 Revolutions/1 (FR, 1931-II:68).

84. Guggenheim to Acting Secretary of State, August 17, 1931, NA 837.113/436 (FR, 1931-II:70).

85. Guggenheim to Acting Secretary of State, September 2, 1931, NA 837.00/3149 (FR, 1931-II:71). Guggenheim congratulated Machado on the handling of the revolt.

86. Memorandum: Conversation between Harry Guggenheim and the Assistant Secretary of State, October 29, 1931, NA 837.51/1481.

87. Memorandum: "Republic of Cuba—Debt Situation," by Adam Geiger (Chase Bank), October 27, 1931, Senate, *Stock Exchange Practices*, Part 5, 2674-2678. Memorandum, conversation between Shepard Morgan and L. S. Rosenthall (both of Chase Bank) and the Assistant Secretary of State, November 6, 1931, NA 837.51/1484.

88. *Ibid.*

89. Memorandum: Conversation between Harry Guggenheim and Secretary Stimson, November 13, 1931, NA 837.00/3207.

90. L. S. Rosenthall to Shepard Morgan, December 12, 1931, Senate, *Stock Exchange Practices*, Part 6, 2774-2775.

91. Guggenheim to Stimson, January 25, 1932, NA 837.00/3227 (FR, 1932-V:533). Memorandum, conversation between Guggenheim and Stimson, November 13, 1931, NA 837.00/3207.

92. Stimson to Guggenheim, March 26, 1932, NA 837.00/3227 (FR, 1932-V:543). Guggenheim to Stimson, March 22, 1932, NA 837.00/3238 (FR, 1932-V:541).

93. Senate, *Stock Exchange Practices*, Part 5, 2542 (Shepard Morgan); G. D. Graves (Vice-president, Chase Grand Central Branch, Cuba) to Shepard Morgan, September 9, 1932, *ibid.*, 2648, reports that the opposition asked the bank not to support Machado.

94. L. S. Rosenthall to Adam Geiger, March 22, 1932, Part 6, 2777. A correct prediction.

95. T. M. Findlay to L. S. Rosenthall, November 9, 1932, Senate, *Stock Exchange Practices*, Part 6, 2784-2785. The Chase Bank discussed its plans for the proposed advance and the sugar tax request with the department. The department had no comment to offer. Memorandum: Telephone conversation between Shepard Morgan and Francis White,

November 4, 1932, NA 837.51 Chase Natl. Bank/87, and, Edwin C. Wilson (Latin American Division) to Shepard Morgan, November 8, 1932, NA 837.51 Chase Natl. Bank/86.

96. Guggenheim to Stimson, November 29, 1932, and Stimson to Guggenheim, December 3, 1932, NA 837.51/1533 (FR, 1933-V:559, 561). Guggenheim to Stimson, December 19, 1932, NA 837.51/1536 (FR, 1933-V:563). Fitzgibbon, *Cuba and the United States*, 242.

97. Memorandum: Conversation between Harry Guggenheim, Shepard Morgan, and the Assistant Secretary, October 20, 1932, NA 837.51 Chase Natl. Bank/81. Guggenheim had suggested much the same thing in August 1932. Guggenheim to Stimson, August 25, 1932, NA 837.51/1521 (FR, 1933-V:554).

98. Shepard Morgan to T. M. Findlay, March 24, 1933, and, Findlay to Morgan, March 25, 1933, Senate, *Stock Exchange Practices*, Part 6, 2789-2790. Morgan stated that the bank was working on a plan to give Cuba assistance in making the June payment provided that there was no moratorium. Machado requested authorization to impose a partial moratorium (which the Cuban Congress granted). He did not utilize the power, but threatened to on several occasions. Guggenheim to Hull, March 23, 1933, NA 837.51/1547 (FR, 1933-V:566); Guggenheim to Hull, March 28, 1933, NA 837.51/1551 (FR, 1933-V:567); Welles to Hull, May 25, 1933, NA 837.51/1567 (FR, 1933-V:571).

99. Guggenheim to Stimson, January 20, 1933, NA 711.37/174. Guggenheim stated that the United States could keep the base at Guantanamo Bay.

100. Findlay to Morgan, March 30, 1933, Senate, *Stock Exchange Practices*, Part 6, 2791.

101. Memorandum: Conversation between Harry Guggenheim, Shepard Morgan and the Assistant Secretary, October 20, 1932, NA 837.51 Chase Natl. Bank/81.

102. Horatio Rubens to J. H. E. (Postmaster General's Office), n.d. (letter sent to the State Department on April 15, 1931), NA 837.00/3038½. The Democrats had been making an issue out of intervention in Latin America. See, for example, Norman H. Davis, "Wanted: A Consistent Latin American Policy," *Foreign Affairs* (July 1931), and, Franklin D. Roosevelt, "Our Foreign Policy," *Foreign Affairs* (July 1928), 583-585.

103. Grosvenor M. Jones revealed another reason for the lack of strict supervision in the latter 1920's (not only in Cuba but in all Latin America): the State Department hoped that loans would cover some of the iniquities in American policy. Senate, *Sale of Foreign Bonds*, Part 2, 724. In 1928 Chargé Curtis was told to talk to the Cuban Government about the prospective loan, but not to base his remarks on the Platt Amendment. White to Curtis, May 5, 1928, NA 837.51/1263.

104. Herbert Hoover, *Addresses Delivered During the Visit of Herbert Hoover to Central and South America, November-December 1928*, (Washington, D. C., 1929). Kellogg to Fletcher, November 23, 1928, NA 033.1110 Hoover, Herbert/149.

105. Hoover to Hughes, February 7, 1929; Hughes to Hoover, February 13, 1929; Hoover to Hughes, February 17, 1929; Charles Evans Hughes Mss.

106. Henry L. Stimson, "Address by Secretary Stimson on May 9, 1931,"

Press Releases (Department of State, May 9, 1931), 390-392. Stimson repeated these arguments in a speech given in October 1932 to the Union League Club in Philadelphia. This speech was entirely dedicated to the proposition that most of American foreign policy was based on the needs of the economy. *The Commercial and Financial Chronicle* (November 26, 1932), 3625. American businessmen expressed similar views; for examples, see Francis R. Hart, "Changes in our Relations With Spanish-America During the Last Quarter Century," *Harvard Business Review* (July 1928)— the author was an official of the Old Colony Trust Company, Boston (reprint sent to the State Department, NA 710.11/1276); Francis Loomis to Kellogg, November 27, 1928, NA 033.1110 Hoover, Herbert/212; Victor M. Cutter, "Relations of the United States Companies with Latin America," *The Annals of the American Academy of Political and Social Science* (July 1930), 130; "Political Agitation and Change in Latin America," *The Commercial and Financial Chronicle* (September 6, 1930), 1472.

107. An article praising this policy was, Thomas H. Healy, "Intervention in Cuba," *America* (March 7, 1931). Reprint sent to the department, NA 837.00/3004.

108. Stimson to Guggenheim, March 26, 1932, NA 837.00/3227 (FR, 1932-V:543).

109. The wife of a *New York Times* correspondent noted that American businessmen in Cuba supported Machado (1933) because they felt that the country needed a "strong hand." Some of them called her husband protesting against the reports of atrocities he had sent to the *Times,* and stated that such stories—whether true or not—would hurt business. Ruby Hart Phillips, *Cuban Sideshow* (Havana, Cuba, 1935), 75.

110. Findlay to Morgan, March 30, 1933, Senate, *Stock Exchange Practices,* Part 6, 2791. Guggenheim later defended the bankers on the grounds that they were trying to preserve stability at all costs, Guggenheim, *The United States and Cuba,* 125-126.

NOTES FOR CHAPTER NINE

1. Similar arguments by Sumner Welles are discussed in, Welles to Hull, September 18, 1933, NA 837.00/3934 (FR, 1933-V:446). For a similar Cuban view, see Cosme de la Torriente, "The Platt Amendment," *Foreign Affairs* (April 1930), 364.

2. Miscellaneous Memos and Data Containing Material on which Secretary Stimson's Speech of February 6, 1931 was based (no date or author indicated), NA 710.11/1518.

3. Wallace Thompson, "The New Age in Our Latin American Relations," *The Annals of the American Academy of Political and Social Science,* (July 1928), 79.

4. Isaac F. Marcosson, "Cuba's Bitter Sweet," *Saturday Evening Post* (June 7, 1930), 3. This article was highly praised in, *The Cuba Review* (July 1930), 18.

5. See, for examples: *Monthly Bank Letter* (April 1929), 58; testimony of Edwin F. Atkins before the Senate Committee on Finance, Senate,

Roosevelt. Secretary of State to Sumner Welles, August 7, 1933, NA 837.00/3603 (FR, 1933-V:338).

12. Sumner Welles to the Secretary of State, August 8, 1933 (Strictly Confidential. Urgent. To be delivered immediately to the President at Hyde Park), NA 837.00/3615 (FR, 1933-V:339).

13. Secretary of State to Sumner Welles, August 9, 1933, NA 837.00/3623 (FR, 1933-V:347).

14. Sumner Welles to the Secretary of State, August 9, 1933, NA 837.00/3622 (FR, 1933-V:344).

15. *Ibid.* Sumner Welles to the Secretary of State, August 9, 1933, NA 837.00/3624 (FR, 1933-V:346).

16. Secretary of State to Sumner Welles, August 9, 1933, NA 837.00/3623 (FR, 1933-V:347).

17. Sumner Welles to the Secretary of State, August 12, 1933, NA 837.00/3650 (FR, 1933-V:358). R. Hart Phillips stated that the officers revolted because they feared American intervention would mean that the greater part of the army would be disbanded. R. Hart Phillips, *Cuba: Island of Paradox* (New York, 1959), 37.

18. Sumner Welles to the Secretary of State, August 12, 1933, NA 837.00/3650. This plan is described in two messages: Sumner Welles to the Secretary of State, August 11, 1933, NA 837.00/3640 (FR, 1933-V:355); Sumner Welles to the Secretary of State, August 11, 1933, NA 837.00/3641 (FR, 1933-V:356).

19. Secretary of State to Sumner Welles, August 12, 1933, NA 837.00/3653a (FR, 1933-V:360).

20. Sumner Welles to the Secretary of State, August 14, 1933, NA 837.00/3648 (FR, 1933-V:363).

21. Sumner Welles to the Secretary of State, August 15, 1933, NA 837.00/3665 (FR, 1933-V:366).

22. Sumner Welles to the Secretary of State, August 19, 1933, NA 711.37/183.

23. *Ibid.*

24. Sumner Welles to the Secretary of State, August 30, 1933, NA 837.00/3739 (FR, 1933-V:376).

25. *Ibid.* Laurence A. Crosby of the law firm of Sullivan and Cromwell—which was the counsel for the Sugar Institute and numerous sugar companies in Cuba—supported the Ambassador's views on this subject. On the whole he believed that the demands of Cuban labor were fair. Memorandum: Conversation between Mr. Laurence A. Crosby and Mr. Duggan, September 1, 1933, NA 837.00/4104.

26. *Ibid.* Sumner Welles to the Secretary of State, August 30, 1933, NA 837.00/3739.

27. Phillips, *Cuba: Island of Paradox*, 57.

28. Sumner Welles to the Secretary of State, September 5, 1933, NA 837.00/3753 (FR, 1933-V:382).

29. Phillips, *Cuba: Island of Paradox*, 69, 72.

30. Cordell Hull to Sumner Welles, September 6, 1933, NA 837.00/3777a. Memorandum of Telephone Conversations between the Secretary of State and the Ambassador in Cuba on September 5, 1933, 5:30 P.M., and between the Assistant Secretary of State (Caffery) and the Ambassador in Cuba, 6:15 P.M. NA 837.00/3764 (FR, 1933-V:385-87). *New York*

The Tariff Act of 1921, 2173-2177; Memorandum, conversation between Shepard Morgan, L. S. Rosenthall, and the Assistant Secretary of State, November 6, 1932, NA 837.51/1484.

6. The American tariff was not the only reason for the poor condition of the Cuban economy. The great increase in the world production of sugar with the subsequent decline in the price of sugar had an adverse effect on Cuba. The American tariff was one of the most important factors in the Cuban economy since the United States was the principal market for Cuban sugar. See Gutierrez, *The World Sugar Problem*, 27, 32.

7. A speaker at the 1926 National Foreign Trade Convention cited Cuba as a good example of how to build trade through foreign loans. Paul J. Kruesi, "Building Foreign Trade Through Foreign Loans," *Official Report of the Thirteenth National Foreign Trade Convention* (New York, 1926), 416-417. G. Butler Sherwell, "Our Investments in Latin American Government Securities," *American Banker's Association Journal* (July 1926).

8. Memorandum: Conversation between Shepard Morgan, L. S. Rosenthall, and the Assistant Secretary of State, November 6, 1931, NA 837.51/1484. *The Cuba Review* (July 1930), 16. *Monthly Bank Letter* (October 1933), 158-160. Howard Mingos, "Sugar and the Tariff," *Commerce and Finance* (November 2, 1932), 1313-1314.

9. Carl W. Linscheid, "Practical Exporting," *Official Report of the Twenty-First National Foreign Trade Convention* (New York, 1934), 93. Linscheid was President of the Export Managers Club of New York. C. E. Bingham, "Recovery for Foreign Trade," *ibid.*, 124. Bingham was Director of the American Exporters and Importers Association. "Final Declaration," *Official Report of the Twentieth National Foreign Trade Convnetion* (New York, 1933), vii, ix, xv.

10. "Cuba and Sugar," *Business Week* (May 3, 1933), 24. See also: H. H. Pike, Jr., "Our Trade with Cuba: An Examination of our Only Reciprocity Treaty," *Official Report of the Twentieth National Foreign Trade Convention* (New York, 1933), 129-134. Robert H. Patchin, "No Fire Sale of Our Foreign Trade Assets," *ibid.*, *Monthly Bank Letter* (October 1933), 160. Howard Mingos, "Sugar and the Tariff," *Commerce and Finance* (November 2, 1932), 1313-1314. *Commerce and Finance* (November 16, 1932), 1356.

11. Carlos Garcia (Cuban Chamber of Commerce in the United States) to the President of the United States, April 4, 1933, NA 611.3731/398; J. L. Mueller (Real Silk Hosiery Company) to Louis Ludlow, April 5, 1933, NA 637.113 Silk Hosiery/1; Newport Rolling Mill Company to the President of the United States, July 6, 1933, NA 611.3731/456; Marietta Paint and Color Company to Senator Simeon Fess, July 11, 1933, NA 611.3731/455; Memorandum: Office of the Economic Advisor, May 5, 1933, NA 611.3731/414, concerns decrease in coal exports to Cuba; Malcolm Stewart (Middle West Foreign Trade Council) to William Phillips (Under Secretary of State), June 29, 1933, NA 611.373 Sugar/198.

12. Memorandum of a Conversation between Phillip Jessup and Mr. Matthews, May 17, 1933, NA 611.3731/416. Memorandum: Office of the Economic Advisor, "Jessup on United States Export Trade with Cuba," September 26, 1933, NA 611.3731/466. Among the companies involved were General Electric, United States Steel, Dupont, and Remington Rand.

13. Cordell Hull, *The Memoirs of Cordell Hull* (2 vols., New York,

1948), I, 357, 358. A. A. Berle, Jr., "America Embarks on a New Trade Policy," *New York Times* (August 26, 1934), 8:1. Sumner Welles, *The Trade Agreements Program* (Department of State, Commercial Policy Series No. 2, Washington, 1934), 5-6. Henry A. Wallace, *America Must Choose* (New York, 1934), 10 ff. Samuel I. Rosenman, *Working with Roosevelt* (New York, 1952), 62. Lloyd Gardner, "New Deal to New Frontiers: 1937-1941," *Studies on the Left* (Fall, 1959), 29-43. There was some difference of opinion within the administration concerning policies, and the general importance of exports—the Peek-Hull controversy being best known—but even with compromises over methods, the export emphasis was most predominant. For discussions of these differences, see George N. Peek, and Samuel Crowther, *Why Quit Our Own* (New York, 1936); Arthur M. Schlesinger, Jr., *The Age of Roosevelt*: *The Coming of the New Deal* (New York, 1958), Chap. 15; Jerome Frank, *Save America First* (New York, 1938), 134-135. The importance of the Latin American trade for certain American products was indicated by these figures for 1935: in that year Latin America accounted for 54.1 percent of U. S. cotton goods exports, 55.3 percent of exports of steel mill products, and almost one-third of the exports of leather goods, rubber manufactures, silk goods, paper products, iron and steel advanced manufactures, and electrical and industrial machinery. Arthur D. Gayer and Carl T. Schmidt, *American Economic Foreign Policy* (New York, 1939), 227.

14. Arthur S. Hillyer, "Current Export Opportunities," *Official Report of the Twentieth National Foreign Trade Convention* (New York, 1933), 75-76.

15. Charles W. Taussig, "Cuba and Reciprocal Trade Agreements," *Official Report of the Twenty-First National Foreign Trade Convention* (New York, 1934), 552-557. See the message from President Roosevelt to the House Committee on Agriculture dated February 19, 1934; U. S., Congress, House of Representatives, Committee on Agriculture, *Hearings on H.R. 7907 (Jones-Costigan) to Include Sugar Beets and Sugarcane as Basic Commodities*, 73rd Cong., 2nd Sess., 1934, 1-2. (Cited hereafter as *Hearings, Jones-Costigan Act*.)

16. Sumner Welles, *Good Neighbor Policy in the Caribbean* (Department of State, Latin American Series No. 12, Washington, 1935), 7-10.

17. *Ibid.* Sumner Welles, *Two Years of the "Good Neighbor" Policy* (Department of State, Latin American Series No. 11, Washington, 1935). Hull, *Memoirs*, I, 342, 344. Charles W. Taussig, "Cuba and Reciprocal Trade Agreements," *Official Report of the Twenty-First National Foreign Trade Convention*, (New York, 1934), 552-557. Sumner Welles, *Relations between the United States and Cuba* (Department of State, Latin American Series No. 7, Washington, 1934).

18. Charles W. Taussig, *Some Notes on Sugar and Molasses* (New York, 1940), 23-24.

19. *New York Times* (September 1, 1933), 27:2 Ernest K. Lindley, "United States Sugar Aid to Pacify Cuba," *New York Herald Tribune* (April 6, 1933). When Berle was appointed financial expert to assist the Cuban Government work out plans for economic rehabilitation the domestic cane sugar refiners requested that he be removed, and charged that he was "prejudiced" in favor of Cuban interests. *New York Times* (August 31, 1933), 7:5.

20. Robert W. Dunn, *American Foreign Investments* (New York, 1926),

127-128. Woodin was President and Director of the American Car a Foundry Company and a dozen other important corporations. He also h a Cuban town named in his honor. *The Cuba Review* (September, 1925),

21. *Congressional Record*, 73rd Cong., 2nd Sess., 1934, Vol. 78, Part 1 11552-11555.

22. *New York Times* (February 26, 1933). Walsh died before takin office.

NOTES FOR CHAPTER TEN

1. The new Ambassador visited the officials of the Chase National Bank prior to departing. Their reaction to him was summed up in a letter to their representative in Havana: ". . . he impresses us as being rather standoff-ish . . . and not inclined to take anyone into his confidence . . . but I am quite sure that you will be able to establish friendly relations." Adam K. Geiger to T. M. Findlay, May 3, 1933, Senate, *Stock Exchange Practices*, Pt. 6, 2792.

2. Sumner Welles, "Is America Imperialistic?" *Atlantic Monthly* (September, 1924), 36-44.

3. Sumner Welles, *Naboth's Vineyard* (2 Vols., New York, 1928), II, 930.

4. *Ibid.*, 930-931. Welles, "Is America Imperialistic?" 36-44. Welles, *Two Years of the Good Neighbor Policy*, 5.

5. *Ibid.* Welles, *Good Neighbor Policy in the Caribbean*, 2. "Statement by Mr. Sumner Welles, Assistant Secretary of State," April 24, 1933, NA 711.37/178. (FR, 1933-V:278). Leading Democrats expressed the same views; see Norman H. Davis, "Wanted: A Consistent Latin American Policy," *Foreign Affairs* (July, 1931), 547.

6. The Secretary of State to the Appointed Ambassador in Cuba, May 1, 1933, NA 711.37/178a (FR, 1933-V:285). These instructions also contained the Root Interpretation of the Platt Amendment, as an expression of policy.

7. Sumner Welles to the Secretary of State, May 13, 1933, NA 837.00/3512 (FR, 1933-V:290).

8. Sumner Welles to the Acting Secretary of State, June 30, 1933, NA 837.00/3566 (FR, 1933-V:316). These groups were the Unión Nacionalista, the ABC, the OCRR, the Conservative opposition, the Liberal opposition, the University, the professors of the normal and high schools, and the women's organizations.

9. Sumner Welles to President Roosevelt, July 17, 1933, NA 837.00 3579½ (FR, 1933-V:325). Sumner Welles to the Secretary of State, Ma 25, 1933, NA 837.51/1567 (FR, 1933-V:572). This message stresse the use of the acute financial needs of the Cuban Government as anoth lever.

10. Sumner Welles to the Acting Secretary of State, July 17, 1933, N 837.00/3579 (FR, 1933-V:322). Sumner Welles to the Acting Secreta of State, July 26, 1933, NA 837.00/3584 (FR, 1933-V:327).

11. Sumner Welles to the Secretary of State, August 7, 1933, N 837.00/3606 (FR, 1933-V:336). This plan was approved by Presid

Times (September 8, 1933). The Marines were still on alert in March 1934. Jefferson Caffery to the Secretary of State, March 14, 1934, NA 837.00/4929.

31. *Ibid.* *New York Times* (September 8, 1933).

32. Memorandum of Telephone Conversations between the Secretary of State and the Ambassador in Cuba on September 5, 1933, 5:30 P.M., and between the Assistant Secretary of State and the Ambassador in Cuba, 6:15 P.M., NA 837.00/3764. Memorandum of Telephone Conversation between the Secretary of State and the Ambassador in Cuba, September 5, 1933, 7 P.M., NA 837.00/3764.

33. Memorandum of Telephone Conversation between the Secretary of State and the Ambassador in Cuba, September 6, 1933, 10 A.M., NA 837.00/3787 (FR, 1933-V:389).

34. *Ibid.* Memorandum of Telephone Conversation between the Secretry of State and the Ambassador in Mexico (Daniels), September 9, 1933, NA 837.00/3940 (FR, 1933-V:412). The Ambassador in Mexico to the Secretary of State, September 6, 1933, NA 837.00/3772 (FR, 1933-V:394). The Mexican Minister for Foreign Affairs (Puig) to the Secretary of State, September 7, 1933, NA 837.00/3775 (FR, 1933-V:394). The Argentine Ministry for Foreign Affairs to the Department of State, September 12, 1933, NA 837.00/3868 (FR, 1933-V:409). Josephus Daniels, *Shirt-Sleeve Diplomat* (Chapel Hill, North Carolina, 1947), 324.

35. Sumner Welles to the Secretary of State, September 7, 1933, NA 837.00/3778 (FR, 1933-V:396).

36. Hull, *Memoirs*, I, 315. Intervention was discussed by the Cabinet on several occasions. The Assistant Secretary of War wanted to "intervene promptly," but the majority were against such a step "unless forced to do so as a matter of absolute necessity." Harold L. Ickes, *The Secret Diary of Harold L. Ickes: The First Thousand Days, 1933-1936* (New York, 1953), 87, 93. Roosevelt's own views had changed since he had helped plan the proposed Mexican intervention in 1919; Franklin D. Roosevelt (Acting Secretary of the Navy) to the Secretary of State, August 7, 1919, NA 711.12/194½ (Secret).

37. Bethlehem Steel Company to the Secretary of State, September 7, 1933, NA 837.00/3891.

38. Sumner Welles to the Secretary of State, September 8, 1933, NA 837.00/3793.

39. M. T. McGovern (American Chamber of Commerce of Cuba) to Sumner Welles, October 6, 1933, NA 837.00/4246. Guy Wellman (Standard Oil Company) to the Department of State, September 11, 1933, NA 837.00/3873. Sumner Welles, *The Time for Decision* (New York, 1944), 196.

40. Memorandum of Telephone Conversation between the Secretary of State and the Ambassador in Cuba, September 6, 1933, NA 837.00/3787.

41. Sumner Welles to the Secretary of State, September 7, 1933, NA 837.00/3780 (FR, 1933-V:400).

42. Phillips, *Cuba: Island of Paradox*, 81.

43. Sumner Welles to the Secretary of State, November 6, 1933, NA 837.00/4343 (FR, 1933-V:513).

44. Sumner Welles to the Secretary of State, September 18, 1933, NA 837.00/3934 (FR, 1933-V:446).

45. *Ibid.*

46. Sumner Welles to the Secretary of State, September 16, 1933, NA 837.00/3915 (FR, 1933-V:440). Sumner Welles to the Secretary of State, September 17, 1933, NA 837.00/3911 (FR, 1933-V:442). Sumner Welles to the Secretary of State, September 17, 1933, NA 837.00/3908 (FR, 1933-V:443).

47. Sumner Welles to the Secretary of State, September 18, 1933, NA 837.00/3934.

48. Sumner Welles to the Secretary of State, September 21, 1933, NA 837.00/3982 (FR, 1933-V:451).

49. Sumner Welles to the Secretary of State, September 25, 1933, NA 837.00/4023 (FR, 1933-V:459).

50. Sumner Welles to the Secretary of State, October 7, 1933, NA 837.00/4146 (FR, 1933-V:477).

51. *Ibid.* Buell, *Problems of the New Cuba,* 182-183. Phillips, *Cuba: Island of Paradox,* 81. *New York Times* (September 20, 1933).

52. Sumner Welles to the Secretary of State, October 18, 1933, NA 837.00/4213 (FR, 1933-V:491). The students were reported to be conspiring to oust Batista. Sumner Welles to the Secretary of State, October 19, 1933, NA 837.00/4236 (FR, 1933-V:492).

53. *Ibid.*

54. Sumner Welles to the Secretary of State, October 24, 1933, NA 837.00/4267 (FR, 1933-V:499).

55. Sumner Welles to the Secretary of State, October 26, 1933, NA 837.00/4281 (FR, 1933-V:501).

56. Sumner Welles to the Secretary of State, October 31, 1933, NA 837.00/4321 (FR, 1933-V:505). Sumner Welles to the Secretary of State, November 4, 1933, NA 837.00/4337 (FR, 1933-V:511).

57. Sumner Welles to the Acting Secretary of State, December 9, 1933, NA 837.00/4488 (FR, 1933-V:536). Batista was again given "full guarantees as to his retention of his present position." Sumner Welles to the Acting Secretary of State, December 10, 1933, NA 837.00/4489 (FR, 1933-V:538). Sumner Welles to the Acting Secretary of State, December 11, 1933, NA 837.00/4498 (FR, 1933-V:539).

58. The Secretary to President Roosevelt (Early) to the Acting Secretary of State, November 22, 1933, NA 837.00/4450 (FR, 1933-V:524).

59. Sumner Welles to the Secretary of State, September 11, 1933, NA 837.00/3830 (FR, 1933-V:422). Secretary of State to Sumner Welles, September 11, 1933, NA 837.00/3830 (FR, 1933-V:424). The Acting Secretary of State to President Roosevelt, at Warm Springs, Georgia, November 23, 1933, NA 837.00/4450/Supp. (FR, 1933-V:525).

60. Cordell Hull, at Montevideo, asked the Department to supply him with the "facts and conditions . . . against recognition" of the regime. Welles was cited as the source for the arguments against recognition. Acting Secretary of State to Cordell Hull, November 28, 1933, NA 837.01/47 (FR, 1933-V:527).

61. Sumner Welles to the Secretary of State, September 17, 1933, NA 837.00/3908 (FR, 1933-V:443).

62. Sumner Welles to the Secretary of State, October 16, 1933, NA 837.00/4206 (FR, 1933-V:487).

63. Sumner Welles to the Acting Secretary of State, December 7,

1933, NA 837.00/4480 (FR, 1933-V:533). M. T. McGovern (President, American Chamber of Commerce of Cuba) to Sumner Welles, November 15, 1933, NA 837.00/4539; this letter had the "unanimous" approval of the members, and argued against recognition. Some examples of these decrees are discussed in, Buell, *Problems of the New Cuba*, 14; many of them concerned labor reforms.

64. Jefferson Caffery to the Acting Secretary of State, December 21, 1933, NA 837.00/4547 (FR, 1933-V:544). Mrs. R. Hart Phillips said that the old electricity rates were "outrageous." Phillips, *Cuba: Island of Paradox*, 127. Caffery divided the Cubans into the "better classes" and the "ignorant masses." Jefferson Caffery to the Acting Secretary of State, January 10, 1934, NA 837.00/4591 (FR, 1934-V:95).

65. Acting Secretary of State to Jefferson Caffery, January 8, 1934, NA 837.01/59 (FR, 1934-V:93).

66. Jefferson Caffery to the Acting Secretary of State, January 10, 1934, NA 837.00/4591.

67. Jefferson Caffery to the Acting Secretary of State, January 14, 1934, NA 837.00/4606 (FR, 1934-V:98).

68. Acting Secretary of State to Jefferson Caffery, January 14, 1934, NA 837.00/4609 (FR, 1934-V:100). Jefferson Caffery to the Acting Secretary of State, January 15, 1934, NA 837.00/4617.

69. Secretary of State to Jefferson Caffery, January 23, 1934, NA 837.01/70 (FR, 1934-V:107). See also, The Charles E. Hires Company to Cordell Hull, January 22, 1934, NA 837.01/69. This company urged recognition in order to prevent labor unrest. Hevia was replaced by Mendieta on January 18.

70. Phillips, *Cuba: Island of Paradox*, 160-161. Buell, *Problems of the New Cuba*, 16-17.

71. Jefferson Caffery to the Secretary of State, March 14, 1934, NA 837.00/4929. *Monthly Bank Letter* (February 1934), 19. Speech by Hamilton Fish in, *Congressional Record*, 73rd Cong., 2nd Sess., 1934, Vol. 78, Part 8, 8416.

72. Cosme de la Torriente, "The Platt Amendment," *Foreign Affairs* (April 1930), 364.

73. Harry F. Guggenheim, "Amending the Platt Amendment," *Foreign Affairs* (April 1934), 448. Sumner Welles to the Secretary of State, November 4, 1933, NA 837.00/4337 (FR, 1933-V:511).

74. Sumner Welles to the Secretary of State, September 18, 1933, NA 837.00/3934. *New York Times* (December 14, 1933), 9:2. The Department stated that the legitimate interests of Americans would be protected. Edwin C. Wilson (Chief, Latin American Division) to the Corn Exchange Bank & Trust Company, December 20, 1933, NA 837.00/4509.

75. Sumner Welles, *Good Neighbor Policy in the Caribbean*, 7.

76. "Final Declaration," *Official Report of the Twentieth National Foreign Trade Convention* (New York, 1933), viii. A similar resolution was passed at the luncheon of the American Manufacturers Export Association, *ibid.*, 246-247. James S. Carson, "Pressing Present-Day Latin-American Problems," *ibid.* Robert H. Patchin, "No Fire Sale of our Foreign Trade Assets," *ibid.*

77. *New York Times* (October 30, 1933), 25:2.

78. Francis B. Sayre, *American Commercial Policy, The Two Alterna-*

tives (Department of State, Commercial Policy Series No. 23, Washington, 1936), 8. Sumner Welles, *The Trade Agreements Program*, 5-6. *Monthly Bank Letter* (October 1933), 158-160.

79. *Ibid.* H. H. Pike, Jr., "Our Trade with Cuba: An Examination of Our Only Reciprocity Treaty," 129-134. For examples see the letters cited in note 11, Chapter IX. The most important letters from such firms were sent to Welles to guide him in the negotiations. Secretary of State to Sumner Welles, June 9, 1933, NA 611.3731/462.

80. These examples were among the recommendations submitted by Phillip Jessup. Memorandum, Office of the Economic Advisor, "Jessup on United States Export Trade with Cuba," September 26, 1933, NA 611.3731/466.

81. Department of State, *Reciprocal Trade Agreement between the United States of America and the Republic of Cuba, Signed at Washington August 24, 1934, as Amended by Supplementary Agreements Signed at Washington, December 18, 1939 and at Habana, December 23, 1941* (Washington, 1942), 10, 33-37, 44. Buell, *Problems of the New Cuba*, 62-63. Department of State, *Analysis of Cuban-American Trade during the First Two Years under the Reciprocal Agreement* (Washington, 1937), Part I, 18.

82. Jessup Memorandum, September 26, 1933, NA 611.3731/466. Secretary of State to Jefferson Caffery, April 3, 1934, *Foreign Relations of the United States: Diplomatic Papers, 1934* (5 vols., Washington, 1952), V, 124-125.

83. Secretary of State to Jefferson Caffery, June 18, 1934, *ibid.*, 140.

84. Buell, *Problems of the New Cuba*, 65. Welles had stated in 1933 that one of the major aims of the trade negotiations was to obtain "a practical monopoly of the Cuban market." Sumner Welles to the Secretary of State, May 13, 1933, NA 837.00/3512.

85. Thomas L. Chadbourne, *Cuba and Sugar Stabilization*, 27-28. Ernest K. Lindley, "United States Sugar Aid to Pacify Cuba."

86. *Hearings: Jones-Costigan Act*, 1-2.

87. Ickes, *Secret Diary*, I, 147.

88. *Hearings: Jones-Costigan Act* (pages are in order of listing in text), 218-219, 226-233, 243-244, 220-221, 71-80, 5, 62-64, *Congressional Record*, 73rd Cong., 2nd Sess., 1934, Vol. 78, Part 6, 6025.

89. *Hearings: Jones-Costigan Act*, 246, 141-142, 201-209. *Congressional Record*, 73rd Cong., 2nd Sess., 1934, Vol. 78, Part 3, 3230-3233; Part 4, 3632-3633.

90. United States Cuban Sugar Council, *Sugar: Facts and Figures* (New York, 1948), 53, 55. Farr & Company, *Manual of Sugar Companies, 1949-1950* (New York, 1950), 260. Roosevelt had asked that Cuba be given 1,944,000 short tons, *Hearings: Jones-Costigan Act*, 1-2. Companies interested in Cuban sugar wanted at least two million tons; Memorandum: Conversation between Mr. Laurence A. Crosby (Sullivan and Cromwell) and Mr. Duggan, September 1, 1933, NA 837.00/4104.

91. The American Sugar Refining Company, *Annual Report: 1934*, (New York, 1935), 11.

92. This trend could also be seen in the AAA and the NRA. For discussions of this see, Schlesinger, *Coming of the New Deal*, Chapters

The Tariff Act of 1921, 2173-2177; Memorandum, conversation between Shepard Morgan, L. S. Rosenthall, and the Assistant Secretary of State, November 6, 1932, NA 837.51/1484.

6. The American tariff was not the only reason for the poor condition of the Cuban economy. The great increase in the world production of sugar with the subsequent decline in the price of sugar had an adverse effect on Cuba. The American tariff was one of the most important factors in the Cuban economy since the United States was the principal market for Cuban sugar. See Gutierrez, *The World Sugar Problem*, 27, 32.

7. A speaker at the 1926 National Foreign Trade Convention cited Cuba as a good example of how to build trade through foreign loans. Paul J. Kruesi, "Building Foreign Trade Through Foreign Loans," *Official Report of the Thirteenth National Foreign Trade Convention* (New York, 1926), 416-417. G. Butler Sherwell, "Our Investments in Latin American Government Securities," *American Banker's Association Journal* (July 1926).

8. Memorandum: Conversation between Shepard Morgan, L. S. Rosenthall, and the Assistant Secretary of State, November 6, 1931, NA 837.51/1484. *The Cuba Review* (July 1930), 16. *Monthly Bank Letter* (October 1933), 158-160. Howard Mingos, "Sugar and the Tariff," *Commerce and Finance* (November 2, 1932), 1313-1314.

9. Carl W. Linscheid, "Practical Exporting," *Official Report of the Twenty-First National Foreign Trade Convention* (New York, 1934), 93. Linscheid was President of the Export Managers Club of New York. C. E. Bingham, "Recovery for Foreign Trade," *ibid.*, 124. Bingham was Director of the American Exporters and Importers Association. "Final Declaration," *Official Report of the Twentieth National Foreign Trade Convnetion* (New York, 1933), vii, ix, xv.

10. "Cuba and Sugar," *Business Week* (May 3, 1933), 24. See also: H. H. Pike, Jr., "Our Trade with Cuba: An Examination of our Only Reciprocity Treaty," *Official Report of the Twentieth National Foreign Trade Convention* (New York, 1933), 129-134. Robert H. Patchin, "No Fire Sale of Our Foreign Trade Assets," *ibid.*, *Monthly Bank Letter* (October 1933), 160. Howard Mingos, "Sugar and the Tariff," *Commerce and Finance* (November 2, 1932), 1313-1314. *Commerce and Finance* (November 16, 1932), 1356.

11. Carlos Garcia (Cuban Chamber of Commerce in the United States) to the President of the United States, April 4, 1933, NA 611.3731/398; J. L. Mueller (Real Silk Hosiery Company) to Louis Ludlow, April 5, 1933, NA 637.113 Silk Hosiery/1; Newport Rolling Mill Company to the President of the United States, July 6, 1933, NA 611.3731/456; Marietta Paint and Color Company to Senator Simeon Fess, July 11, 1933, NA 611.3731/455; Memorandum: Office of the Economic Advisor, May 5, 1933, NA 611.3731/414, concerns decrease in coal exports to Cuba; Malcolm Stewart (Middle West Foreign Trade Council) to William Phillips (Under Secretary of State), June 29, 1933, NA 611.373 Sugar/198.

12. Memorandum of a Conversation between Phillip Jessup and Mr. Matthews, May 17, 1933, NA 611.3731/416. Memorandum: Office of the Economic Advisor, "Jessup on United States Export Trade with Cuba," September 26, 1933, NA 611.3731/466. Among the companies involved were General Electric, United States Steel, Dupont, and Remington Rand.

13. Cordell Hull, *The Memoirs of Cordell Hull* (2 vols., New York,

1948), I, 357, 358. A. A. Berle, Jr., "America Embarks on a New Trade Policy," *New York Times* (August 26, 1934), 8:1. Sumner Welles, *The Trade Agreements Program* (Department of State, Commercial Policy Series No. 2, Washington, 1934), 5-6. Henry A. Wallace, *America Must Choose* (New York, 1934), 10 ff. Samuel I. Rosenman, *Working with Roosevelt* (New York, 1952), 62. Lloyd Gardner, "New Deal to New Frontiers: 1937-1941," *Studies on the Left* (Fall, 1959), 29-43. There are some difference of opinion within the administration concerning policies, and the general importance of exports—the Peek-Hull controversy being best known—but even with compromises over methods, the export emphasis was most predominant. For discussions of these differences, see George N. Peek, and Samuel Crowther, *Why Quit Our Own* (New York, 1936); Arthur M. Schlesinger, Jr., *The Age of Roosevelt: The Coming of the New Deal* (New York, 1958), Chap. 15; Jerome Frank, *Save America First* (New York, 1938), 134-135. The importance of the Latin American trade for certain American products was indicated by these figures for 1935: in that year Latin America accounted for 54.1 percent of U. S. cotton goods exports, 55.3 percent of exports of steel mill products, and almost one-third of the exports of leather goods, rubber manufactures, silk goods, paper products, iron and steel advanced manufactures, and electrical and industrial machinery. Arthur D. Gayer and Carl T. Schmidt, *American Economic Foreign Policy* (New York, 1939), 227.

14. Arthur S. Hillyer, "Current Export Opportunities," *Official Report of the Twentieth National Foreign Trade Convention* (New York, 1933), 75-76.

15. Charles W. Taussig, "Cuba and Reciprocal Trade Agreements," *Official Report of the Twenty-First National Foreign Trade Convention* (New York, 1934), 552-557. See the message from President Roosevelt to the House Committee on Agriculture dated February 19, 1934; U. S., Congress, House of Representatives, Committee on Agriculture, *Hearings on H.R. 7907 (Jones-Costigan) to Include Sugar Beets and Sugarcane as Basic Commodities*, 73rd Cong., 2nd Sess., 1934, 1-2. (Cited hereafter as *Hearings, Jones-Costigan Act*.)

16. Sumner Welles, *Good Neighbor Policy in the Caribbean* (Department of State, Latin American Series No. 12, Washington, 1935), 7-10.

17. *Ibid.* Sumner Welles, *Two Years of the "Good Neighbor" Policy* (Department of State, Latin American Series No. 11, Washington, 1935). Hull, *Memoirs*, I, 342, 344. Charles W. Taussig, "Cuba and Reciprocal Trade Agreements," *Official Report of the Twenty-First National Foreign Trade Convention*, (New York, 1934), 552-557. Sumner Welles, *Relations between the United States and Cuba* (Department of State, Latin American Series No. 7, Washington, 1934).

18. Charles W. Taussig, *Some Notes on Sugar and Molasses* (New York, 1940), 23-24.

19. *New York Times* (September 1, 1933), 27:2 Ernest K. Lindley, "United States Sugar Aid to Pacify Cuba," *New York Herald Tribune* (April 6, 1933). When Berle was appointed financial expert to assist the Cuban Government work out plans for economic rehabilitation the domestic cane sugar refiners requested that he be removed, and charged that he was "prejudiced" in favor of Cuban interests. *New York Times* (August 31, 1933), 7:5.

20. Robert W. Dunn, *American Foreign Investments* (New York, 1926),

127-128. Woodin was President and Director of the American Car and Foundry Company and a dozen other important corporations. He also had a Cuban town named in his honor. *The Cuba Review* (September, 1925), 9.

21. *Congressional Record,* 73rd Cong., 2nd Sess., 1934, Vol. 78, Part 11, 11552-11555.

22. *New York Times* (February 26, 1933). Walsh died before taking office.

NOTES FOR CHAPTER TEN

1. The new Ambassador visited the officials of the Chase National Bank prior to departing. Their reaction to him was summed up in a letter to their representative in Havana: ". . . he impresses us as being rather standoff-ish . . . and not inclined to take anyone into his confidence . . . but I am quite sure that you will be able to establish friendly relations." Adam K. Geiger to T. M. Findlay, May 3, 1933, Senate, *Stock Exchange Practices,* Pt. 6, 2792.

2. Sumner Welles, "Is America Imperialistic?" *Atlantic Monthly* (September, 1924), 36-44.

3. Sumner Welles, *Naboth's Vineyard* (2 Vols., New York, 1928), II, 930.

4. *Ibid.,* 930-931. Welles, "Is America Imperialistic?" 36-44. Welles, *Two Years of the Good Neighbor Policy,* 5.

5. *Ibid.* Welles, *Good Neighbor Policy in the Caribbean,* 2. "Statement by Mr. Sumner Welles, Assistant Secretary of State," April 24, 1933, NA 711.37/178. (FR, 1933-V:278). Leading Democrats expressed the same views; see Norman H. Davis, "Wanted: A Consistent Latin American Policy," *Foreign Affairs* (July, 1931), 547.

6. The Secretary of State to the Appointed Ambassador in Cuba, May 1, 1933, NA 711.37/178a (FR, 1933-V:285). These instructions also contained the Root Interpretation of the Platt Amendment, as an expression of policy.

7. Sumner Welles to the Secretary of State, May 13, 1933, NA 837.00/3512 (FR, 1933-V:290).

8. Sumner Welles to the Acting Secretary of State, June 30, 1933, NA 837.00/3566 (FR, 1933-V:316). These groups were the Unión Nacionalista, the ABC, the OCRR, the Conservative opposition, the Liberal opposition, the University, the professors of the normal and high schools, and the women's organizations.

9. Sumner Welles to President Roosevelt, July 17, 1933, NA 837.00/3579½ (FR, 1933-V:325). Sumner Welles to the Secretary of State, May 25, 1933, NA 837.51/1567 (FR, 1933-V:572). This message stressed the use of the acute financial needs of the Cuban Government as another lever.

10. Sumner Welles to the Acting Secretary of State, July 17, 1933, NA 837.00/3579 (FR, 1933-V:322). Sumner Welles to the Acting Secretary of State, July 26, 1933, NA 837.00/3584 (FR, 1933-V:327).

11. Sumner Welles to the Secretary of State, August 7, 1933, NA 837.00/3606 (FR, 1933-V:336). This plan was approved by President

Roosevelt. Secretary of State to Sumner Welles, August 7, 1933, NA 837.00/3603 (FR, 1933-V:338).

12. Sumner Welles to the Secretary of State, August 8, 1933 (Strictly Confidential. Urgent. To be delivered immediately to the President at Hyde Park), NA 837.00/3615 (FR, 1933-V:339).

13. Secretary of State to Sumner Welles, August 9, 1933, NA 837.00/3623 (FR, 1933-V:347).

14. Sumner Welles to the Secretary of State, August 9, 1933, NA 837.00/3622 (FR, 1933-V:344).

15. *Ibid.* Sumner Welles to the Secretary of State, August 9, 1933, NA 837.00/3624 (FR, 1933-V:346).

16. Secretary of State to Sumner Welles, August 9, 1933, NA 837.00/3623 (FR, 1933-V:347).

17. Sumner Welles to the Secretary of State, August 12, 1933, NA 837.00/3650 (FR, 1933-V:358). R. Hart Phillips stated that the officers revolted because they feared American intervention would mean that the greater part of the army would be disbanded. R. Hart Phillips, *Cuba: Island of Paradox* (New York, 1959), 37.

18. Sumner Welles to the Secretary of State, August 12, 1933, NA 837.00/3650. This plan is described in two messages: Sumner Welles to the Secretary of State, August 11, 1933, NA 837.00/3640 (FR, 1933-V:355); Sumner Welles to the Secretary of State, August 11, 1933, NA 837.00/3641 (FR, 1933-V:356).

19. Secretary of State to Sumner Welles, August 12, 1933, NA 837.00/3653a (FR, 1933-V:360).

20. Sumner Welles to the Secretary of State, August 14, 1933, NA 837.00/3648 (FR, 1933-V:363).

21. Sumner Welles to the Secretary of State, August 15, 1933, NA 837.00/3665 (FR, 1933-V:366).

22. Sumner Welles to the Secretary of State, August 19, 1933, NA 711.37/183.

23. *Ibid.*

24. Sumner Welles to the Secretary of State, August 30, 1933, NA 837.00/3739 (FR, 1933-V:376).

25. *Ibid.* Laurence A. Crosby of the law firm of Sullivan and Cromwell—which was the counsel for the Sugar Institute and numerous sugar companies in Cuba—supported the Ambassador's views on this subject. On the whole he believed that the demands of Cuban labor were fair. Memorandum: Conversation between Mr. Laurence A. Crosby and Mr. Duggan, September 1, 1933, NA 837.00/4104.

26. *Ibid.* Sumner Welles to the Secretary of State, August 30, 1933, NA 837.00/3739.

27. Phillips, *Cuba: Island of Paradox*, 57.

28. Sumner Welles to the Secretary of State, September 5, 1933, NA 837.00/3753 (FR, 1933-V:382).

29. Phillips, *Cuba: Island of Paradox*, 69, 72.

30. Cordell Hull to Sumner Welles, September 6, 1933, NA 837.00/3777a. Memorandum of Telephone Conversations between the Secretary of State and the Ambassador in Cuba on September 5, 1933, 5:30 P.M., and between the Assistant Secretary of State (Caffery) and the Ambassador in Cuba, 6:15 P.M. NA 837.00/3764 (FR, 1933-V:385-87). *New York*

Times (September 8, 1933). The Marines were still on alert in March 1934. Jefferson Caffery to the Secretary of State, March 14, 1934, NA 837.00/4929.

31. *Ibid. New York Times* (September 8, 1933).

32. Memorandum of Telephone Conversations between the Secretary of State and the Ambassador in Cuba on September 5, 1933, 5:30 P.M., and between the Assistant Secretary of State and the Ambassador in Cuba, 6:15 P.M., NA 837.00/3764. Memorandum of Telephone Conversation between the Secretary of State and the Ambassador in Cuba, September 5, 1933, 7 P.M., NA 837.00/3764.

33. Memorandum of Telephone Conversation between the Secretary of State and the Ambassador in Cuba, September 6, 1933, 10 A.M., NA 837.00/3787 (FR, 1933-V:389).

34. *Ibid.* Memorandum of Telephone Conversation between the Secretry of State and the Ambassador in Mexico (Daniels), September 9, 1933, NA 837.00/3940 (FR, 1933-V:412). The Ambassador in Mexico to the Secretary of State, September 6, 1933, NA 837.00/3772 (FR, 1933-V:394). The Mexican Minister for Foreign Affairs (Puig) to the Secretary of State, September 7, 1933, NA 837.00/3775 (FR, 1933-V:394). The Argentine Ministry for Foreign Affairs to the Department of State, September 12, 1933, NA 837.00/3868 (FR, 1933-V:409). Josephus Daniels, *Shirt-Sleeve Diplomat* (Chapel Hill, North Carolina, 1947), 324.

35. Sumner Welles to the Secretary of State, September 7, 1933, NA 837.00/3778 (FR, 1933-V:396).

36. Hull, *Memoirs*, I, 315. Intervention was discussed by the Cabinet on several occasions. The Assistant Secretary of War wanted to "intervene promptly," but the majority were against such a step "unless forced to do so as a matter of absolute necessity." Harold L. Ickes, *The Secret Diary of Harold L. Ickes: The First Thousand Days, 1933-1936* (New York, 1953), 87, 93. Roosevelt's own views had changed since he had helped plan the proposed Mexican intervention in 1919; Franklin D. Roosevelt (Acting Secretary of the Navy) to the Secretary of State, August 7, 1919, NA 711.12/194½ (Secret).

37. Bethlehem Steel Company to the Secretary of State, September 7, 1933, NA 837.00/3891.

38. Sumner Welles to the Secretary of State, September 8, 1933, NA 837.00/3793.

39. M. T. McGovern (American Chamber of Commerce of Cuba) to Sumner Welles, October 6, 1933, NA 837.00/4246. Guy Wellman (Standard Oil Company) to the Department of State, September 11, 1933, NA 837.00/3873. Sumner Welles, *The Time for Decision* (New York, 1944), 196.

40. Memorandum of Telephone Conversation between the Secretary of State and the Ambassador in Cuba, September 6, 1933, NA 837.00/3787.

41. Sumner Welles to the Secretary of State, September 7, 1933, NA 837.00/3780 (FR, 1933-V:400).

42. Phillips, *Cuba: Island of Paradox*, 81.

43. Sumner Welles to the Secretary of State, November 6, 1933, NA 837.00/4343 (FR, 1933-V:513).

44. Sumner Welles to the Secretary of State, September 18, 1933, NA 837.00/3934 (FR, 1933-V:446).

45. *Ibid.*

46. Sumner Welles to the Secretary of State, September 16, 1933, NA 837.00/3915 (FR, 1933-V:440). Sumner Welles to the Secretary of State, September 17, 1933, NA 837.00/3911 (FR, 1933-V:442). Sumner Welles to the Secretary of State, September 17, 1933, NA 837.00/3908 (FR, 1933-V:443).

47. Sumner Welles to the Secretary of State, September 18, 1933, NA 837.00/3934.

48. Sumner Welles to the Secretary of State, September 21, 1933, NA 837.00/3982 (FR, 1933-V:451).

49. Sumner Welles to the Secretary of State, September 25, 1933, NA 837.00/4023 (FR, 1933-V:459).

50. Sumner Welles to the Secretary of State, October 7, 1933, NA 837.00/4146 (FR, 1933-V:477).

51. *Ibid.* Buell, *Problems of the New Cuba,* 182-183. Phillips, *Cuba: Island of Paradox,* 81. *New York Times* (September 20, 1933).

52. Sumner Welles to the Secretary of State, October 18, 1933, NA 837.00/4213 (FR, 1933-V:491). The students were reported to be conspiring to oust Batista. Sumner Welles to the Secretary of State, October 19, 1933, NA 837.00/4236 (FR, 1933-V:492).

53. *Ibid.*

54. Sumner Welles to the Secretary of State, October 24, 1933, NA 837.00/4267 (FR, 1933-V:499).

55. Sumner Welles to the Secretary of State, October 26, 1933, NA 837.00/4281 (FR, 1933-V:501).

56. Sumner Welles to the Secretary of State, October 31, 1933, NA 837.00/4321 (FR, 1933-V:505). Sumner Welles to the Secretary of State, November 4, 1933, NA 837.00/4337 (FR, 1933-V:511).

57. Sumner Welles to the Acting Secretary of State, December 9, 1933, NA 837.00/4488 (FR, 1933-V:536). Batista was again given "full guarantees as to his retention of his present position." Sumner Welles to the Acting Secretary of State, December 10, 1933, NA 837.00/4489 (FR, 1933-V:538). Sumner Welles to the Acting Secretary of State, December 11, 1933, NA 837.00/4498 (FR, 1933-V:539).

58. The Secretary to President Roosevelt (Early) to the Acting Secretary of State, November 22, 1933, NA 837.00/4450 (FR, 1933-V:524).

59. Sumner Welles to the Secretary of State, September 11, 1933, NA 837.00/3830 (FR, 1933-V:422). Secretary of State to Sumner Welles, September 11, 1933, NA 837.00/3830 (FR, 1933-V:424). The Acting Secretary of State to President Roosevelt, at Warm Springs, Georgia, November 23, 1933, NA 837.00/4450/Supp. (FR, 1933-V:525).

60. Cordell Hull, at Montevideo, asked the Department to supply him with the "facts and conditions . . . against recognition" of the regime. Welles was cited as the source for the arguments against recognition. Acting Secretary of State to Cordell Hull, November 28, 1933, NA 837.01/47 (FR, 1933-V:527).

61. Sumner Welles to the Secretary of State, September 17, 1933, NA 837.00/3908 (FR, 1933-V:443).

62. Sumner Welles to the Secretary of State, October 16, 1933, NA 837.00/4206 (FR, 1933-V:487).

63. Sumner Welles to the Acting Secretary of State, December 7,

1933, NA 837.00/4480 (FR, 1933-V:533). M. T. McGovern (President, American Chamber of Commerce of Cuba) to Sumner Welles, November 15, 1933, NA 837.00/4539; this letter had the "unanimous" approval of the members, and argued against recognition. Some examples of these decrees are discussed in, Buell, *Problems of the New Cuba*, 14; many of them concerned labor reforms.

64. Jefferson Caffery to the Acting Secretary of State, December 21, 1933, NA 837.00/4547 (FR, 1933-V:544). Mrs. R. Hart Phillips said that the old electricity rates were "outrageous." Phillips, *Cuba: Island of Paradox*, 127. Caffery divided the Cubans into the "better classes" and the "ignorant masses." Jefferson Caffery to the Acting Secretary of State, January 10, 1934, NA 837.00/4591 (FR, 1934-V:95).

65. Acting Secretary of State to Jefferson Caffery, January 8, 1934, NA 837.01/59 (FR, 1934-V:93).

66. Jefferson Caffery to the Acting Secretary of State, January 10, 1934, NA 837.00/4591.

67. Jefferson Caffery to the Acting Secretary of State, January 14, 1934, NA 837.00/4606 (FR, 1934-V:98).

68. Acting Secretary of State to Jefferson Caffery, January 14, 1934, NA 837.00/4609 (FR, 1934-V:100). Jefferson Caffery to the Acting Secretary of State, January 15, 1934, NA 837.00/4617.

69. Secretary of State to Jefferson Caffery, January 23, 1934, NA 837.01/70 (FR, 1934-V:107). See also, The Charles E. Hires Company to Cordell Hull, January 22, 1934, NA 837.01/69. This company urged recognition in order to prevent labor unrest. Hevia was replaced by Mendieta on January 18.

70. Phillips, *Cuba: Island of Paradox*, 160-161. Buell, *Problems of the New Cuba*, 16-17.

71. Jefferson Caffery to the Secretary of State, March 14, 1934, NA 837.00/4929. *Monthly Bank Letter* (February 1934), 19. Speech by Hamilton Fish in, *Congressional Record*, 73rd Cong., 2nd Sess., 1934, Vol. 78, Part 8, 8416.

72. Cosme de la Torriente, "The Platt Amendment," *Foreign Affairs* (April 1930), 364.

73. Harry F. Guggenheim, "Amending the Platt Amendment," *Foreign Affairs* (April 1934), 448. Sumner Welles to the Secretary of State, November 4, 1933, NA 837.00/4337 (FR, 1933-V:511).

74. Sumner Welles to the Secretary of State, September 18, 1933, NA 837.00/3934. *New York Times* (December 14, 1933), 9:2. The Department stated that the legitimate interests of Americans would be protected. Edwin C. Wilson (Chief, Latin American Division) to the Corn Exchange Bank & Trust Company, December 20, 1933, NA 837.00/4509.

75. Sumner Welles, *Good Neighbor Policy in the Caribbean*, 7.

76. "Final Declaration," *Official Report of the Twentieth National Foreign Trade Convention* (New York, 1933), viii. A similar resolution was passed at the luncheon of the American Manufacturers Export Association, *ibid.*, 246-247. James S. Carson, "Pressing Present-Day Latin-American Problems," *ibid.* Robert H. Patchin, "No Fire Sale of our Foreign Trade Assets," *ibid.*

77. *New York Times* (October 30, 1933), 25:2.

78. Francis B. Sayre, *American Commercial Policy, The Two Alterna-*

tives (Department of State, Commercial Policy Series No. 23, Washington, 1936), 8. Sumner Welles, *The Trade Agreements Program*, 5-6. *Monthly Bank Letter* (October 1933), 158-160.

79. *Ibid.* H. H. Pike, Jr., "Our Trade with Cuba: An Examination of Our Only Reciprocity Treaty," 129-134. For examples see the letters cited in note 11, Chapter IX. The most important letters from such firms were sent to Welles to guide him in the negotiations. Secretary of State to Sumner Welles, June 9, 1933, NA 611.3731/462.

80. These examples were among the recommendations submitted by Phillip Jessup. Memorandum, Office of the Economic Advisor, "Jessup on United States Export Trade with Cuba," September 26, 1933, NA 611.3731/466.

81. Department of State, *Reciprocal Trade Agreement between the United States of America and the Republic of Cuba, Signed at Washington August 24, 1934, as Amended by Supplementary Agreements Signed at Washington, December 18, 1939 and at Habana, December 23, 1941* (Washington, 1942), 10, 33-37, 44. Buell, *Problems of the New Cuba*, 62-63. Department of State, *Analysis of Cuban-American Trade during the First Two Years under the Reciprocal Agreement* (Washington, 1937), Part I, 18.

82. Jessup Memorandum, September 26, 1933, NA 611.3731/466. Secretary of State to Jefferson Caffery, April 3, 1934, *Foreign Relations of the United States: Diplomatic Papers, 1934* (5 vols., Washington, 1952), V, 124-125.

83. Secretary of State to Jefferson Caffery, June 18, 1934, *ibid.,* 140.

84. Buell, *Problems of the New Cuba*, 65. Welles had stated in 1933 that one of the major aims of the trade negotiations was to obtain "a practical monopoly of the Cuban market." Sumner Welles to the Secretary of State, May 13, 1933, NA 837.00/3512.

85. Thomas L. Chadbourne, *Cuba and Sugar Stabilization*, 27-28. Ernest K. Lindley, "United States Sugar Aid to Pacify Cuba."

86. *Hearings: Jones-Costigan Act*, 1-2.

87. Ickes, *Secret Diary*, I, 147.

88. *Hearings: Jones-Costigan Act* (pages are in order of listing in text), 218-219, 226-233, 243-244, 220-221, 71-80, 5, 62-64, *Congressional Record*, 73rd Cong., 2nd Sess., 1934, Vol. 78, Part 6, 6025.

89. *Hearings: Jones-Costigan Act*, 246, 141-142, 201-209. *Congressional Record*, 73rd Cong., 2nd Sess., 1934, Vol. 78, Part 3, 3230-3233; Part 4, 3632-3633.

90. United States Cuban Sugar Council, *Sugar: Facts and Figures* (New York, 1948), 53, 55. Farr & Company, *Manual of Sugar Companies, 1949-1950* (New York, 1950), 260. Roosevelt had asked that Cuba be given 1,944,000 short tons, *Hearings: Jones-Costigan Act*, 1-2. Companies interested in Cuban sugar wanted at least two million tons; Memorandum: Conversation between Mr. Laurence A. Crosby (Sullivan and Cromwell) and Mr. Duggan, September 1, 1933, NA 837.00/4104.

91. The American Sugar Refining Company, *Annual Report: 1934*, (New York, 1935), 11.

92. This trend could also be seen in the AAA and the NRA. For discussions of this see, Schlesinger, *Coming of the New Deal*, Chapters

6 & 7; Richard Hofstadter, *The American Political Tradition and the Men Who Made It* (New York, 1954), 325-336.

93. Senate, *Sale of Foreign Bonds*, I, 64 (Charles Mitchell of the National City Bank), II, 619-620 (James Speyer), II, 447 (Clarence Dillon). John Abbink, "The Relation to Sales Policy of Longer Term Credits," *Official Report of the Twentieth National Foreign Trade Convention* (New York, 1933), 224. See also the statement by Palmer Pierce at the Latin American Session, *ibid.*, 92.

94. Georges St. Jean. "Putting an Edge on the 'Edge Act,'" *Official Report of the Eighteenth National Foreign Trade Convention* (New York, 1931), 251-253.

95. *Ibid.* Reginald F. Chitter, "Government Credit Aid for Foreign Trade," *Official Report of the Twentieth National Foreign Trade Convention*, 240-241. Remarks by Eugene P. Thomas, *ibid.*, 305-306; Palmer Pierce, *ibid.*, 92; Grosvenor Jones (Bureau of Foreign and Domestic Commerce), *ibid.*, 310-311; "Final Declaration," *ibid.*, ix. *The Commercial and Financial Chronicle* (January 23, 1932), 601. Palmer Pierce (Chairman, Committee on Inter-American Relations) to Henry L. Stimson, September 19, 1931, NA 800.51/648½. George N. Peek, "Foreign Trade Credits," *Official Report of the Twenty-First National Foreign Trade Convention* (New York, 1934), 444. John Abbink, "Financing for Exports," *ibid.*, 451-457. This discussion of the development of the Export-Import Banks is of necessity only a brief summary of a much more involved story of business-government cooperation.

96. Remarks of Grosvenor Jones, *Twentieth National Foreign Trade Convention*, 310-311. Speech by George N. Peek, *Twenty-First National Foreign Trade Convention*, 444.

97. "Final Declaration," *ibid.*, x-xi. Remarks by Eugene P. Thomas (President of the Council), *Official Report of the Twenty-Second National Foreign Trade Convention* (New York, 1935), 145-147.

98. John Abbink, "Financing for Exports." Abbink was called in to advise the government on the bank.

99. Sumner Welles to the Secretary of State, June 30, 1933, NA 837.51 Chase National Bank/97 (FR, 1933-V:576). Sumner Welles to the Secretary of State, August 30, 1933, NA 837.00/3685 (FR, 1933-V:578).

100. *Ibid.*

101. Preliminary Report on Cuban Finances Prepared by American Financial Experts, September 5, 1933, NA 837.51/1612½ (FR, 1933-V:583).

102. Memorandum: Plan for the Relief and Future Economic Recovery of Cuba, Submitted by Dr. Cyrus F. Wicker, November 1933, NA 837.00/4403. Memorandum: Cuba, by Jefferson Caffery, December 4, 1933, NA 711.37/198. This memo contains one of the rare references to the need for agrarian reform.

103. Export-Import Bank, *Second Annual Report of the Export-Import Bank* (Washington, 1935). U. S., Congress, Senate, Committee on Banking and Currency, *Hearings on Increasing the Lending Authority of the Export-Import Bank*, 76th Cong., 3rd Sess., 1940 (Washington, 1940), 33. Warren Lee Pierson, "Export-Import Bank Operations," *The Annals of the American Academy of Political and Social Science* (Philadelphia, 1940), 35-40.

104. *New York Times* (February 28, 1934), 29:8. Senator Pittman was of the leading silverites in the Democratic Party. He considered silver to be closely tied to the export trade, *Congressional Record,* 72nd Cong., 1st Sess., 1931, Vol. 75, Part 1, 286. See also Wayne S. Cole, "Senator Key Pittman and American Neutrality Policies, 1933-1940," *The Mississippi Valley Historical Review* (March, 1960), 645-646.

105. *Twenty-First National Foreign Trade Convention,* 413-414. "Final Declaration," *ibid.,* vii, xiv. Similar expressions can be found in: *Monthly Bank Letter* (September 1934), 136-137; James S. Carson, "New Approaches in Inter-American Commercial Relations," *The Annals of the American Academy of Political and Social Science* (Philadelphia, 1939), 66-71; Otto T. Kreuser, "Some Inter-American Financial Problems," *ibid.,* 164-168.

NOTES FOR CHAPTER ELEVEN

1. Department of Commerce, *Investment in Cuba,* 10.

2. Department of State, *Analysis of Cuban-American Trade during the First Two Years under the Reciprocal Agreement,* I, 1.

3. Department of Commerce, *Investment in Cuba,* 138-139. U. S., Bureau of the Census, *Statistical Abstract of the United States: 1954* (Washington, 1954), 924. *Ibid., Statistical Abstract of the United States: 1959,* 898. 1958 amount was $545.9 million; the estimated 1959 amount was $435 million, *Wall Street Journal* (April 6, 1960), 4.

4. Gayer and Schmidt, *American Economic Foreign Policy,* 228. Department of Commerce, *Investment in Cuba,* 138.

5. *Ibid.*

6. *Ibid.,* 10.

7. *Ibid.* See also Buell, *Problems of the New Cuba,* 227-229.

8. *Ibid.* U. S., Department of Commerce, *U. S. Investments in the Latin American Economy* (Washington, 1957), 175.

9. *Ibid.*

10. *Ibid.,* 175. Department of Commerce, *Investment in Cuba,* 10.

11. *Ibid.* The apparent increase in public utility investments between 1929 and 1936 was probably due to a change in the basis of valuation, since United States capital did not flow into Cuban utilities during this period.

12. *Ibid.*

13. *Ibid.,* 10-11. Bureau of the Census, *Statistical Abstract: 1959,* 871. Department of Commerce, *U. S. Investments in the Latin American Economy,* 112.

14. U. S., Senate, Committee on Finance, *Hearings on Sugar Act Extension,* 84th Cong., 2nd Sess., 1956 (Washington, 1956), 279.

15. U. S., Tariff Commission, *Economic Controls and Commercial Policy in Cuba* (Washington, 1946), 33. United States Cuban Sugar Council, *Sugar: Facts and Figures,* 52.

16. *Ibid.,* 63-64. Department of Commerce, *Investment in Cuba,* 136-138.

All former trade agreements are inoperative for such time as the United States and Cuba are contracting parties to GATT.

17. United States Cuban Sugar Council, *Sugar: Facts and Figures*, 53-55.

18. *Ibid.*, 57-63. The increase in the conditional payment was initially made during the war.

19. *Wall Street Journal* (March 16, 1960), 24; and March 17, 1960), 7.

20. United States Cuban Sugar Council, *Sugar: Facts and Figures*, 63, 70-71. *Wall Street Journal* (March 9, 1960), 1, 10.

21. *Ibid.*

22. Senate, *Hearings on Sugar Act Extension*, 75-78. In 1954, each of thirty-nine sugar cane producers received over $100,000 in payments; the largest payment was for $1,085,000 and went to the Hawaiian Commercial and Sugar Company (p. 80-81). See J. Fred Rippy, "Sugar in Inter-American Relations," *Inter-American Economic Affairs* (Spring, 1956), 50-64. Cuba markets much of the remainder of the sugar produced under the International Sugar Agreement of 1953.

23. Senate, *Increasing the Lending Authority of the Export-Import Bank*, 33. Graham H. Stuart, *Latin America and the United States* (New York, 1943), 244-245. Henry C. Wallich, *Monetary Problems of an Export Economy*, 139.

24. Foreign Bondholders Protective Council, *Report: 1955-1957* (New York, 1958), 112.

25. Hubert Herring, *A History of Latin America: From the Beginnings to the Present* (New York, 1955), 408. It was rumored that Batista held elections in deference to a personal request from Roosevelt.

26. The new government was recognized by the United States on March 27: Phillips, *Cuba: Island of Paradox*, 262.

27. *Ibid.*, 223, 246.

28. The United States continued to ship arms to Batista until the spring of 1958; the British did not halt their shipments of arms to Batista. *Ibid.*, 386.

29. *Ibid.*, 324-325.

30. *Ibid.*, 335-336, 338-339.

31. *Ibid.*, 388.

32. U. S., Senate, Special Committee to Study the Foreign Aid Program, *Central America and the Caribbean Area: Report on United States Foreign Assistance Programs*, 85th Cong., 1st Sess., 1957 (Washington, 1957), 9, 21.

33. Ickes, *Secret Diary*, I, 553. A similar view was expressed in, Phillips, *Cuban Sideshow*, 315-316.

34. For a complete list of the various issues see, Foreign Bondholders Protective Council, *Report for Years 1941-1945* (New York, 1945).

35. Buell, *Problems of the New Cuba*, 388-389.

36. Secretary of State to Jefferson Caffery, June 30, 1934, NA 837.51 Chase National Bank/195. The Foreign Bondholders Protective Council had been formed in 1933 upon the request of Cordell Hull and William H. Woodin. Hull wanted a private group to handle the negotiations over defaulted bonds so the State Department would not have to become directly involved; Foreign Bondholders Protective Council, *Report: 1955-1957*, xv.

37. Moody's Investors Service, *Government Securities, 1938*, Part III of *Moody's Manual of Investments: American and Foreign* (New York, 1938), 2669-2671.

38. Department of State, *Foreign Relations of the United States: Diplomatic Papers, 1938* (5 vols., Washington, 1956), V, 483-484; The Under-Secretary of State (Welles) to the Chargé in Cuba (Beaulac), October 13, 1938. Williard Beaulac to the Secretary of State, October 7, 1938, *ibid.*, 481. Warren Brothers Company held $9,800,000 in gold notes, and $1,050,000 in port notes. Purdy and Henderson held $1,500,000 in bonds.

39. Williard Beaulac to the Secretary of State, October 6, 1938, *Foreign Relations: 1938*, V, 481.

40. Memorandum of Conversation by the Ambassador in Cuba (Wright), August 30, 1939, Department of State, *Foreign Relations of the United States, 1939* (5 vols., Washington, 1957), V, 549-550. The promise was kept.

41. Memorandum of Conversation by the Ambassador in Cuba, April 18, 1939, *ibid.*, 526-527. No memoranda of these conversations have been found in Department files. In a speech given on his return, Batista cited the sugar duty reduction as one of the concessions promised. Phillips, *Cuba: Island of Paradox*, 188.

42. Memorandum of Conversation by the Ambassador in Cuba, February 25, 1939, *Foreign Relations, 1939*, V, 522. Memorandum by the Assistant Chief of the Division of the American Republics (Briggs) to the Under-Secretary of State (Welles), April 13, 1939, *ibid.*, 525.

43. The American Ambassador to the Cuban Secretary of State (Angel Campa), July 30, 1939, *ibid.*, 531-532.

44. Memorandum of Conversation by the Ambassador in Cuba, August 31, 1939, *ibid.*, 552-553. Exporters of sugar had to surrender 20 percent of their proceeds to the Currency Stabilization Fund against payment in pesos at par; other exporters had to surrender 10 percent, but this latter group was never required to comply with the law. Wallich, *Monetary Problems of an Export Economy*, 125. This was a form of exchange control, but the United States did not consider it too rigid. Tariff Commission, *Economic Controls and Commercial Policy in Cuba*, 20.

45. J. Butler Wright to the Secretary of State, September 12, 1939, *Foreign Relations, 1939*, V, 529. Memorandum of Telephone Conversation by the Assistant Chief of the Division of American Republics (Briggs), September 13, 1939, *ibid.*, 567.

46. *Ibid.*

47. *Ibid.*

48. Memorandum of Conversation by the Ambassador in Cuba, August 31, 1939, *ibid.*, 552-553.

49. The Cuban Secretary of State to the American Ambassador, September 13, 1939, *ibid.*, 568-569.

50. James S. Carson, "New Approaches in Inter-American Commerical Relations," *The Annals of the American Academy of Political and Social Science* (Philadelphia, 1939), 68. William S. Culbertson, "Economic Defense of the Americas," *ibid.*, (1940), 186-196. The American Rice Millers Association was pressuring the Department to work out an agreement with Cuba containing more benefits for rice. Memorandum of Conversation

by the Assistant Chief of the Division of Trade Agreements (Deimel), December 13, 1939, *Foreign Relations, 1939*, V, 574-575.

51. Foreign Bondholders Protective Council, *Report for Years 1941-1944*, 364-367. *New York Times* (June 24, 1940), 6:6 (June 27, 1940), 37:8.

52. Department of Commerce, *Investment in Cuba*, 5, 163-164.

53. Lowry Nelson, *Rural Cuba* (Minneapolis, 1950), 240-241. Department of Commerce, *Investment in Cuba*, 181.

54. *Ibid.*, 139.

55. *Wall Street Journal* (March 9, 1960), 1.

56. Department of Commerce, *Investment in Cuba*, 31. Nelson, *Rural Cuba*, 134.

57. Harold H. Martin, "Can Castro Save Cuba?" *Saturday Evening Post* (August 1, 1959), 40. This figure cited by an editor of the *Post* may be rather low. Robert Taber says that 700,000 people were landless. Robert Taber, "Castro's Cuba," *The Nation* (January 23, 1960).

58. For an example, see Raul Lorenzo, *El Empleo en Cuba* (Habana, 1955).

59. Columbia Broadcasting Company Television Presentation entitled, *World-Wide 60: Report on Cuba*, televised in February 1960. Taber, "Castro's Cuba." Martin, "Can Castro Save Cuba?" Harry B. Murkland, "Cuba: The Evolution of Revolution," *Current History* (March 1960), 129-133. Carleton Beals, "Cuba's Revolution: The First Year," *The Christian Century* (March 9, 1960), 284-286. Mary E. Furleigh, "A Missionary Looks at the Cuban Revolution," *Christian Herald* (April 1960), 13. The first-hand report of a University of Texas student who spent several weeks hiking around Cuba to find out what was happening, *The Austin American* (April 27, 1960), 1. *Wall Street Journal* (February 24, 1960), 1, 6. "Visitor Finds Cuba Relaxed, Friendly," *The Christian Century* (January 20, 1960), 69.

60. Quoted in, Taber, "Castro's Cuba." For earlier statements concerning Castro's plans see: Fidel Castro, "Why We Fight," *Coronet* (February 1958); Andrew St. George, "A Visit with a Revolutionary," *ibid.*; Andrew St. George, "Inside Cuba's Revolution," *Look* (February 4, 1958).

61. Taber, "Castro's Cuba." CBS, *Report on Cuba*.

62. Department of Commerce, *Investment in Cuba*, 155, 159.

63. Taber, "Castro's Cuba." *Wall Street Journal* (March 8, 1960), 1, 6; (April 6, 1960), 4. See also Ruby Hart Phillips, "Castro Gets the Bill," *The Reporter* (October 29, 1959), 23-24. Import reduction is part of the "austerity" program designed to accumulate capital for industrial expansion.

64. Taber, "Castro's Cuba." Department of Commerce, *Investment in Cuba*, 32. Five estates were expropriated in 1947 under this law.

65. CBS, *Report on Cuba*.

66. *Ibid.*, *Wall Street Journal* (March 8, 1960), 1; (April 6, 1960), 3, 4. Since April the Cuban Government has taken over—"intervened"—other American property, including the Texaco and Standard refineries.

67. *Wall Street Journal* (March 8, 1960), 1. CBS, *Report on Cuba*.

68. In a filmed interview a manager of the King Ranch admitted that they were not in a very good position to protest the valuation used by the Cubans: CBS, *Report on Cuba*.

69. *Wall Street Journal* (February 24, 1960), 1, 6. Tad Szulc, "Cuba's

Future is Written in Sugar," *The New York Times Magazine* (July 24, 1960); 13; Szulc reported that most of the construction activities have been centered in the rice, cattle, and vegetable cooperatives.

70. Phillips, *Cuba: Island of Paradox,* 397-401.

71. CBS, *Report on Cuba.*

72. Martin, "Can Castro Save Cuba?" 40. For a discussion of the crimes of the Batista regime see Phillips, *Cuba: Island of Paradox,* 285, 292, 316, 375. Furleigh, "A Missionary Looks at the Cuban Revolution," 14.

73. Martin, "Can Castro Save Cuba?" 40. Furleigh, "A Missionary Looks at the Cuban Revolution," 14.

74. *Wall Street Journal* (March 8, 1960), 6.

75. *Ibid.* (April 11, 1960), 1, 8.

76. After a prolonged debate in the House Agriculture Committee, the President's request was granted in a quick move by Congress early in July 1960 and the President announced the quota suspension on July 6, 1960.

77. *Wall Street Journal* (April 8, 1960), 8. The opinions of several beet producers were given, *ibid.* (March 9, 1960), 1, 10.

78. *Clovis News Journal* (June 21, 1960), New Mexico. *Friona Star* (June 24, 1960), Texas. Cooley, the Democratic chairman of the House Agriculture Committee, held out for a renewal of the old sugar act.

79. Theodore Draper, "The Runaway Revolution," *The Reporter* (May 12, 1960), 14-20.

80. Martin, "Can Castro Save Cuba?" 41. Phillips, *Cuba: Island of Paradox,* 207, 350-351; Mrs. Phillips writes that Batista really coddled the Communists. She cannot confirm the rumor that he had made a deal with them but she says that it seems probable.

81. Phillips, *Cuba: Island of Paradox,* 352-353. Draper, "The Runaway Revolution," 15-18.

82. Draper, "The Runaway Revolution," 19.

83. *Ibid.,* 16.

84. *Ibid.,* Martin, "Can Castro Save Cuba?" The moral fanaticism of the movement is discussed in, H. S. Trevor-Roper, "Puritans—From Calvin to Castro," *New York Times Magazine* (March 20, 1960), 28. Revolution and the cult of "personalista" is discussed in, Frank Tannenbaum, "The Political Dilemma in Latin America," *Foreign Affairs* (April 1960), 497-515. Harold Lavine, "Social Revolution in Cuba," *Commentary* (October 1959), 324-328.

85. Szulc, "Cuba's Future is Written in Sugar," 31.

86. Demand for intervention in, *Human Events* (April 7, 1960), 4. Most business publications continue to cite the need for caution; for example, *Wall Street Journal* (June 21, 1960) stated that military intervention and U. S. sponsored counterrevolution should not be considered.

87. Matt. 12: 43-45.

88. *The Reporter* (March 20, 1958), 8. For a penetrating analysis of the "open door empire" theme see William A. Williams, *The Tragedy of American Diplomacy* (Cleveland, 1959), 14-20, 204-212.

89. Columbia Broadcasting Company Television Presentation, *World Wide 60: Trujillo—Portrait of a Dictator,* televised in March 1960.

90. U. S., Senate, Committee on Finance: *Hearings on H.R. 1, Trade Agreements Extension,* 84th Cong., 1st Sess., 1955 (Washington 1955), Part 4, 2049.

91. For a discussion of this theme see "Instead of Intervention," *Christian Century* (March 16, 1960), 307-308.

92. Quoted in, Taber, "Castro's Cuba." See also, William P. Glade, Jr., "Castro and Cuba—The Politics of Economic Development," *Social Order* (March 1960), 123-124: this is the publication of the Jesuit Social Science Center.

Bibliography

Archival and Manuscript Sources

National Archives of the United States. General Records of the
Department of State (Record Group 59).

> Most of the files dealing with Cuban-American rela-
tions were covered for the period 1917–1934. In addition,
many files on Central American and Latin American policy,
and the activities of business organizations were utilized for
the same period.

National Archives of the United States. General Files of the
Senate (Record Group 46).

> The files used in this group were: Finance Committee
Files on the Parcel Post Convention (70th Cong., 1st Sess.,
1927–28); Foreign Relations Committee Files on the Isle of
Pines Treaty (68th Cong., 2nd Sess, 1924–25). Other files
were examined, but many of these Senate files contain
little information.

Charles Evans Hughes Papers. Library of Congress. Washington, D. C.

Chester Lloyd Jones Papers. University of Wisconsin Library.
Madison, Wisconsin.

Public Documents

I. Congressional

Congressional Record. 1917–1934.

House of Representatives, Committee on Agriculture. *Hearing
on H.R.7907, to Include Sugar Beets and Sugarcane as Basic
Commodities*. 73rd Cong., 2nd Sess., 1934.

————. Committee on Immigration and Naturalization. *Hearing on the Restriction of Immigration*. 68th Cong., 1st Sess.,
1924.

————. Committee on Ways and Means. *Act to Amend Sections 2804 and 3402 of the Revised Statutes of the United States.* Report No. 636, 70th Cong., 1st Sess., 1928.

————. Committee on Ways and Means. *Hearings on General Tariff Revision.* 66th Cong., 3rd Sess., 1921.

————. Committee on Ways and Means. *Hearings, Tariff Readjustment—1929.* 70th Cong., 2nd Sess., 1929.

————. Committee on Ways and Means. *Hearing on H.J. Res. 371 Limiting Importation Packages of Cigars.* 70th Cong., 2nd Sess., 1930.

Senate. *American Property Interests in the Isle of Pines,* 67th Cong., 4th Sess., 1923, S. Document No. 295.

————. Committee on Banking and Currency, *Hearings on Increasing the Lending Authority of the Export-Import Bank.* 76th Cong., 3rd Sess., 1940.

————. Committee on Banking and Currency, *Hearings on Stock Exchange Practices.* 73rd Cong., 2nd Sess., 1933 and 1934.

————. Committee on Finance. *Hearings on H.R. 1, Trade Agreements Extension.* 84th Cong., 1st Sess., 1955.

————. Committee on Finance. *Hearings on the Proposed Tariff Act of 1921.* 67th Cong., 2nd Sess., 1922.

————. Committee on Finance. *Hearings, Tariff Act of 1929.* 71st Cong., 1st Sess., 1929.

————. Committee on Finance. *Hearings, Sale of Foreign Bonds or Securities in the United States.* 72nd Cong., 1st Sess., 1931 and 1932.

————. Committee on Finance. *Hearings on Sugar Act Extension.* 84th Cong., 2nd Sess., 1956.

————. Committee on Finance. *Hearings, to Include Sugar Beets and Sugarcane as Basic Agricultural Commodities under the Agricultural Adjustment Act.* 73rd Cong., 2nd Sess., 1934.

————. Committee on Foreign Relations. *Adjustment of Title to Isle of Piñes.* Report No. 1. 67th Cong., 4th Sess., 1922.

————. Subcommittee of the Committee on Foreign Relations. *Hearings on Foreign Loans.* 68th Cong., 2nd Sess., 1925.

————. Committee on Immigration. *Hearings, Restriction of Western Hemisphere Immigration.* 70th Cong., 1st Sess., 1928.

————. Select Committee on Investigation of the Tariff Com-

mission. *Investigation of the Tariff Commission*. 69th Cong.,
1st Sess., 1926.

————. Special Committee to Study the Foreign Aid Program.
*Central America and the Caribbean Area: Report on United
States Foreign Assistance Programs*. 85th Cong., 1st Sess.,
1957.

————. Subcommittee of the Committee on the Judiciary.
Hearings, The Lobby Investigation. 71st Cong., 1st Sess.,
1929 and 1930.

————. Subcommittee of the Committee on Manufactures.
Hearings, Shortage of Sugar. 65th Cong., 2nd Sess., 1918.

————. *Papers Relating to the Adjustment of Title to the
Ownership of the Isle of Pines*. Document No. 166. 68th
Cong., 2nd Sess., 1924.

HUGHES, CHARLES EVANS. *Some Aspects of the Work of the Department of State*. Senate Document No. 206. 67th Cong.,
2nd Sess., 1922.

II. Other

Department of Commerce. *Annual Report of the Secretary of
Commerce*. 1919–1933.

————. Bureau of Foreign and Domestic Commerce. *Cuban
Readjustment to Current Economic Forces*. Trade Information Bulletin No. 725. 1930.

————. *Investment in Cuba, Basic Information for United
States Businessmen*. 1956.

————. Bureau of Foreign and Domestic Commerce. *United
States Trade with Latin America in 1930*. Trade Promotion
Series No. 124. 1930.

————. *U. S. Investments in the Latin American Economy*.
1957.

Export-Import Bank, *Second Annual Report of the Export-Import
Bank*. 1935.

Department of the Interior. Bureau of Education. *Practices and
Objectives in Training for Foreign Service*. Bulletin No. 21.
1924.

Department of the Navy. Office of Naval Intelligence. *The United
States Navy as an Industrial Asset*. 1923.

————. Information Section. *Some of the Unusual Peacetime
Activities of the United States Navy*. 1923.

————. Office of Naval Intelligence. *Information Concerning the United States Navy and Other Navies.* 1925.

————. *The United States Navy in Peacetime.* 1931.

PORTER, ROBERT P. *Report on the Commercial and Industrial Condition of the Island of Cuba.* Treasury Department Document No. 2072. 1898.

Department of State. *Foreign Relations of the United States.* 1917–1940.

————. *Analysis of Cuban-American Trade during the First Two Years under the Reciprocal Agreement.* 1937.

————. *Press Releases.* May 9, 1931 (Address by Secretary Stimson).

————. *Reciprocal Trade Agreement between the United States of America and the Republic of Cuba, Signed at Washington August 24, 1934, as Amended by Supplementary Agreements Signed at Washington December 18, 1939 and at Habana December 23, 1941.* 1942.

————. *Right to Protect Citizens in Foreign Countries by Landing Forces.* 3rd revised edition w/supplemental appendix. 1934.

SAYRE, FRANCIS B. *American Commercial Policy, The Two Alternatives.* Commercial Policy Series No. 23. 1936.

STIMSON, HENRY L. *The United States and the Other American Republics.* Latin American Series No. 4. 1931.

WELLES, SUMNER. *"Good Neighbor" Policy in the Caribbean.* Latin American Series No. 12. 1935.

————. *Relations between the United States and Cuba.* Latin American Series No. 7. 1934.

————. *The Trade Agreements Program.* Commercial Policy Series No. 2. 1934.

————. *Two Years of the Good Neighbor Policy.* Latin American Series No. 11. 1935.

Tariff Commission. *The Effects of the Cuban Reciprocity Treaty of 1902.* 1929.

————. *Economic Controls and Commercial Policy in Cuba.* 1946.

————. *The Foreign Trade of Latin America.* Part I. 1940.

SELECTED READING LIST ON CUBA AND
CUBAN-AMERICAN RELATIONS

ATKINS, EDWIN F. *Sixty Years in Cuba.* Cambridge, 1926.

ALIENES Y UROSA. *Caracteristicas Fundamentales de la Economia Cubana.* Habana, 1950.

BEALS, CARLETON. *The Crime of Cuba.* Philadelphia, 1933.

BEMAN, LAMAR T. (ed.). *Selected Articles on Intervention in Latin America.* New York, 1928.

BUELL, RAYMOND L., *et. al. Problems of the New Cuba.* The report of the Commission on Cuban Affairs of the Foreign Policy Association. New York, 1935.

CALLCOTT, WILFRID H. *The Caribbean Policy of the United States, 1899–1920.* Baltimore, 1942.

CHAPMAN, CHARLES E. *A History of the Cuban Republic,* New York, 1927.

DE CONDE, ALEXANDER. *Herbert Hoover's Latin American Policy.* Stanford, 1951.

DUNN, ROBERT W. *American Foreign Investments.* New York, 1926.

FARR & COMPANY. *Manual of Sugar Companies, 1949–1950.* New York, 1950.

FERGUSSON, ERNA. *Cuba.* New York, 1946.

FEUERLEIN, WILLY, and HANNAN, ELIZABETH. *Dollars in Latin America.* New York, 1941.

FITZGIBBON, RUSSELL H. *Cuba and the United States 1900–1935.* Menasha, Wis., 1935.

GUERRANT, EDWARD O. *Roosevelt's Good Neighbor Policy.* Albuquerque, 1950.

GUGGENHEIM, HARRY F. *The United States and Cuba.* New York, 1934.

GUTIERREZ, GUSTAVO. *El Dessarrollo Economico de Cuba.* Habana, 1952.

GUTIERREZ, VIRIATO. *The World Sugar Problem, 1926–1935.* London, 1935.

JENKS, LELAND H. *Our Cuban Colony.* New York, 1928.

JONES, CHESTER LLOYD. *Caribbean Interests of the United States.* New York, 1919.

LOCKMILLER, DAVID A. *Enoch H. Crowder, Soldier, Lawyer, and Statesman.* Columbia, Mo., 1955.

LORENZO, RAUL. *El Empleo en Cuba.* Habana, 1955.

MORRIS, CHARLES. *Our Island Empire.* Philadelphia, 1898.

NELSON, LOWRY. *Rural Cuba.* Minneapolis, 1950.

PRATT, JULIUS. *Expansionists of 1898.* Baltimore, 1936.

PHILLIPS, RUBY HART. *Cuban Sideshow.* Havana, 1935.

————. *Cuba: Island of Paradox.* New York, 1959.

PORTER, ROBERT P. *Industrial Cuba.* New York, 1899.

PRINSEN GEERLIGS, H. C., and PRINSEN GEERLIGS, R. J. *Cane Sugar Production, 1912–1937.* London, 1938.

SCHATTSCHNEIDER, ELMER E. *Politics, Pressures and the Tariff.* New York, 1935.

TAUSSIG, CHARLES W. *Some Notes on Sugar and Molasses.* New York, 1940.

United States Cuban Sugar Council. *Sugar—Facts and Figures, 1952.* Washington, 1952.

VERRILL, A. HYATT. *Cuba of Today.* New York, 1931.

WALLICH, HENRY C. *Monetary Problems of an Export Economy: The Cuban Experience, 1914–1947.* Cambridge, Mass., 1950.

WELLES, SUMNER. *The Time for Decision.* New York, 1944.

WINKLER, MAX. *Foreign Bonds—An Autopsy.* Philadelphia, 1933.

————. *Investments of United States Capital in Latin America.* Boston, 1928.

WRIGHT, PHILLIP G. *The Cuban Situation and Our Treaty Relations.* Washington, 1931.

————. *Sugar in Relation to the Tariff.* New York, 1924.

Index

Index

Abbink, John, 162
A.B.C. (political party), 225
Agrarian Reform, 176, 177, 178, 179, 180, 181, 231, 235, 236
Agrarian Reform Institute, 178
Agriculture Adjustment Act, 160
Agriculture Department, 142, 160, 236
American and Foreign Power Co., 196
American Banker's Association, 162
American Bottler's of Carbonated Beverages, 54, 60, 62, 202, 203
American Car and Foundry Co., 45, 114, 225
American Chamber of Commerce of Cuba, 36, 45, 49, 50, 51, 52, 54, 55, 68, 75, 76, 77, 79, 81, 83, 87, 92, 95, 109, 113, 115, 117, 119, 140, 151, 199, 213, 229
American Committee on Cuban Emergency, 45, 143
American Exporters and Importers Association, 62, 64
American Farm Bureau Federation, 45, 55, 64, 67, 160
American Federation of Labor, 62, 63, 116, 217
American Food Administration, 20, 21
American Manufacturers Export Assn., 44, 158, 162, 198, 229
American Molasses Company, 142
American Producers of Cuban Sugar, 45
American Relief Administration, 56
American Rice Miller's Association, 234
American Steel Co. of Cuba, 45
American Sugar Refining Company, 20, 29, 30, 47, 161, 191
American Trading Co., 45
Anti-United States sentiment, 27, 57, 68, 77, 79, 103-4, 106-10, 111-12, 121, 176, 181, 205, 214
Arbuckle Brothers Refinery, 20, 45, 200
Associated American Interests of Cuba, 23
Association of Mill Owners of Cuba, 54
Atkins, Edwin F., 31, 43, 45, 52, 191, 199
Atlantic Fruit and Sugar Company, 202
Austin, Harry, 61

Babst, Earl, 20, 21, 161
Bacharach, Isaac, 60, 203
Bacon, Elliot C., 101
Baldwin Locomotive Works, 45
Baldwin, William, 60, 62, 63, 71, 202
Baltimore Association of Commerce, 160
Banking moratorium, 84-85, 86-87
Barkley, Alben, 117
Barlow Claim, 217
Batista, Fulgencio, 144, 149, 152, 153, 154, 155, 156, 170, 172, 173, 176, 179, 181, 183, 184, 185, 228, 233, 234, 236
Beaulac, Williard, 172
Beet sugar producers (domestic), 24, 42-48, 52, 53-62, 64-69, 140, 160, 163, 168-69, 180-81, 200, 204, 205
Behn, Hernand, 114
Behn, Sosthenes, 115, 197
Berle, Adolph A., Jr., 141, 142, 152, 163, 189, 224
Berwind-White Coal Mining Co., 45
Bethlehem Steel Company, 151
Bingham, Hiram, 109, 110
Blaine, John J. (Senator, Wis.), 66

247

"This excellent book will probably become a standard source of information on U.S.-Cuban relations . . . highly recommended. . . ."
—*Library Journal*

THE UNITED STATES AND CUBA

Business and Diplomacy, 1917-1960

by ROBERT F. SMITH

This is a carefully documented examination of the historical relationship between business interests in Cuba and the United States. The history of Cuban-American relations centers about a complicated interaction of political and economic motives and methods intended to provide specific economic benefits and to preserve a friendly, stable Cuban government, thus protecting American business interests in Cuba. This book, the first in this century to utilize material from the State Department archives, provides the detailed background necessary for a full understanding of the failure of United States business diplomacy and the resulting current Cuban-American difficulties.

ABOUT THE AUTHOR

Dr. Robert F. Smith teaches history at the University of Rhode Island. A member of Phi Beta Kappa, Phi Alpha Theta, The American Historical Association, Dr. Smith has written numerous articles that have appeared in historical journals. In addition to Dr. Smith's scholarly research into Cuban-American relations, he has good reason to be conscious of anti-American sentiment, for as a seaman in the United States Naval Reserve in 1948, he narrowly escaped capture by an anti-American mob in Santiago, Cuba. Dr. Smith has prepared another volume, *What Happened in Cuba?*, soon to be published.

 COLLEGE AND UNIVERSITY PRESS
263 Chapel Street   New Haven, Conn.